AMERICA'S
LOST TREASURES

by Michael Paul Henson

Jayco Publishing Co.
PO Box 1511, South Bend IN 46634

Library of Congress Cataloging in Publication Data

Henson, Michael Paul.
    America's lost treasures.

    1. United States—Antiquities—Miscellanea.
2. Treasure-trove—United States—Miscellanea.
3. Archaeology—United States—Field work—Miscellanea.
4. Excavations (Archaeology)—United States—Miscellanea.
I. Title.
E159.5.H46 1984   930.1'0973   84-5750
ISBN 0-9607728-1-2

Litho in U.S.A.

THE SEEKERS

Hidden gold, lost mines and buried treasures, because they are the material of which dreams are made, have attracted and fascinated man for thousands of years. Almost without exception, all men have sought treasure in one form or another. But the greatest treasure hunt of all time began almost 500 years ago when the first bearded and steel helmeted adventurers landed in a wild new world and started a search for gold and glory that is still going on.

Following in their footsteps have been thousands of others of every race and color, marching through incredible odds in their search. Today, more than ever, the daring ones are still marching, armed with instruments that the Spanish Conquistadors would have thought were the tools of witchcraft.

Those that still march seek not only glory, but the golden promises of hidden riches, some of which have disappeared into the pages of history, while others have been caught up in the backwash of time or became lost in the retelling of legends.

But the search goes on and will continue as long as man has the ability to dream, for without dreams he cannot exist.

Michael Paul Henson
Jeffersonville, Indiana

1-812 283 4164

Author, Michael Paul Henson, using his favorite metal detector, A Fisher M-Scope 1265-X.

For more information on the Fisher line of products, contact:
Fisher Research Laboratory
1005 "I" Street, Dept. MH
Los Banos, CA 93635-4398

FOREWORD

This Question and Answer approach for information on treasure sites and methods of recovery has never before been attempted in book form. It will be of interest and assistance to amateurs and professionals alike.

Admittedly, in several instances the answer to a question is limited but enough information is given to assist the treasure hunter in further research and possible recovery.

The material herein listed encompasses the entire United States and answers almost any question an interested person will have concerning the entire scope of the treasure hunting hobby.

DEDICATION

This book is dedicated to those that want and need to ask questions concerning all phases of treasure hunting but do not know where to start, or how to obtain the answers.

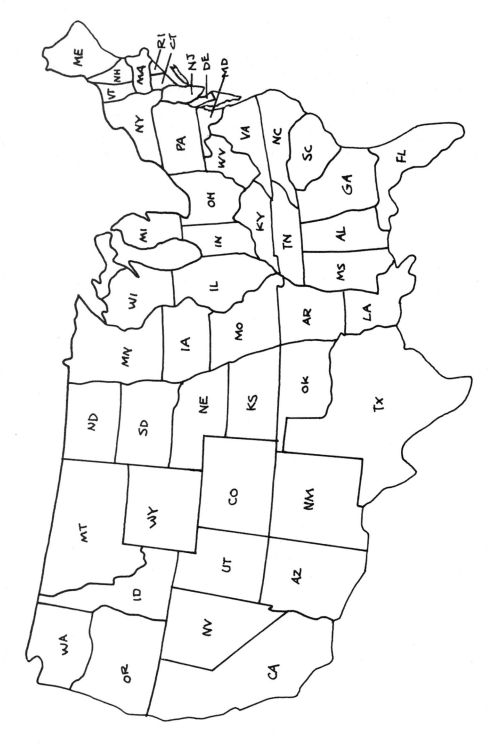

VIII

TABLE OF CONTENTS

CHAPTER ONE

In this chapter there will be several instances in which there are more questions and answers on one state than on others. This is because some states have a larger number of known locations that have been researched. It would be impossible for any author to completely investigate all of the treasure locations ghost or near-ghost towns, lost mines, metal detector sites, gem locations, places of interest, et cetera, for persons interested in the treasure hunting hobby throughout the United States. Even if an author could compile such a work it would comprise hundreds of pages and be too voluminous for the average person to read.

The following alphabetical listing of states giving over 500 questions and answers is actually a volume of different treasure sites within the United States. The purpose of this work is to furnish information that will be of interest and help to treasure hunters on vacation, that travel to different states, also to weekenders that want to visit and search within their own or surrounding states, and for the "arm-chair adventurers" (who for various reasons cannot travel) it will, if nothing more, make interesting reading.

In a large number of answers the names of towns, counties, mountains, rivers, et cetera, are given instead of the state's name. This is done in order that the name of the state will not become too repetitious.

ALABAMA

Q: I would like information on several locations of pirate treasure in Alabama.

A: Here are three: In the area south of Fort Morgan in Baldwin County, the pirate Lafitte is supposed to have buried over $200,000 in gold and silver coins, somewhere on the beach.

The pirate Gasparilla is supposed to have buried part of his loot in different locations around Mobile Bay.

There are local stories of pirate treasure being buried on the tip of a long peninsula that separates Box Secour Bay from the Gulf of Mexico. This is approximately 33 miles south of Mobile. Coins have been found along the beach of the time period when pirates infested these coastal waters.

Q: Is there a location of lost treasure in west central Alabama?

A: There is an old story of a strongbox being dropped into the Tombigbee River, south of Myrtlewood in Marengo County. This money, $30,000 in gold, was being transported by a tax collector in 1860, when outlaws tried to rob him. He threw the strongbox into the water close to the ford that was operated there at that time. The bandits killed the collector but research reveals that they did not get the money.

Q: I have heard of a box of gold that was buried in Newton. Do you have any information on this?

A: In December of 1864, when a band of guerrillas and outlaws under the command of an ex-Confederate colonel named Joseph Sanders, attacked the town of Newton, in Dale County, Alabama. The townspeople had a major problem: what to do with a box filled with a small fortune in coins that belonged to the town. The problem was solved by selecting three men to bury the box. When the fight was over, four of Newton's citizens were dead, and as fate would have it, three of them were the ones that had buried the town's treasury. There is enough evidence (a large plaque near the courthouse and court records) to prove that this incident occurred, to warrant a treasure hunter's investigation.

Q: Has silver ever been found in Alabama?

A: Yes, in 1832, an epidemic of measles broke out among a small tribe of Indians living in Talladega County. A white man named Issac Stone treated the Indians so that most of them lived. While living with the redmen, Stone noticed that they had numerous silver trinkets. He tried in vain to learn the source of the silver but all he was ever told by the Chief was, the silver came from Wolf Creek in St. Clair County, Alabama. All Stone could obtain was a piece of silver ore that assayed 70 percent silver and 30 percent lead. Somewhere on Wolf Creek there is an Indian silver mine waiting to be found.

Q: Did you ever hear of the Savannah Jack Treasure?

A: Around 1812, in Montgomery County, Alabama, there was a Shawnee Indian village known as Souvanogee. It was located near a corner formed by the Tallapoosa River and Likasa Creek.

The leader of this village was a half-breed, Indian prophet called savannah Jack. He and his band of braves robbed, murdered and pillaged this section of Alabama for six years.

There is no known or itemized record of the amount of plunder that fell into the hands of Captain Jack and his renegades. Jack had been exposed to the ways of white men and knew well the values they placed on gold and silver. Certainly anything of monetary value was gathered up by Jack on these raids and carried back to the village.

Savannah Jack and his band of renegade Indians were finally pursued and caught up with by General Dale and his troops in 1818. In the running gun battle that followed, several of the Indians were killed on the spot. It is believed that Savannah Jack was severely wounded in the gun battle and died a short time later in Sipsey Swamp.

It is obvious that there should still be several caches of Savannah Jack's loot buried near the old Indian camp of Souvanogee. He had six years to accumulate it in. The village was taken by surprise in the attack and there was not sufficient time to dig up his various caches. The campground covered quite an area but traces of it can still be found.

Q: Where can I pan for gold in Alabama?

A: Gold has been found by panning in Cleburne and surrounding counties in Alabama. However, no large deposits have ever been discovered. Write the State Geology Department, in Montgomery, Alabama, for information on the known locations of gold within the state. This information is usually free.

Q: Has Railroad Bill's missing loot in Alabama ever been found?

A: Here briefly is the story of Railroad Bill, whose real name was Morris Slater. During the early 1890's, he systematically robbed the Louisville and Nashville railroad in southwestern Alabama. It is not known how much money was taken, but the robberies went on for six years, so the amount was considerable. After about three years of the bandit's activities, the railroad put a reward of $1,250 cash on Bill's head. In 1895, Bill killed Sheriff Ed McMillan, then left Alabama. However,in 1896, he returned and started robbing trains again.

This continued for several months until one day Bill went into a store in Atmore where two men killed him. None of the money Bill obtained through his robberies was ever recovered. Since he couldn't put the money into banks and never married, there is no doubt but that the money was hidden somewhere between Atmore and Bay Minette, Alabama. Newspapers of the time carried accounts of Bill's robberies so there could be a clue in them.

Q: Could you give me several locations of hidden Civil War treasure in Alabama that I can do research on?

A: It would be impossible to give all the locations of Civil War loot that was hidden (in some manner) in Alabama from 1861 to 1865, or say if the stories are true. However, here are three sites worth further research:

The gold and silver treasure of the Whitfield family was buried on their farm near Demopolis during the Civil War.

A Confederate treasure of $900,000 in gold coins and bars is buried in the area of Birmingham.

Three wagon loads of gold and silver coins, worth $285,000, were buried on a fence line at Tallassee during the Civil War.

Q: Have diamonds eve been found in Alabama?

A: Yes, it is known that diamonds have been found, while panning for gold, in Shelby and Lee Counties, Alabama. Several of these stones were quite valuable. Write the Department of the Interior, Washington, D.C. 20240, they will send literature (usually free) on all the diamond locations in the United States.

Q: What is the story, briefly, on the Henry Nunez Treasure?

A: Henry Nunez operated a ferry on the Perdido river, about where US Highway 90 now crosses the river, about 16 miles northwest of Pensacola, and buried a fortune somewhere on the Alabama side near his house. Two caches were discovered, but rumors persist of a third, worth $110,000, that was buried during the Civil War.

Q: One of the largest treasures in the United States, called "The Treasure of Red Bone Cave," is supposed to be in Alabama. What is it and where is the general location?

A: If the story of the Red Bone Cave treasure is true, and there are several facts to support it, then this treasure is indeed one of the largest in the United States. Here is the basic story:

There are many theories about the incredible fortune hidden in one of the huge caverns that pock the limestone cliffs along the north side of the Tennessee River near Muscle Shoals, Alabama. The theory most historians endorse is that this is the final resting place of the fabulous lost trove of Hernando de Soto—which contains a substantial portion of the $200 million Inca treasure taken by Pizarro in Central America. Recently, in March 1971, a Spanish gold brick was found in the area as well as several Spanish coins.

One witness, a trapper, actually saw the treasure in the cave when he was, briefly, a prisoner of the Chickasaws in about 1720. As he descirbed it later, the gold and silver bars, neatly stacked, reached from the floor to the ceiling. Chests rotten with age had split open and golden "sun" medallions, golden animals with jeweled eyes, and Spanish coins were scattered on the sandy floor. After his escape from the Indians, the trapper searched for this cave but could never relocate it.

Q: I realize pirates are supposed to have buried treasure in several different places in Alabama, but could you give me a bona-fide location?

A: From old records there seems little doubt but that Jean Lafitte buried treasure near the mouth of the Tombigbee river. Coins and jewelry have been found along the beach that was identified as being of the time period in which Lafitte operated. This is a good location to spend a vacation in searching.

Q: I know Civil War loot was hidden all over Alabama, but I am interested int he large cache near Athens. Can you help me?

A: Here is a location where no find has been reported: In the closing months of the Civil War, a wealthy man named Hansen, assisted by other citizens, decided to turn over to the Confederate government a large amount of gold and silver coins that they had accumulated in various ways. Two wooden boxes measuring two feet by three feet by four feet were made to hold the coins. A plan to deliver the money to Montgomery, Alabama, had to be discarded because of Union forces in the area. It was decided to try to get this large shipment to Confederate General Hood in Columbia, Tennessee, where it seemed likely that the Confederates would win a major battle.

Hansen and two Rebel soldiers disguised as farmers started the journey but near Athens the heavily loaded wagon became mired in a bog-hole. While Hansen and the two soldiers were trying to remove the wagon four Union scouts appeared and demanded that it be unloaded, suspecting that it was loaded with arms and ammuniton. Hansen killed one Union soldier with a pistol, the Confederate soldiers killed two more but were themselves killed. The fourth wounded Union scout managed to escape.

Hansen used the horses to overturn the wagon so that the boxes of money went into the quicksand-like mud and sank. He then ran the horses around so that it would look like a Confederate patrol had camped there. Taking the wagon, Hansen made it to a Southern symphathizer's house to whom he told the story of the money in the bog-hole. As Hansen and a Confederate soldier were on their way later to obtain help in removing the money they were

3

both killed by a Union patrol. The Southern sympathizer was the only one left that knew the general location of the money. He searched unsuccessfully for it then moved to California after the war.

It would help your search if you could obtain an 1865 map that shows an old stream crossing, approximately four miles north of Athens, Alabama.

ALASKA

Q: Can you tell me of a tresure location in Alaska where I might find something?

A: Here is one you can look into:

Cortez D. Thompson, better known in Denver as "Cort," was the card-playing, free wheeling husband of Martha A. (Mattie) Silks, a madam during Denver's lurid red-light district days. Cort went to Alaska during the gold rush and is said to have accumulated a fortune of $50,000 in gold through crooked card games. When he became involved in a brawl with Jefferson Randolph (Soapy) Smith, Cort fled Alaska leaving his gold buried somewhere in or near the town of Chitina.

Q: Can you tell me, briefly, the history of gold in Alaska?

A: Alaska, the fourth largest gold producing state, yielded a total of 29,872,981 ounces from the first discovery in 1848 through 1965. More than half of this total was mined from placers in the Yukon region and the Seward Peninsula. The important lode-mining area has been in the southeastern part of the state, where mines in the Juneau and Dhichagof districts produced more than 7 million ounces of gold through 1959.

Q: I have heard of a location in Alaska called the Lake of the Golden Bar. Where is it located?

A: Among the most fascinating of Alaskan stories is the tale of the "Lake of the Golden Bar." According to the legend, in August of 1884, three prospectors started across the St. Elias Mountains near the Yukon River. One evening the men came to a small lake and saw golden rays beaming in the sunlight from a bar only a few feet from the shore. Throwing down their packs, the men swam to the bar and found it paved with gold nuggets.

The prospectors built a cabin and remained at the lake for weeks, picking up golden nuggets and stowing them in a nearby cave. They estimated their hoard at a half ton or more of the precious metal.

Indians, probably some of the fierce Tlinghet tribes who inhabited the area, burned the cabin and killed one of the parnters. The other two prospectors escaped but became separated. Without provisions, each started alone for civilization, finally reaching the United States.

One prospector was paralyzed as a result of the hardships he had undergone during the trip. The other started back for Alaska the next summer in the hope of recovering the gold the three had accumulated. He was never heard from again, and his fate remains a mystery. The lost gold laden river bar has never been relocated.

Q: I have heard of a treasure in Alaska called the Seal Pirates Missing Gold. Do you have any information on this?

A: It has been estimated that over one million dollars was buried on Adak Island by the captain of the Hitslap, a ship engaged in killing seals. Captain Gregory Dwargstof had taken this gold from the Sealing Association, then buried it somewhere on Red Bluff Hill on Adak Island in 1892. Several coins have been found but the $1,000,000 waits for some lucky treasure hunter.

Q: Where can gold be panned in Alaska? I need the names of rivers (other than the Yukon) where gold has already been found.

A: Gold has been found in the following rivers: Tanana, Chena, Porcupine, Kuskokwin and Kayukuk. If you search for gold along these rivers, be sure and check their tributaries. Sometimes this is where you find the mother lode.

Q: Is there a lost mine on or near the Prince of Wales Island group?

A: Yes, in the 1880's, a Frenchman would come to the general store at Howkan, on Long Island, one of the group that make up the Prince of Wales Islands, and buy supplies. He always paid with raw gold. The storekeeper tried to persuade the Frenchman to tell where he obtained his gold, but this request was refused. Finally several Indian trackers were hired to trail the Frenchman and learn where his mine was located. But somehow the miner always eluded them.

One day in 1889, the Frenchman boarded a steamer and was never seen again. A few years later one of the original Indian trackers found the Frenchman's camp and a sluice box, used in extracting gold, on the north side of Dall Island. This island would be a very good place to prospect for gold and search for this lost gold mine.

Q: Do you have the story of 18 sacks of stolen gold ore, hidden on the Harris River?

A: In 1927, a highgrader (this was a man who stole gold ore from a mine) secreted 18 sacks of rich ore in an abandoned mine shaft about three miles up and on the north side of the Harris river. This would be a good place to search, since the old mine shafts can probably still be seen.

Q: I need information on the Lukey cache at Nome, Alaska. Can you help me?

A: All I have on this is, a large amount of gold coins was buried near Nome in 1900 by a prospector named Silas Lukey, who was later killed before he could retrieve his cache. Write the Historical Society, Pouch G., Division of State Libraries and Museums, Juneau, Alaska 99801. They can probably help you since they have most of the early records concerning Alaska.

Q: Would you tell me where it is and what is the Lost Swede Mine?

A: Two prospectors named Olaf Swendson and Antonio Pauzza found nine mineral-bearing ledges in the Talkeetna Mountains, north of Anchorage, Alaska. They mined and carried out, on a packhorse, enough gold to retire them for life. The gold was so rich it could be chopped out with an axe.

Indians had known of this deposit for centuries. The two prospectors, having suffered untold hardships during their stay in the mountains, never returned to their gold bearing ledges.

Q: Is there a treasure ship that sank anywhere in Alaskan waters?

A: Yes, the British steamer Islander sank in Taku Inlet near Icy Point in the Stevens Passage, nine miles from Juneau on August 15, 1901. She was carrying over $3,000,000 in gold dust, nuggets and bullion. Several salvage attempts have been made on this ship and to date $240,000 has been brought up.

Q: Is there any truth to the lost gold of Thomas Bay?

A: No one can say if it is true until the gold is found. Here are the exact directions given by an aged Indian to a white man in 1900. "You go to the Bay of Death (Thomas Bay), camp on the right side of Patterson River. Travel up river about eight miles, turn up to high country. Walk one mile and a half. See half-moon lake there. I find plenty yellow stone there."

This location is near Patterson Glacier, with the half-moon lake nearby. This is one site that needs further investigation.

Q: What is the cache known as the Swede's Treasure?

A: This is a cache of $50,000 in gold coins that was buried in the 1890's somewhere between Dawson, Canada, and Eagle, Alaska. You can contact the Eagle Historical Society, Eagle, Alaska 99738. Perhaps they will have more information on this cache.

Q: I have heard of a lost mine in Alaska called the "Lost Sourdough Sailor's Mine." Can you help me on this?

A: The story is that a sailor named Shaun Casey jumped ship and started to prospect for gold on the Yukon River. Finding a fabulously rich vein, Casey packed out enough to last him for life. The location of the mine is believed to be near Fortymile, an abandoned frontier town at the junction of Bullion Creek and the north fork of Forty Mile River.

Type of tavern "Fat Patty" Cannon operated.

Marked tree may be symbol.

Replica of pioneer fort.

Rumored cache of coins near Ky. graveyard.

Silver bars found in Ariz.

Remains of old stage station.

Landmark may be treasure guide.

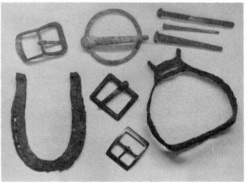

Found around N.M. stage station.

ARIZONA

Q: Have diamonds ever been found in Arizona?

A: When a meteor crashed onthe Coconino Plateau near Winslow, Arizona, an estimated 22,000 years ago, it created a crater 4,000 feet across and 570 feet deep, and scattered fragments over an area 2½ miles in diameter. It is believed that the main body of the meteor, perhaps a mile deep, may be worth as much as $20,000,000 because of the many diamonds it might contain.

Dolph Cannon, a mysterious character who lived the life of a recluse in the caves of Canyon Diablo, spent many years gathering meteor fragments, breaking them apart and extracting the tiny diamonds. When he appered in Winslow on frequent trading trips, he always carried a large roll of bills. Some thought this money was secured from selling the diamonds he recovered, but some believed he had entered the country with a supply of money which he kept cached in one of the caves.

One day Cannon disappeared and was never seen again in his canyon haunts. It was speculated that he had accumulated a fortune in diamonds and had left the country. But some ten years later, it was learned that he had been murdered, supposedly by someone attempting to force him to tell where his accumulation of meteor diamonds was cached. Many subsequent searches of Canyon Diablo revealed the caves in which the recluse had lived, but no diamonds or cash have ever been reported found.

Q: What do you have on a Mexican wagon load of gold in Cochise County?

A: A Mexican wagon train loaded with a vast amount of gold bound for Sana Fe, camped one night at the springs near what is now the near ghost town of Dos Cabezas. Because of the fear of robbery, the treasure was customarily unloaded each night and buried near the camp. Early on the next morning the camp was attacked by Indians, and only a seven-year-old boy managed to escape. Hiding in the bushes throughout the day, he was found by an aged Mexican, and finally made his way back to Mexico.

He made a search for the treasur esome 45 years later, looking for it between two hills where the dry bed of the Willcox could be seen to the west. Believed never found, the treasure is said to have included a life-sized gold statue of the Virgin Mary, a huge gold crucifix and a great quantity of gold dust and nuggets.

Q: Did an Indian trader bury a fortune in coins on the Little Colorado River near Flagstaff?

A: Indian trading post operator, Herman Wolf, buried his 30 years accumulation of profits, estimated at $250,000 in gold coins, somewhere near his store on the Little Colorado River, northwest of Leupp, just off the California/Santa Fe Trail near Canyon Diablo. A bucket of Mexican silver and 20 U.S. gold coins have been found in 1901 and 1966, respectively. It is but a small portion of Wolf's 1869 to 1899 hoard.

Q: Did soldiers, while fighting Indians, ever find gold in Arizona?

A: In the early 1870's a troop of soldiers from Fort Tucson were engaged in chasing a band of Apaches toward the Mexican border. If the Indians succeeded in crossing over into Mexico, they could not be brought tack to their reservation, so in spite of the terrific heat the soldiers pressed hard to overtake them.

Somewhere in the Baboquivari Mountains the troops were brought to a halt in a small canyon where a pool of cool water had collected at the foot of a rocky ledge. A second pool was found ner the first and the men split into two groups so that they could all gather around the welcome water. As one of the soldiers kneeled to fill his canteen, he noticed that the bottom of the pool was covered iwth bright shining pebbles. He scooped up a handful and showed them to his companions. Someone recognized the pebbles as gold nuggets and there was a wild scramble to fill their pockets. More nuggets were found along the ledge and the men, forgetting their tiredness, rushed madly to gather as many as they could before being ordered to resume the chase.

When the officer in charge gave the command to mount, several of the men expressed their desire to abandon the chase and collect the gold, but the order stood and their request was denied. As the soldiers rode away, the men tried to locate landmarks in their minds so they could return at a later date. But in a country where all the landscape looks remarkably alike, it takes an extremely experienced man to retrace his steps weeks or months later.

Eventually the fleeing Indians were headed off, captured and returned to Tucson, but the soldiers did not forget the gold. Some asked to be discharged but were denied. Two of the more determined, deserted, stole mounts and rode away to the south. they eventually found the ledge, but the water in the pools they depended upon had dried up. Nevertheless, they gathered all the gold they could carry, and loaded their horses so heavily that they were forced to walk and lead the animals. Before long the extreme heat began to take its toll nd they had to lighten their animals' burdens. Time and time again they discarded some of the gold. One of the horses fell and could not rise. Before long the second horse dropped of thirst and exhaustion.

When a search party found the deserters, one was dead and the other was dying. Before death claimed him he managed to gasp out an account of their experiences. It is said that several of the men who had seen the gold in the two "tanks" in the Baboquivari Mountians, made several searches after they were discharged from the army. If any ever found it the news was kept a secret.

Q: Do you have any information on George Casner's treasure, southwest of Flagstaff?

A: Not far from his cabin at the foot of Casner Mountains, and up the Mooney trail, just south of Flagstaff, George Mose Casner bored holes in several pine trees and cached hoards in his "tree banks," then plugged the holes. In one such tree near the cabin, $1,000 in gold coins were found, and another, in Beaver Creek Canyon, contained rolls of currency. it is also believed he buried five dutch ovens, each containing $20,000 in gold coins, in separate locations, but near each other in Sycamore Canyon, below Casner Mountain.

Q: Could you give me the names of several ghost towns in Gila County?

A: Here are a few you might want to check into. Information concerning their exact locations can possibly be obtained in the county seat.

McMinnenville, where once was the great Stonewall Jackson shaft mine; Los Adobes, a Mexican village now abandoned; Burch, which still is a small copper mining camp; Wheatfields, which once had a silver mill; Christmas; Chrysolite; Chilito, once a copper mining camp; Copper Hill,once a very important camp that even had a hospital; Nugget, once a silver mining camp; Pioneer; Bellevue; Armer; Catalpa; Little Giant; Reno; Salt River and Tonto.

Q: Has silver been found in Arizona?

A: Yes, this location dates back to the days of the Spanish Consquistidors. The fabulously rich silver deposits were found on top of the ground in balls ranging from ounces to several hundred pounds by the early Spaniards, Bolas de Plata and Planchasde Plata, and are located on the Mexican United States border near Nogales. Spanish records reveal the location as 10 to 15 miles southwest of present day Arivaca, near the Baboquivara Mountains. These mines are known as the Lost de Plata Mines.

Q: Do you have any inforation on John Glanton's hidden treasure?

A: John Glanton, ex-scalp hunter, operated a ferry crossing at the junction of the Gila and Colorado Rivers, near where Yuma is today, during the gold rush of 1849. He averaged $20,000 a month in cash and his accumulated hoard was buried at the base of a mesquite tree close to the junction of the two rivers. He was killed by Yuma Indians and his hoard of coins was never recovered.

Q: I have heard of two safes that were lost when a dam broke in te 1880's near Wagoner. Do you have anything on this?

A: A huge dam was built in a gorge on the Hassayampa river to provide water for placer mining. It collapsed during a cloudburst and the mining camp below was washed away. Somewhere downstream are two packed safes from the 1880's assay office and saloon.

Q: Do you have any information on the treasure hidden by the outlaw gang known as the "Benders?"

A: Upwards of $75,000 is beieve hidden around Cienaga Station by a gang of outlaws known as the "Benders." One night, the Apaches who had been getting the blame for the outlaws depredations, swooped down and eliminated the entire Bender gang. This cache has never been reported found.

Q: Is there a lost Spanish gold mine in Sants Cruz County?

A: This story was given to me by Thomas Penfield (deceased) who write the book "A Guide to Treasure in Arizona."

One of the first Mexican families to follow Father Euxebio Kino northward into Pimeria Alta was the Valverdes. They settled in the Santa Cruz Valley in the vicinity of Guevavi Mission (now only a mound of rubble, but its site can be located). With their ranch established, the Valverdes took to the surrounding mountains in search of gold which they knew the Indians had secured. They found gold at some spot lost to history and developed a rich mine. Employing Indian laborers, the Valverde mine produced enough gold each year that a large pack train was required to carry it out to Mexico. The Valverdes prospered immensely, and to store the wealth from their mine between pack trips to Mexico, they built a stone vault under the main house of the ranch.

Stinging under the harsh treatment of their Spanish masters, the Indians of Pimeria Alta rose in revolt in 1772, destroyed missions and ranches, and killed all white men who did not flee their wrath. Among the families managing to escape to Mexico were the Valverdes, but they had to leave behind their horses and cattle, and about a year's accumulation of gold.

Wealthy from the gold they had already sent to Mexico, the Valverdes never returned to Arizona. In time, all traces of the ranch were reduced to rubble, and today not even a low mound remains to indicate its site, which is probably overgrown with mesquite and cottonwood trees.

Q: I know the Alvord gang hid gold from a robbery in Arizona, could you tell me where?

A: $60,000 in gold bullion and coin was secreted somewhere along the old trail between Cochise and Wilcox, a few miles out of Cochise by this outlaw gang in the 1800's.

ARKANSAS

Q: Do you have any information on Black Cave or Spanish Treasure Cave?

A: Black Cave, or Spanish Treasure Cave as it is often called, is just off State Highway 59, between the towns of Gravette and Sulphur Springs in northwestern Benton County. It is thought to be the location of a mine excavated by the Spaniards during one of their early expeditions to this region. The cave was in the side of a cliff. Near it stood a large oak tree on which was carved a map.

In the early 1900's, a strange Spaniard appeared in the county, claming to have information about a treasure buried in the cave. Quoting $3,000,000 as the value of the treasure, he interested a group of men who formed an exploration company. After examining the cave for a distance of about a mile and finding nothing, the search for the mysterious Spaniard's gold was abandoned.

Q: Did Spaniards find silver in Arkansas during the 1540's?

A: When Hernando de Soto and his men left the Hot Springs area they journeyed southward along the Ouachita river. On the way, the Spaniards met a party of friendly Ouachita Indians near what is now the town of Camden. Noting the armlets and other ornaments of pure silver the Indians were wearing, De Soto demanded to know where the silver came from. The Indians shrewdly refused to disclose the source of the metal so De Soto ordered his men to search for the mine, especially along the Ouachita and its tributaries.

Old-time prospectors say that many years after De Soto's death, a band of Spanish adventurers located the Indians' mine and actually took silver from it, thus giving it the name of the Lost Spanish Mine. The Spaniards worked the mine for several years and before returning to Mexico, they sealed its entrance with a huge rock and destroyed their crude smelting apparatus.

Q: What is the story concerning eleven mule loads of gold near Hot Springs?

A: At about 1900, an Indian who gave his age as the late 90's, came to Hot Springs seeking 11 mule loads of gold. He was suffering from an illness and got around with great difficulty. He said that his father, Running Horse, had told him that the gold came from the Lost Indian Mine, which the Indians had recovered after the Spanish abandoned it. The gold was said to have been taken away by the Indians and buried along the old Indian Trail between Hot Springs and Lick Skillet, now called Hollywood. So far as is known, the aged Indian died before he could make his find.

Q: Is there really a diamond mine in Arkansas?

A: Yes, you can pay a fee and search for diamonds near Murfreesboro, Arkansas.

Q: I know Belle Starr cached money in Arkansas, but where is the general location.

A: Jesse and Frank James, Belle Starr, and her husband, Pony Starr, are said to have robbed a bank in Missouri of $34,000. Fleeing into northwestern Arkansas over the old Butterfield Stage route, they stopped at Shiloh (now Springdale) and made camp nearby. Several years later, an old woman appeared in Shiloh and spent some time there, apparently picking berries. She confided to an acquaintance that she was really looking for a cave in a bluff flecked with reddish colored rock. She said the cave entrance was closed with a large rock on which was depicted the figure of an Indian head and that another rock below the large rock bore the figure of a ladder. After several days of searching, without success, the old woman left and was never seen in the area again.

Q: Is there any truth to the story that there is a lost silver mine in northern Arkansas?

A: All anyone can do on any treasure location before searching, is try to obtain all the information they can, pertaining to it. As to the exact truth, no one can say for sure until the treasure is found. There is a local legend of a lost silver mine, called the Tabor Mine, on Tomahawk creek in Searcy County.

Q: Do you have a treasure location in Boone County that I can search for?

A: Here are two:

Near Coweta Falls is a cave under a large rock bluff. Mounds in the vicinity, many arrowheads and other relics indicate that the place was once the site of a large Indian settlement, and legend says that the Indians buried a large pot of gold in the walls of the bluff. The history of the cave, recorded in pictographs on a deerhide, was once brought by an Indian to Harrison, Boone County seat. Drawn on the deerhide were the falls, a spring, an Indian moccasin, a snake and a pot of gold. The symbols are said to have duplicated those on the walls of the cave. The Indian was never able to locate the gold.

Sometime during the Civil War, a party of four or five Indians were on their way from Missouri to Indian Territory. They traveled in three wagons and were said to be transporting a large quantity of gold and silver coins, thought to have been secured by guerrilla-type raids on midwestern communities. While passing through Arkansas, they suspected they were being followed by a party of white men. Fearful that they were about to be robbed, they stopped long enough to bury their treasure along Bee Creek in the northern part of Boone County. Burning their wagons over the spot, they continued on their journey, intending to recover the money when the country had quieted down. It is said that two of the original party returned years later, but failed to find the treasure.

Q: How many lost gold mines do you have information on in Arkansas?

A: Here is what I have:

A lost gold mine is located in the vicinity of the Caddo river, just south of Norman.

A lost Indian gold mine is near the Cosatot River.

The Lost Fred Conley Gold Mine is north of Bear Creek Springs.

The Lost Louisiana Gold Mine is southeast of Fayetteville.

The Lost LaHarpe Gold Mine is located near Morrillton.

A lost Indian gold mine is located in the vicinity of St. Joe.

The Spanish Diggings Gold Mine is near Elkins.

Q: Is there a treasure close to Fayetteville that I can check into?

A: William Flynn is believed to have buried a keg of gold and silver coins on his farm near Fayetteville, worth $115,000.

The Hermann family buried five jars of gold coins in separate locations during the Civil War, on their farm at Dutch Mills, southwest of Fayetteville. After the war they recovered three of the jars but failed to find the other two.

Q: Do you have any research on the Edgar Mason cache?

A: $62,000 in gold and silver coins was buried in an old washtub by Edgar Mason north of his cabin. He became crippled and senile and could never relocate the exact spot. The cabin site is about 20 miles east of Morrilton, Arkansas.

Q: Could you give me information on treasure locations within 100 miles of Pine Bluff?

A: Here are several:

Clarendon is an old river town in Monroe County. During the Civil War a Federal gunboat was on its way upstream with a safe full of gold to pay troops. The citizens of Clarendon (southern sympathizers) mounted an old cannon on the levee, overlooking the river. Concealing the cannon, they waited. As the gun boat swung inshore toward Clarendon the hidden men fired the cannon. It was a direct hit. The boat began to sink but the ship's crew shelled the town until the vessel disappeared. The ship's rusted smokestack was visible for years. It was an acepted fact that the safe, containing $150,000 in gold, was still aboard. So far as is known, the Yankee gold is still there.

A lost lead mine is believed to be two miles up from the mouth of Thodes Canyon. Chunks of pure lead have been found along the mountain sides in the area.

South of Little Rock, two boys killed an old man, R. F. Leigh, in 1933, in an effort to make him tell the location of his money, which they did not find. The two young men were later caught. The old man's money is rumored to be still buried where he put it.

A treasure known as the Spanish Galleons, supposedly consisting of $45,000,000 in gold bars is believed hidden near Kelso in Desha County.

Q: What treasure is supposed to be hidden near Avants Mountain?

A: Sometime after the Civil War, John Avants homesteaded a piece of land along the Cosatot River north of De Queen. The area can be located by Avants Mountain, named for the pioner settler. Some ten to twelve years later, a stranger came to Avants place and asked the assistance of the father and his several sons. The stranger was seeking a landmark, he said, near two springs close together. If he could locate the springs, he declared, they would lead him to a vast treasure. Father and sons all said they were thoroughly familiar with the vicinity but had never seen such a place as the stranger described.

Before departing in defeat, the stranger revealed that a party of Spaniards with seven jack loads of gold had once made camp near the two springs. Here they were attacked by Indians, and the Spaniards realized that they would have to dispose of their treasure if they were to escape with their lives. The gold—and one of the Spaniards who had been killed—were hastily buried. Then the Spaniards took flight, closely followed by the Indians. Only a few of them managed to escape to Mexico where they told their story. One by one the survivors died or were killed before they could return and recover the gold.

It was two or three years after the stranger's dejected departure that two of the Avants' boys happened upon a pair of springs exactly as had been described to them. They found spikes driven into some trees and strange markings carved on others. Not realizing the significance of the signs, they made no search for the treasure. Many years later, one of the Avants' boys happened to relate the story of the stranger to a nephew, who immediately recalled that he had plowed up a skelton near the twin springs. A search was then made for the buried gold, but without success. Subsequent searches for the treasure have been made over the years, but all have failed.

Q: Any possible source of information that you have on the lost treasures and mines of Arkansas will be greatly appreciated.

A: An excellent source of information on the lost treasures and mines of Arkansas is Fred W. Allsopp's "Folklore of Romantic Arkansas" published by the Grolier Society in 1931. You will need only Volume 1, and this should be available in any large library in Arkansas.

CALIFORNIA

Q: I would like to know if there is anything lost or buried near the head of the Gulf of California.

A: Dig into the history of Southern California and especially the Colorado River and you've got a surprise awaiting you. Some of the old boats that sank in the Colorado still show above the water at the confluence of the river and the Gulf, but these have been searched. There are others, not so well known, that justify a lot of investigation. Not all of the gold from mines in Arizona went across the desert, as many people believe. Lots of it went down the Colorado and not all of it got to its destination. There are several recorded caches of gold and silver along this river.

Q: Is there really a place called the Lake of Gold in California?

A: In the fall of 1853, Francis Lingard, well known around the Feather River mining camps, walked into John Carrington's store at Nelson Point and paid for $100 worth of provisions and supplies with a single gold nugget. At the gasp of surprise from the spectators, Lingard displayed several other nuggets of equal size. Lingard returned a second time to Carrington's store, made more purchases, and again paid for them with nuggets. But on his third trip to the store, Lingard made no purchases, and when the opportunity arose, he told Carrington that he was flat broke. This is the story Lingard told.

While looking for water in the High Sierras the year before, Lingard had found a small stream where it fell over a ledge into a lake. Kneeling at the lake's edge, he noted that the bed of the stream's channel, and for some distance out into the lake, was covered with large nuggets of pure gold. Obviously they had been carried there by the stream from some source above. All he had to do was pick the nuggets up.

That night Lingard made camp near the bed of gold, gathered all he could carry the next morning, and headed to Nelson Point for supplies. Along the way he found he had more gold than he could carry and cached most of the nuggets at the base of a large pine tree. When he returned to the region after his first trip to Carrington's store, he could find neither the lake nor the cache of nuggets at the pine tree. Nor could he find them on his second return, made necessary because he had to go to Nelson Point again for supplies.

Carrington believed Lingard and grubstaked him for a third search for the bed of gold. He continued the search until winter forced a halt. The following spring, Lingard led a party of half a dozen men in search of the golden lake and the cache of nuggets. After several weeks of failure, the search was abandoned. Lingard guessed that the heavy rains preceding the organized search had raised the level of the lake to a point where it concealed the bed of gold. The fate of Lingard is unknown, although some claim he was killed by the angry gold seekers. Although searches for Lingard's storied lake of gold have all but ceased, the region searched in the past has generally been in the lakes area of eastern Nevada County.

Q: Could you give me a little information on mercury and has it ever been found in California?

A: The chief ore of mercury (quicksilver) is cinnabar, mercury sulfide (HgS). Low grade deposits are often deceiving because a thin crust of the bright red mineral gives a false appearance of richness. Impure cinnabar may be dark red, almost black. Cinnabar forms near hot springs and is found near the earths surface in areas of recent volcanic rocks. The most extensive occurance in the world is at Almaden, Spain. Another large one is at Idria, Italy. Named after these ancient localities are the important California mines at New Almaden and New Idria. The mercury produced at New Almaden is credited with having made possible the tremendous gold productions that took place during the California gold rush immediately after 1848.

Q: Is there any truth to the story that $780,000 taken from a wealthy Chinaman is buried, in a safe, near Gonzales, California?

A: The only way to say that a treasure ever actually existed is to find it. There is a story that gold worth $780,000 in an iron safe, was stolen from Tom Sing of Monterey in 1875. It is believed to be cached on the banks of the Salinas River, at a point midway between Gonzales and Chualar. The men who buried the cache followed an old cattle trail and secreted the safe amid a group of pine trees a few hundred yards from the riverbed. They were killed by a sheriff's posse before the safe was ever recovered.

Q: I would like a treasure location in Modac County that I can search for.

A: In Modac County, north of Alturas near Chimney Rock, on the banks of the Piedra River, is the location of several sacks of gold dust and nuggets which were put into a narrow wash and then covered with dirt and rocks. This cache was hidden by the Ute Indians after they had attacked and killed five prospectors. This would be worth over $50,000 today.

Q: Is it possible that Errol Flynn ever hid any of his fabulous wages in California?

A: It is very likely that Flynn buried, or hid in some manner, thousands of dollars. It is known that he would put back "syphon off" money so that his lawyers, agents and ex-wives couldn't get it. He once hid $5,000 in his yard at Mulholland and couldn't find it later. He buried another $17,000 in Tapango Canyon, not far from Santa Monica, California. It has been estimated that well over $50,000 was hidden on his property in Jamaica.

Q: What is the story of the sunken ship Brother Jonathan?

A: Here is the story, briefly: The most publicized sunken treasure on the west coast is that of the Brother Jonathan. A large ship in her day, the side wheeler was loaded with 700 tons of freight (including 300 barrels of whiskey), 192 passengers, 54 crew members, and a reported $800,000 to more than $1,000,000 in gold coins and bullion when she sailed from San Francisco on July 28, 1865, bound for Portland, Oregon, and Victoria, British Columbia. Pushed along by gentle seas, she covered half the distance in good time.

On July 30, fighting heavy seas and high winds that developed overnight, the captain headed the Brother Jonathan shoreward as she neared Crescent City. Here he was to stop for the purpose of placing ashore a chest containing upward of $200,000 in gold coins for the pay of federal troops in the area. But coastal currents pulled the vessel off course, and a sudden cloudburst darkened the sky. Lurching wildly, the Brother Jonathan scraped her bottom on a submerged rock, opening a gash in her hull below the water line. Overloaded, the vessel went to the bottom in a reported 12 minutes. All but 19 of the 246 persons aboard perished.

Where does the treasure wreck lie? Almost certainly on one of the rocks of St. George Reef. There seems to be no evidence that her hulk was ever located.

Q: Has silver ever been found in California?

A: Here is a good location to check out. About 1932, a long freight train was slowly pulling across the desert between the way stations of Homer and Bannock. From the cab window of the locomotive, the engineer saw the figure of a man stretched out in the sparse shade of a bush along the rails ahead. Obeying the custom of trains stopping to give aid to people in distress in the desert, the engineer brought the freight to a grinding halt. The unconscious man, near death from heat and exposure, was taken aboard and hospitalized in Barstow when the train reached that point.

Without ever speaking a work, the man soon died. When his heavy knapsack was opened, police officials found 35 pounds of black silver ore. An immediate effort was made to trail the dead man from the spot where he had been picked up. Along the seven miles the trackers were able to follow, other pieces of the same ore were found, apparently discarded to lighten his burden. Eventually his trail was lost among the rocks in the mountains to the north, where he is believed to have made his find on the slopes of Homer Mountain. All efforts to locate the source of this rich silver ore have failed.

Q: I need a location of buried treasure in San Bernardino County.

A: In the late 1880's, a band of four or five outlaws held up the Bradshaw Route stage office in Beaumont, then known as San Goronio, and made off with $20,000 in gold coins. Heading west across the Moreno Badlands, they holed up in a mesquite grove on the outskirts of the little town of Moreno. On the following morning they were surprised by a posse and all were killed. No gold coins were found on their bodies or in the area searched, so it was presumed that the treasure was buried or hidden some distance away from where they made camp and were killed.

Q: Have diamonds been found in California?

A: When the diamond fields of America are mentioned, most people think of the well-known fields in Arkansas and North Carolina. They overlook California entirely.

Diamonds have been found in California in widely separated areas, and over a long period of time. The California State Division of Mines says diamonds were found in that state shortly after placer mining began in 1849. In the gold washings of the Mother Lode area, good diamonds were found, though the discovery did not create any widespread interest.

These diamonds were never traced conclusively to their source, but geologists believe they were washed down from the dark volcanic rock in the Sierra Mountains.

Q: What do you have on the Jim Savage treasure?

A: A fortune in raw gold dust and nuggets was placed in a flour barrel by Jim Savage who operated a trading post on the south fork of the Merced River. He secreted the barrel somewhere nearby and was shot to death in an argument. The site is in the area of Coarsegold.

Q: I read of an epidemic of smallpox that killed several Indians and when the dead were buried, treasure was put into the graves with them. Where is this site?

A: Indians buried gold, silver, weapons and a hoard of valuable artifacts with their dead when an epidemic hit their camp, killing over half the Indians. The site is above the Kern River on Greenhorn Mountain, near the Davis Ranger Station on the banks of Freeman Gulch.

Q: I have heard of a "river of gold" in California. Could you give me any information on this?

A: Yes, there is such a story with facts to support its authenticity. Found in the late 1890's, Earl Dorr's underground river of gold is believed by prospectors who knew Dorr, to be the richest deposit of gold in the world. This natural Fort Knox was blasted shut after Dorr discovered it and when he went to stake a claim, found that it belonged to someone else.

The cave has been explored recently and the "Spelunkers" reported finding the passage deep inside the cave where Dorr had blasted shut the only opening to this natural vault and burned his name on the rocks with his carbide lamp. This "lost river of gold" in a cavern, is believed somewhere along the California-Arizona border.

COLORADO

Q: I have heard that treasure is buried at the old Virginia Dale Stage Station in Colorado. Can you tell me where it is located?

A: On U.S. 287, about five miles south of the Wyoming line, is the small village of Virginia Dale. Just north of the town, also on U.S. 287, is the Virginia Dale Monument, which points to the old Virginia Dale Stage Station. Located about one mile east of the monument, this station was established in 1862, when Indian trouble in Wyoming forced the Overland Stage to operate through northern Colorado. The station is now in ruins, but easily located. It was once the hangout of outlaws, who are said to have left loot buried there in several places.

Q: Do you have a location of a lost Spanish gold mine in Colorado?

A: Almost everyone in southern Colorado, through five generations, has heard of the rich lost gold mine high in the nearby mountains. Spaniards came up from Mexico, a few years after the American Revolutinary War, and discovered, in a rugged mountain peak, somewhere near what is now the state's southern border, an immensely rich deposit of gold.

The Spaniards began preparations for mining, timbering a shaft, making melting ovens and a cleaning trough. They had little more than started taking out ore, when something, never explained, occurred to call them away. They ordered their peons and Indian slaves to cover the mouth of the shaft and remove all evidence of their labor. Then destroying their trail down the mountainside, the Spaniards and their train of horses, mules and servants, left that region forever.

There is no question that the mountains and mesas of Colorado are teeming with gold, but of the hundreds who have heard this legend, many have not believed it, thinking it wouldn't hold water. According to tradition, the Spaniards discovered the gold by accident, under conditions in which they were not equipped to undertake extensive and long continued mining operations.

Most oldtimers who have hunted this lost lode believe it lies in the rugged peaks rising west of Trinidad as the southern point and Walsenburg as the northern point. Trinidad is in Las Animas County; Walsenburg is in Huerfano County.

Q: Do you have any information on the Reynolds Gang's robberies in Colorado?

A: Jim Reynolds and his gang of outlaws stashed the spoils of several robberies in the mid 1860's, worth $175,000 in gold and silver coins, a short distance (4 to 10 miles) up Handcart Creek at its junction with the South Platte River in the Pike National Forest. Many substantiating clues have been found but the loot is still there.

The Reynolds gang also robbed a stage at McLaughlin Station near present day Como and took $63,000 in loot. The gang was surprised by a posse at Handcart Gulch on the north fork of the South Platte River where the money was buried. So far as is known the gang never returned for any of their caches.

Q: I know Colorado is rich in lost mine history. How many, according to legend, would you say are lost?

A: Here are the names of fifteen lost gold mines in Colorado: Yampa river mine in Moffatt County; Jim Baker mine in the area of Hahn's Peak; Lost Phantom mine near Steamboat Springs; Los Cache La Pundre in Black Mountain near old Fort Collins; The Lost Dutchman of Colorado; La Borgeaus; Dying Prospector; Bierstadt; Barber; Issac Alden; Slate; Brush Creek; Crazy Woman; Len Pollard; John La Foe; and the Brush Creek Lost Mine is near Eagle, Colorado.

All of these lost mines, and others, are located within the state. The actual number of lost mines within Colorado alone, is unknown. Since there are so many, I cannot give more locations because of limited space. However, historical societies and libraries might be of help to the interested searcher.

Q: I have heard of $15,000 taken in a robbery, that was hidden near Golden. Do you have any information on this?

A: On the road that leads from Golden to Lookout Mountain, $15,000 in loot taken in a 1960 robbery is buried. The man who hid the loot died of a heart attack after police broke the case.

Q: I heard a story of an abandoned gold mine being found, several years ago, near Salida, Colorado. Do you have anything on this?

A: Sometime between the years 1938 to 1940, three men were working on the highway a few miles north of Salida, Colorado. Work shut down for a few days, so they decided to do a little prospecting in the nearby mountains, just to kill time.

They stumbled on an abandoned mine which looked as though the owner had either met with violence, or just walked off without ever returning. They wondered what had actually happened. Some badly rusted tools were lying in the excavation. Had Indians killed the mine owner? Maybe some prospector had just made the excavation and failing to locate ore rich enough, had walked off looking for a better vein.

Something didn't add up, so the three workers searched for some kind of clue that might explain why the mine had been abandoned. There were no close graves to indicate the previous miner had died. Each tool was an antique, so whoever left them there, had done it a long time ago.

The three men took samples of ore. It looked good to them, however, an assay would soon tell whether it was worth working. For reasons unknown, the samples weren't sent to the assay office right away and when the returns came back, they proved the ore to be rich in gold.

However, not being miners and having good jobs which they did not want to lose, the men followed another highway project to another area and soon forgot about the gold. They later told the story but never searched for the mine.

Q: Is there a cache of highgraders gold ore in the Falls Creek area?

A: Near the head of Falls Creek in Falls Creek Valley, northwest of Durango, is a cache of 12 sacks of highgraded gold ore, each weighing 60 lbs., secreted by Hank Somers.

Q: I need information on a lost gold mine in southern Colorado, can you help me?

A: A prospector came into Durango, Colorado, one day in 1905, bowed down by the weight of a sack, full of extremely rich ore. He was in urgent need of some ready money and could not wait for the ore to be smelted and returned from the Denver mint as coin. After having the specimens of the ore assayed, he showed the assayer's reports and offered the sack of ore for sale. While displaying it to possible cash customers, he related how he came by it.

When prospecting in the Bear Creek region, of the eastern Nettleton district, he said, about 30 miles from Durango, he had accidently found the tunnel of an old mine. He realized some mystery hovered over the mine, for there was evidence that it had been abandoned suddenly, and probably involuntarily, many years ago.

All around on the floor, and on the ground outside the tunnel, were heaps of gold ore, of the same kind he had in the sack. The ore was very high grade, and the vein, which he did not take time to locate, being short of food, must have been only a few feet away.

Inside the tunnel were the skeltons of three men, bleached snow-white, and covered with dust. The prospector cagily avoided telling any land marks to get back to the tunnel.

The prospector was eager to sell the ore quickly so he could return to the mine with an adequate supply of provisions and the necessary equipment to make a thorough survey as to the extent of the gold vein.

In the late spring of 1918, Pedro Martinez visited Durango with a quantity of the same kind of ore, teeming with gold. He had the same story to tell; tunnel, skeltons and all. Before Martinez could return to the mine, or file a claim on it, he fell ill with the flu and died.

In the fall of 1938, a sheepherder brought into Durango a sack of gold ore which was recognized by old-timers as the same sort of rich ore brought in by Martinez. The sheepherder told the same tale, identical in all details.

Local people decided that a story checking three ways and standing up through so many years must have some basis in fact so several townsmen grubstaked the sheepman to lead them to the Three Skeleton mine. The expedition was quickly begun and as quickly abandoned. The guide could not find the way back. The mine is believed to be around Bear Creek where it flows through the eastern Nettleton district, about thirty miles from Durango.

Q: Could you tell me of a cache of gold in Pool Canyon, Moffat County?

A: In a canyon, possibly Pool Canyon, near the Utah border, is a rich gold mine, believed to hold 25 pounds of raw gold in its tunnel. The Hanson brothers who worked the mine were killed and they took the secret of the location to the grave with them.

Q: Has platinum been found in Colorado?

A: Yes, there is a story of lost platinum in Colorado, but this is all the information I have on it:

A large platinum deposit is located north of Dinosaur National Monument against the Wyoming border and not far from Utah. it is in an extremely rugged area and is supposed to be very rich.

Q: How many lost silver mines are there in Colorado?

A: No one can say for sure, but here are several with their general locations:

The Lost Clay Peterson Silver Mine is in the vicinity of Fort Collins.

A lost silver mine is in the area of Maybell.

A lost silver mine and cache of silver bullion is in the vicinity of Rabbit Ears Pass in Jackson County.

Hill's Lost Silver Mine is near Heeney.

There is a lost silver mine in the area of Fruita.

Alex Kalobetski had a secret silver mine in the Baldy or Silver Mountains north and west of La Veta. He mined his private lode from 1900 to 1936, when he was killed suddenly in an automobile accident.

A lost Spanish silver mine is close to Walsenburg.

White's Lost Silver Mine is in the area of Culebra Peak.

Q: Do you have any information on a train robbery that took place near Trinidad?

A: In 1890, a train was robbed of $250,000 in gold coins at a railroad station five miles west and ten miles north of Trinidad. The posse killed the outlaws and the money was never recovered.

CONNECTICUT

Q: Can you tell me about any lost mines or treasure books on Connecticut?

A: Try looking for a lost gold mine in the hills near New Haven. Three Italians obtained gold from the mine in 1900 and camouflaged it when they went away.

Gold ore has been found on rocky hillsides around Litchfield. You could try searching for a lead mine near Harwinton. The mine produced lead for the Colonies, but was lost about 1732.

I do not know of any treasure books on Connecticut. Your best bet would be to search county histories in public libraries for more information.

Q: Is there treasure buried on Pilot and Goose Islands near Norwalk, Connecticut?

A: For more than a century and a half, legends telling of Captain Kidd and other pirates burying treasure on Pilot and Goose islands have been circulated. It is doubtful whether pirates buried treasure on Goose Island, but they certainly did on Pilot Island.

Norwalk River steamboat pilot Captain Joseph Merrill, while walking among the sand dunes, found an unspecified number of gold coins on Pilot Island. Merrill did not make the amount known and it is not known if he found any other treasure, such as jewels.

There have been rumors of more pirate caches being found in recent years, but so far I have not been able to trace them down.

Nearby, on the Fort Molly Rocks, stands the ruins of a Civil War fort which should make interesting searching with a metal detector.

Q: Is there any treasure buried in the central part of Connecticut, say around Hartford?

A: A few miles south of Hartford is the reputed burial site of a pirate treasure. There is a well authenticated story that Captain William Kidd buried two chests of gold, silver and jewels somewhere in the area.

His sloop had been anchored for a while off Oyster Bay on Long Island but he slipped the hook one dark night, sailed to the mouth of the Connecticut River and continued upstream. On a small peninsula jutting into the river near what is now the town of Weatherford on the west bank, and the town of Naubuc on the east bank, Kidd went ashore. He selected a hillside and buried the chests.

Kidd then returned to Oyster Bay. His wife and a lawyer, James Emmot, whom he had sent for, came on board. On Emmot's promise to defend him against charges of piracy, Kidd agreed to surrender in Boston. Kidd was at first allowed his freedom, but on July 6, 1699, he was arrested and confined in chains. He was sent to England for trial and subsequently hanged.

Kidd had told Emmot where the chests were buried and asked him to dig them up for the benefit of his wife. However, Emmot waited until after Kidd's execution before trying to recover the treasure. He then found the markers but not the treasure. Thinking that Kidd had double-crossed him, Emmot revealed the secret location before he died.

Narrowing the search area down enough so that metal detectors could be used, requires careful research. The area was practically wilderness in 1699, with no towns or settlements of any kind—just primeval forests reaching to the water's edge. Also, the river has changed course many times. Figure these things out and proceed from there.

Q: Is there a location of lost jewelry near Norwalk?

A: Yes, on May 6, 1853, a New Haven Railroad train headed for Boston, raced blindly around a sharp bend, and shot through an open drawbridge outside Norwalk, Connecticut. It was the worst single American railroad disaster up to that time. Lost amid the smoking splintered rubble were the lives of 46 people and a fortune in fine jewelry worth a quarter of a million dollars (at that time).

One of those who died on that ill-fated journey was Thaddeus Birke, a jeweler from New York City. An Englishman, he had arrived in the United States only two months earlier. He had opened a shop as an independent importer-salesman-distributor for the London's Tawny Gems, Ltd. The firm supplied him with exquisite jewelry from France, Bavaria and of their own manufacture in England. He had been invited to Boston by shipping magnate Nigel Massey, who was interested in buying some jewels for his wife.

Two days before Birke was to leave, he packed away dozens of his finest specimens into two stout, leather-covered hardwood trunks. There were heavy gold bracelets, earrings, and finger bands all studded with precious and semi-precious stones. There were large brooches and pins of gold mounted with pearls and diamonds, with necklaces to match. Two pendants, one a 30-carat diamond and the other an oval slab of emerald, were included. Altogether, over $50,000 in exotic jewelry was packed in the trunks for the trip.

When Birke boarded the train, the two trunks were with him and were placed in the seat across from where he sat.

As the train neared a drawbridge across the Norwalk River, about three hundred yards from the South Norwalk Depot, the engineer failed to notice that the red spheres used to alert any oncoming train of the bridge's opening were out. Just as the tender prepared to close the bridge, the train thundered around the curve towards the opened bridge and the train plunged headlong into the river below. Birke and his two trunks were in the first passenger car which followed the engine, tender and two mail cars. All landed in the river below, killing some 46 people instantly.

The stacked debris was cleared from the channel, but most of the baggage and smaller chunks of wreckage were strewn through the river's depths, never to be recovered. Birke's twin trunks of bejeweled treasure were never found.

Q: What is the story of $50,000 being buried in Fairfield County?

A: All I have on this is that a man buried $50,000 worth of gold coins and jewelry near Greenwich. He was later caught and sent to the penitentiary. After being released he could never retrieve his cache because the police watched him. Contact the Fairfield Historical Society, 636 Old Post road, Fairfield, Connecticut 06430, or the police department at Greenwich. They could have more information of this treasure cache.

Q: I am a beginning treasure hunter and need help on any known treasure locations in the Connecticut area.

A: Here is one that has been searched for but never reported found: During the Revolutionary War, a Captain Lemuel Bates operated a tavern about one mile north of East Granby. The tavern was the headquarters for a group of patriots. One night 13 wagons en route from Boston to Philadelphia stopped at the tavern. They were heavily guarded and loaded with wooden boxes containing several million in newly-minted gold coins borrowed from France to aid in the cause of the Revolution. During the night the guards were overpowered by a band of Tories, who drove the gold-laden wagons away. The wagons were later found in a pasture a short distance from the tavern, giving support to the belief that the gold was hastily hidden nearby.

About a century later, Richard H. Phelps of East Granby wrote a book, generally accepted as factual, in which he stated that one Henry Wooster, a Tory, making his escape from Old Newgate Prison, fled to England. He wrote his mother from there that he had left a great fortune buried near East Granby Center, and that his companions in the crime had been killed by the Indians. The crime he referred to was supposed to have been the robbery of the wagon train.

Q: Would you give me a list of pirate treasures supposedly hidden in Connecticut?

A: Here are several: Pirate treasure is believed buried on Fishers Island off Mystic. Coins of the 1600's have been found on this island.

In Windham County it is said that the pirate Blackbeard buried a large treasure in the area of Brooklyn.

A crew member of Captain Kidd's is believed to have hidden part of his share of treasure in the vicinity of Middletown.

A Negro slave witnessed the burial of a pirate chest of treasure in the sand at Stratford Point in Fairfield County in 1699. He was afraid to tell about it until years later. He then could not find the exact spot.

On Money Island, in the Thimble Island group off Stoney Point, Captain Kidd is believed to have buried a treasure in the fissures of a large rock formation connected to the island. This rock is underwater at high tide.

Q: I am an underwater salvager, could you give me several locations of wrecks or sites that I can work on along the coast of Connecticut?

A: The steamer Larchmont sank in 1907. Some articles have been recovered by divers, but $150,000 remains underwater.

The supply ship Onondega sank in 1918, with dishes and other items of value aboard. The propellor sold for $6,000 when it was salvaged. Many other items have been salvaged, but there is more down there.

The privateer Defense sank in 1799, loaded with loot, just off Barlett's Reef. Some estimates say that as high as 500,000 continental dollars were aboard the Defense when it sank.

An unknown wreck was found by two divers and they recovered three silver bars just off old Saybrook. Might be more there.

The pivateer Hermione sank just off New London in 1782, with an unknown quantity of silver on board.

An unidentified frigate sank off Savin Rock. Clam diggers have found some of the brass cannon that were on board.

A French frigate sank off Thimbles Isles in 1875. The cargo consisted of $20,000 in gold and brandy.

Blackbeard landed at New Haven in 1716, and is said to have buried treasure near there.

Gold coins and a bracelet were found by boys on Tuxis Island in 1903 and there could be more pirate loot buried there.

Q: What is the story on $175,000 that is suposed to be buried near Litchfield?

A: I have nothing on this location. I suggest that you check the libraries in Litchfield or Torrington, Connecticut, for material on this site.

Q: Do you have the story of $50,000, called the Old Leatherman's Treasure?

A: One day in 1858, a leather-clad figure showed up in Harwinton, Connecticut, and although he made regular appearances over the ensuing years, it was quite some time before the populace learned his identity and the fact that he was carrying a large treasure. His name was Jules Bourglay and he was a Frenchman that had gone insane because of a crash in the leather business in France. He came to the United States and became an itinerant plumber. It wasn't until after his death that it was learned he had hidden $40,000 he had inherited from his family somewhere in or near a cave he used for a home, close by Lake Saltonstall, East Haven, Connecticut. Although it has been searched for, this cache has never been reported found.

DELAWARE

Q: I am a scuba diver and need information on any shipwreck I can search for in Delaware. Can you help me?

A: In October 1837, Boston citizens spilled their tea cups in shock as they read in the Boston "Times" that $60,000 to $120,000 in gold specie had been stolen off the packetship Susquehanna.

Within a short time of the robbery, the ship loaded with the stolen gold vanished, and it is believed to have gone down with its rich haul near the mouth of the Delaware River. No trace of the treasure has ever been found.

The Susquehanna was bound for Liverpool from Philadelphia that brisk October afternoon. At two o'clock, near Five Fathom Bank, off the Delaware Capes, a freshly painted black clipper fore-topsail schooner sailed in close to the packetship. Suddenly grappling lines were thrown and more than a dozen heavily-armed pirates swarmed aboard the Susquehanna. Within ten minutes they had loaded the gold cargo aboard their vessel and set sail.

The schooner had sailed a short distance when it mysteriously vanished for all time, apparently going to the bottom with its rich cargo.

Q: Would you tell me how many places pirate loot was buried in Delaware?

A: There would be no way I could tell all of the places where pirates cached something, but here are several locations where pirate loot is believed to be:

In 1699 pirate treasure taken in Madagascar was buried near New Castle.

On the banks of Blackbird Creek, in New Castle County, Blackbeard is believed to have buried a treasure.

It is rumored that Captain Kidd's $400,000 treasure is buried on the windswept island of Bombay Hook in Kent County.

A member of a pirate crew buried a treasure near a huge boulder between two trees on Kelly Island.

Loose coins that have been found along the beaches of Sussex County shoreline, indicate there could be treasure buried or sunk nearby.

The Great Sand Hill in Sussex County, at the tip of Cape Henlopen, is believed to have several pirate caches of treasure buried in it.

Q: Could you give me two or three treasure sites in Delaware that I can research? I am retired and free to travel.

A: Here are three you might like to work on:

There is believed to be a treasure buried on Fenwick Island.

In the area of Taylor's Bridge in New Castle County, is a treasure of gold coins known as the Dominique You. Local residents probably remember the story.

$100,000 in silver coins and bullion is believed to be about the Count Durant, a vessel that sank at the Indian River inlet.

Q: I have heard that many coins have been found along the Delaware Coast. Can you tell me in what area and explain where the coins came from?

A: After heavy easterly storms, many coins have been found—and are still being found—along the Delaware Coast near the Indian River Coast Guard Station. These coins are mostly Irish half-pence coppers of the period 1780-1783, although a few gold and silver coins have been found.

Though a half-pence isn't particularly valuable, it's tantalizingly possible you'll find other old coins. In 1972, diver Doug Keefe found over 100 coins in a few feet of water just offshore. Most were half-pence coins, but he also discovered five Spanish silver reals, fifteen Spanish gold coins, and several other silver coins.

It is supposed that the coins came from the strong-box of a vessel wrecked off the coast, and some believe the vessel to be the Faithful Steward, which foundered in 1785 while bound for Philadelphia. Her cargo consisted of barrels of English and Irish half-pence copper coins dated from 1740 to 1783. Local residents forgot about the vessel until 1930, when the Indian River Inlet was dredged. This changed the offshore currents and coins began washing up on the beach. Literally hundreds have been found since.

Recent information says that the Faithful Steward went down at about 38 degrees, 44 minutes and 40 seconds Latitude. It now lies at about 38 degrees, 39 minutes, and 30 seconds Latitude. The depth at the original sinking was 19 feet at low tide. At the present location it would be about 50 feet deep.

Q: Do you have any information on the "Patty Cannon" treasure?

A: From 1819 to 1929, "Fat Patty" Cannon and two male partners ran a tavern near Reliance, a small town on the Delaware/Maryland border. During this time the murderous trio robbed and killed dozens of wealthy slave dealers and buyers. When they were caught, over 37 bodies were found nearby.

When authorities finally got a lead on the murders and captured Fat Patty, the murderess swallowed poison to avoid trial. She had already disposed of one partner and the other was soon hanged.

Local residents estimate she cached between $75,000 and $150,000 in gold double eagles somewhere near her two-acre tract of land. Since 1910, local farmers have found over $12,000 hidden in small, scattered caches. Many more of the valuable double eagles could still be hidden nearby.

The site is close to the state lines of Maryland and Delaware but no one can definitely pinpoint its location. The location is claimed by various treasure hunters to be in both states.

Q: Could you give me, briefly, the story of the De Braak, a treasure ship that sank off the Delaware coast?

A: In May of 1798, the British privateer De braak sailed into Delaware Bay. She carried plunder from a years' sail in the Caribbean preying on Spanish shipping. During that time she had sacked five very rich galleons and was carrying gold, silver, and copper valued at some $15,000,000.

On the 25th of May, she was off Cape Henlopen about a mile from the light-ship in Old Kiln Roads and was ready to drop anchor. It was then that a squall occurred, filling her mainsail, capsizing her, and sending her to the deep.

It is estimated that she is still there in some fifteen fathoms of water, waiting for the right party to recover her treasure.

Q: Do you have any information on a treasure in Delaware in what was called the "Purgatory Woods?"

A: In an area bounded by White Clay Creek and St. Georges Creek, between Newark and a place known as Cooch's Bridge, is a marshy, wooded section known in 1777 as "Purgatory Woods." In these woods between charred roots and rotting vegetation is buried a large wooden bowl holding about a peck of English gold and a few silver coins which at today's prices would represent a small fortune. This money was hidden by Thomas Cooch in 1777, to keep it from falling into the hands of the British when they took over his grist mill, which they later burned.

Q: Is it true that a German submarine was sunk off the coast of Delaware by the U. S. Navy in 1945?

A: Naval records show that U (U-boat) 853 sank off Block Island, May 6, 1945, in 130 feet of water. The U-boat was depth charged by USN destroyer escort Atherton and frigate Meberly. This was the last U-boat sunk in the Battle of the Atlantic. $1,000,000 in mercury (worth a fortune today) was aboard. No record can be learned of the mercury being recovered.

Q: Did you ever hear of an area called the "Wedge" in Delaware and are there any treasure locations there?

A: The area known as the "Wedge" about 70 years ago, was located where Pennsylvania, Maryland and Delaware meet. This approximately 800 acres was a no-man's-land, claimed by both Pennsylvania and Delaware. Bootleggers, gamblers, moonshiners, et cetera all took advantage of the absence of enforced laws. There are several stories of money and jewelry being buried during the periods from 1893 to 1921 within the "Wedge." Here is where local research might pay off for you.

Q: Could you give me the map coordinates of where the Three Brothers treasure ship sank off the coast of Delaware?

A: The wreck of the Three Brothers was located at 38 degrees, 38 minutes and zero seconds in 1785. It is now believed to be at 38 degrees, 38 minutes and 39 seconds latitude. The original depth at sinking was 24 feet, and it now lies at about 28 feet.

Q: Could you tell me where I can obtain a map showing sunken ships along the coast of Delaware?

A: The most extensive listing of maps I know of is in the Library of Congress. Write: Map Division, Reference Dept., Library of Congress, Washington, D.C. 20540. Tell them what you're looking for.

DISTRICT OF COLUMBIA

Q: Can you tell me if there is any treasure buried in Washington, D.C.?

A: There is a story that a treasure of $25,000 is buried somewhere on the grounds of the official home of the commandant of the U. S. Marine Corps in Washington, D.C. Often referred to as the oldest official residence in Washington, work was begun on this house in 1804 and completed a year later. In those days each government department was its own banker, and the Marine Corps normally kept about $50,000 in its military chest, guarded by two marine sergeants. When these two sergeants were suddenly called to duty to defend the city from British attack in the War of 1812, they hurriedly buried the residue of the funds—about $25,000—and hurried off to war. Both were killed, taking with them the secret of the treasure.

Q: Is there a lot of graft money hidden in our nation's capitol?

A: There are several stories of political payoff money and campaign funds being hidden in the District of Columbia. These rumors would have to be checked through newspaper files, police reports, national records, et cetera, since I am sure the polititicians involved are not going to tell about them.

Q: Did Bernarr McFaddan ever hide any money around Washington?

A: There is a story that McFaddan buried $100,000 in a metal container on the banks of the Potomac River, in the District of Columbia. This is highly possible since McFadden was a rich man for his time. He owned "True Story" magazine and its subsidiaries. For some reason, unknown to his family, McFaddan distrusted banks and hid large amounts of money in different states. His widow has estimated that her husband might have concealed as much as $6 million to $10 million. Rumors would indicate that approximately $1,000,000 of McFaddan's hidden money has been recovered on Long Island, New York, alone. It could pay a treasure hunter to research the New York and Washington, D. C. newspapers on the life of Bernarr McFaddan.

FLORIDA

Q: I would like to know more about the story of a cache of $500,000 in gold bullion reportedly buried in the Everglades of Florida by a group of Confederate soldiers.

A: Rumors of this buried gold have persisted for more than a hundred years, and many searches have been made for it. Here is the story:

In 1865, a Captain Riley and a detachment of Confederate troops were sent from Kentucky with a half-ton of gold bullion to be transported to Ft. Mead, Florida, and then on to Havana, Cuba. As Union troops advanced through Florida, the Confederate band fled into the Everglades, buried the gold at their last camping place and continued their flight.

In September, 1944, it was reported that State Game Officer L. P. Harvey led a small party into the Everglades and located what they believed to have been the last camping place of the Confederates, almost hidden by undergrowth, but identified by Confederate relics found there. The site was described as being located at the point of an angle formed by running a line 40 miles due west of Ft. Lauderdale, and another line due northwest of the Miami City Hall until it met the first line.

This would place the treasure on a Seminole Indian reservation in west central Broward County.

Q: Was the Ashley gang treasure in Florida ever found?

A: If this treasure, amounting to $150,000 in currency, taken by the Ashley's in a series of Florida bank robberies in the 1920's, was ever found it was not publicized. It is commonly believed in Florida that the Ashley's had a secret hideout on an island in the Everglades, and that their loot was hidden there.

Q: Could you tell me of a treasure buried by the pirate, "Billy Bowlegs" Rogers, in northwestern Florida?

A: It is believed that several millions of dollars worth of gold plate and silver bullion were buried on the north side of an island (could be Santa Rose) in Choctawhatchee Bay by Rogers in 1838. Another cache is supposed to be buried on the nearby mainland.

Q: I live in St. Johns County, Florida, near St. Augustine. I have a metal detector and would like to know some sites where I can use it.

A: There are several good sites around St. Augustine where, with a little research you might have some luck. The Galleon Treasure Fleet, consisting of 11 Spanish ships that sank in 1714 off Matanzas Inlet, the Richard Crowe treasure that is believed buried in St. Augustine, the Fort Marion treasure in St. Augustine, and the Gasparilla treasure on Anastasia Island.

Q: Do you have any information on the Calusa Indian treasure in Florida?

A: Yes, Calusa Indians salvaged treasure from some Spanish galleon wrecks and stored it in secret hiding places. The chief of the Calusas, Carlos, traded the precious gold and silver for trinkets with the Spanish on the west coast of Florida at the present-day site of Charlotte Harbor. The Calusa tribe was killed by the Spaniards and the treasure sites, somewhere in the harbor area, were never revealed.

Q: Could you give me information on several shipwrecks along the coast of Florida?

A: Here are four: North of Fort Lauderdale and on the Hilsboro Rocks, several treasure ships were lost. One of the many unidentified wrecks have already given up a cache of silver bars to some divers.

An unidentified wreck carrying war cargo worth $5 million, sank prior to World War II, five miles east of Pompano. It is resting in 65 feet of water.

Treasure from a Spanish galleon wreck was buried by the survivors about 13 miles north of Fort Lauderdale along the beach.

An unidentified vessel carrying a load of $5 million in silver bars was reported wrecked off the New River Sound in Broward County.

Q: I know Florida is rich in sunken treasure, but can you give me a location on land, near where I live, that I can search for.

A: Try this one: The Seminole Indians are supposed to have buried seven pony loads of English and American coins, plus other booty, in a few feet of swamp silt, on the extreme Florida and Georgia border near the Chattahoochie River in what is now Jackson County. These Indians were trying to escape Andrew Jackson's soldiers during the seminole War in the 1830's.

Q: Would you give the story, briefly, of the sinking of a Spanish convoy in 1715, off the coast of Florida?

A: During the early years of the eighteenth century, it was the custom of Spanish ships laden with gold and silver mined in Mexico and Peru to gather in mid-summer off the Florida coast near Sebastian Inlet, about 40 miles south of the present-day space center at Cape Kennedy.

The purpose of this rendezvous was to form a convoy for protection against attacks from pirates. Undoubtedly some late arrivals in July of 1715 delayed formation of the fleet, and it was not until the start of the hurricane season that the homeward journey of 11 galleons was begun. Setting sail on July 13, 1715, the Spanish convoy was hit by a violent hurricane that sank all but one of the ships and scattered fabulous treasures on the ocean floor some 2000 feet from shore.

Q: What can you tell me about the ghost town of St. Joseph, Florida?

A: St. Joseph was once the largest town in Florida, and is notable among Florida's several ghost towns as having been abandoned almost overnight.

The town owed its existence to a bitter dispute over homestead claims. Between 1804 and 1811, the Spanish granted a company of Indian traders a large tract of land on the Apalachicola River and St. George Sound, which included the settlement of Apalachicola. When the United States acquired Florida in 1822, a legal battle over the validity of the title developed. the U. S. Supreme Court upheld the company's claims, making squatters of those who held property there. Many refused to come to terms with the company and founded a new town site on St. Joseph Bay and named it St. Joseph. The first constitutional convention of Florida was held there, and the town boomed.

In 1841, a ship from Africa tied up in St. Joseph and brought yellow fever. Within a matter of weeks, three-fourths of the estimated population of 7,000 had died. Panic stricken survivors abandoned their homes and fled. Ships avoided the port and hotels and business houses closed. For three years, the town was deserted, with only a few venturesome fishermen daring to approach the spot.

In 1844, a hurricane and tidal wave leveled the spot. Devastating storms followed at intervals until, bit by bit, all remains of the town were obliterated. Today, the site is covered by a jungle growth of pines, matted creepers and palmettos.

23

Q: I would like information on a man named Thompson that cached a large amount of money in Tampa, Florida.

A: In the early 1920's, Thompson, a lumberman from Michigan, retired and settled in Tampa. Through shrewd investments he is believed to have accumulated a large fortune. After he died in 1928, his wife could never find his money. Thompson apparently buried it somewhere near his home on Zake Street in Tampa.

Q: Do you have any information on a sunken ship near Boca Raton, Florida?

A: Here is a quote from the booklet, "A Romance of the Past, a Vision of the Future."

"Many years ago a fisherman was cruising over the outer reef off Boca Raton Inlet and saw what appeared to be an ancient ship, partly covered with sand. After telling the story to his friends, a company was formed and a diver engaged.

"There, lying on the bottom of the sea in about sixty feet of water, they located the wreck of an old ship, undoubtedly uncovered by the hurricane of the previous fall. The diver went down and chipped a hole in the hull of the ship and brought up what appeared to be a bar of iron, reporting that the wreck was filled with those bars.

"A more careful examination proved that the bar was pure silver. Additional equipment was secured and plans made to remove the entire treasure, but severe weather prevented immediate return and they were forced to wait for a calm sea.

"When the old ship was finally located once more, it had sunk deeper in the sand. Dynamite was used in an attempt to break up the wreck, but this blast only caused it to sink deeper, and it was finally swallowed up and no more silver was obtained.

"All traces of the wreck had long since disappeared, and unless it may be uncovered by another storm, somewhere off Boca Raton, buried in the depths of the ocean, is a fortune that may never be recovered."

Q: What do you know about a treasure supposedly buried on Amelia Island?

A: Amelia Island, off the east coast of Florida, just south of the Georgia line, was for years, a convenient pirate rendezvous. Like all such areas, local stories of pirate treasure abound, and it may be true in the case of Amelia Island. A few gold doubloons have been picked up from time to time and it is presumed by natives that about $170,000 worth of treasure has been recovered after much digging.

Amelia Islanders point out that more than one poor family has suddenly stopped digging and started to live like kings. Also there are those who insist that more treasure is to be found on Amelia Island.

Q: Where in Florida is the best place to find sea shells that I can sell for money?

A: Off the Florida coast, at Fort Myers, there is an island known as Sanibel. On sunshiny, still days, the island's long, sandy beaches are largely deserted. But let it turn stormy and the wind kick up a surf, and the beaches are suddenly thronged. Surfers? No, shell hunters. And what they find is worth real money!

It isn't too likely these shell hunters of Sanibel will find one of the most valuable of all shells, the Glory-of-the-Seas, worth about $1,000 because the home waters of this Cone shell are the East Indies rather than the West.

So precious are the shells to be found on Sanibel's beaches that collectors, agents and dealers flock from all over the world to the island's Shell Fair and Auction each spring.

Treasure can come in many forms other than silver and gold, and the beaches of Sanibel are free to all.

Q: Have coins been washed up on the shore at Honey-moon Island?

A: Yes, coins are washed up on the beach on the south shore of Honey-moon Island and on the shore at the north end of Caladesia Island. Both are located a little north of Clearwater and the finds indicate either an offshore wreck or treasure chest.

Q: Are there any treasure sites near Coopers Point, south of Tampa?

A: Cooper's Point, north of the Courtney Campbell Causeway, was once a pirate camp in the late 1700's and markings on trees and rocks in this area tend to indicate treasure is buried nearby. (This is a location where a knowledge of treasure symbols could help.)

Old Ct., stone building.

Early fort or trading post.

Old iron smelter in Maryland.

Author with jar of found coins.

Old reconstructed inns in N.C.

Old graveyards may be markers pointing to treasure buried nearby.

GEORGIA

Q: I have heard the story that the Spanish brought Aztec gold to Georgia. This is supposed to be near Lone Mountain, do you have anything on this?

A: Here is all the information I have on this location: In early times Stone Mountain was known as "Lone Mountain" and was so called by the Cherokee and Creek Nations. According to the present Chief of the Cherokee Indian Reservation in North Carolina, there is a fabulous Spanish treasure amounting to many millions in gold bullion concealed or buried in the vicinity of Lone Mountain. According to his story, the Spanish, loaded with many wagon loads of Aztec gold from Mexico, were camping near Lone Mountain one night when they were suddenly attacked by a large group of Indians who massacred them to the last man. The supplies and provisions were taken by the Indians but the gold was concealed by them somewhere near Lone Mountain.

Q: Did the Indians have any gold when they were forced to leave Georgia, Alabama and South Carolina in 1838? Where are some likely locations to search?

A: When the Indians left in 1838, the United States Army estimated that they buried or hid in caves $50,000,000 in gold. Most of this was never retrieved because for years the Indians were kept on reservations and not allowed to return. Almost every county in the northern half of Georgia has numerous stories of lost gold. Contact the county clerks or historical societies in this area. They almost always have information on local history.

Q: Where was the first "gold rush" in Georgia and how much gold has been mined in the state?

A: No one can say for certain how much gold was been panned or mined in Georgia. The following information is on a historical marker at Auraria in Lumpkin County: "Auraria, (gold), in 1832 the scene of Georgia's first gold rush, was named by John C. Calhoun, owner of a nearby mine worked by Calhoun slaves. Auraria and Dahlonega were the two gold towns in the United States before 1849. Between 1829 and 1839, about $20,000,000 in gold was mined in Georgia's Cherokee County. From Auraria, in 1858, the "Russell Boys," led by Green Russell, went west and established another Auraria near the mouth of Cherry Creek, that later became Denver, Colorado. Green Russell uncovered a fabulous lode called Russell Gulch near which was built Central City, Colorado, called 'the richest square mile on earth.'

Q: I am told that people are still looking for Confederate gold that is supposed to be buried at Washington, Georgia. Can you tell me anything about it?

A: There is a story that a Confederate treasure of gold was buried in Washington. This story doubtless originated from the fact that Jefferson Davis held the last meeting of the Confederate Cabinet there on May 5, 1865. The meeting took place in the old Heard House, the site of which is now occupied by the Wilkes County Courthouse, on the public square. When this courthouse was built in 1904, an extensive search was made on the site for buried Confederate gold, but so far as is known, nothing was found.

Q: Is there any truth to the story that De Soto buried treasure in America, and where?

A: The only treasure De Soto is known to have found in America was pearls —some 350 pounds of them. Like all other Spanish explorers in the country, De Soto was looking for gold. At the Indian village of Cofitachequi, along the Savannah River in Georgia, when De Soto demanded gold, he was shown the strings of pearls which were used as decorations in a big house where the mummified bodies of the dead were kept. These were not fine pearls, as the Indians used fire in opening the shells, but the explorer helped himself to 350 pounds of them.

As the burden of carrying 350 pounds of pearls became too great, they were buried somewhere along De Soto's route through Georgia.

Q: I have heard of a location in Georgia where several Confederate cannons were thrown into a river. Could you tell me where this site is and how many guns there were?

A: When General Robert E. Lee surrendered on April 9, 1865, the Union Army pushed on to the last Confederate stronghold at Columbus, Georgia. After the ensuing battle, which the Union won, all Confederate equipment was destroyed. This included 60 cannons that were thrown into the Chattahooche River, on April 16, 1865.

The existence of the guns can be verified by the Georgia Department of Archives and History. A detailed listing of the guns can be obtained from the federal archives in Washington, D.C., and from military maps used by General Winslow, the approximate sites where the guns were dumped can be determined.

The sunken cannons of the Chattahoochee are probably worth $200,000 at today's prices.

Q: Can you tell me something about the Jeremiah Griffin Treasure in Georgia?

A: About 1830, the property of the Columbia Gold Mines near Thompson, in McDuffie County, was acquired by Jeremiah Griffin, a wealthy plantation owner. He set up Georgia's first stamp mill and took out $80,000 in gold bullion during the first year of operation. Before his death by accident in 1847, Griffin had accumulated a sizable fortune in gold, and a search was made for $100,000 he is thought to have buried along a creek bank near the town of Little River, in Wilkes County. It is believed that this treasure has not been recovered.

Q: Someone has told me that there is a tunnel in downtown Columbus, with treasure in it. Is there any truth to this?

A: I don't know how true the story is, but such a story does exist. At 1316 Third Avenue, in Columbus, is a house with two large, black lions guarding the doors. This is known as the Lion House to tourists, but is better known locally as the Ralston-Cargill House. It is believed that a subbasement led to an underground tunnel that emerged on a lake once occupying the present site of the Racine Hotel.

According to a story, a drove of mules was once hidden in this secret chamber during the Federal occupation of Columbus in 1865, and that a considerable treasure was concelaed here at the same time and never retrieved. Whether there is any truth to this story is anybody's guess, but in the 1870's an appreciable hoard of gold coins was found in a window casing of the old house. The site would certainly bear checking out.

Q: Could you tell me some of the areas in Georgia where gold has been found?

A: A slave owned by Major Logan of Loudsville discovered gold on the Lovelady place in White County in 1828. At about the same time, another slave discovered gold on Bear Creek near Dahlonega and there is some evidence that the Spaniards had mined gold in White County.

There are several areas for gold panners in the Dahlonega region. Other places to pan are located in Dawson County, four miles south of Dawsonville, in McDuffie County, 11 miles northwest of Thompson, and in Cherokee County, four miles west of Hot Springs and seven miles south of Canton.

Gold has also been reproted in Bartow, Fannin, Newton, Paulding, Rabun and Walton Counties.

Q: Do you know of any treasure locations in Georgia?

A: Here are a few that with searching and local researching, can keep you busy for a while:

A huge store of gold bars are buried in a cave, located behind a waterfall and partially submerged in the water, on the north bank of the Coosawattee River to the east of the bridge near Fort Coosawattee, in the vicinity of Carters Quarters, just off Highway 411.

$18,000 in currency, contained in fruit jars, is buried near the McKnight trailer house, about five miles south of Ellijay.

A rich Indian silver mine is located at the mouth of Flat Creek near the Coosawattee River in Gilmer County.

A store of Indian gold is secreted in a cave close to the confluence of Scarecorn and Talking Rock Creeks. In other caches in this area, Indians hid many pots of gold before leaving the land.

Q: An Indian named George Welch is said to have buried a treasure in Georgia. Can you tell me where this treasure is supposed to be?

A: George Welch, a Cherokee tribal chief, lived on Sitting Duck Creek near the Etowah River in the extreme northeastern corner of Forsyth County. He owned many slaves and a lot of property, including a tavern that stood on the old Alabama Road and very close to the Forsythe-Cherokee county line. When the Cherokees were removed from this area, Welch is said to have left behind a sizeable fortune buried near the tavern, which was destroyed by fire in 1930.

Q: Could you tell me anthing about the Pumpkinsville Creek Treasure or mine in Bartow County?

A: On May 29, 1938, the Atlanta Journal Sunday Magazine published the following story: "Gold is alleged to have been buried on the C. M. Jones Farm on Pumpkinsville Creek. As late as 1932, Indians were still coming back to search for this buried treasure and gold mines. David Quarles is the only white man said to have seen the Indian mines and he was blindfolded on the way to the place where the Indians led him." The gold mine or treasure is believed to be in Alatoona Cut in Bartow County.

Q: Have diamonds ever been found in Georgia?

A: Yes. Likely places to search, or pan, for diamonds are around the Harshaw Mine area in the Acooche Valley of White County, Morrow Staion area in Clayton County and the Gainesville area in Hall County.

HAWAII

Q: Do you have any information on a cache of coins buried near a volcanic cone close to Maui, Hawaii?

A: In 1883, a Japanese schooner put into Maui to take on water and supplies, and three young sailors jumped ship and later robbed a runner that worked for several local gamblers. After taking the money, the three men went inland to the lava beds. At the base of a conical upthrust called a "spatter cone" they buried the coins. Making three maps, one for each of them, the three returned to Maui, where they tried to get into one of the local criminal gangs.

Realizing that such amateurs could cause them trouble, the gang leader had two of the ex-sailors killed and the third one died a little later. One of the maps was found on the third sailor, but search as they might, the authorities were never able to locate the coins (or tokens).

Worth only a few dollars in 1883, today the coins are extremely rare and sought after by collectors—each one worth as much as $500.00. No record exists indicating discovery of the coins and apparently the cache near the spatter cone in Hawaii, worth $350,000, still waits.

Q: What is the largest treasure in Hawaii that you have information on?

A: There is one very big and important treasure in the Hawaiian Islands. This treasure is the burial chamber of Hawaii's most famous ruler, King Kamehamaeha, who died about 1810. It's a vast treasure of jewels, pearls, diamonds, and rare artifacts. It is reported to also contain his warrior robes ornately decorated with feathers from two colorful and now extinct birds.

Legend has it that the burial is in a cave in a rain forest. Not much is actually known about the circumstances of his burial, except that when he died, there was a great ceremony; then a great burial party departed to bury their beloved king in a secret place.

Also, it's possible that he wasn't buried in a cave as some think, because many Hawaiians buried their dead in hand-dug underground chambers. Much research will be required for this one. A good place to start might be the Bishop Museum on Oahu; also, the History and Archaeology Departments of the University of Hawaii.

Q: Do you have the story on the sunken $100,000 in gold coins that was aboard the ship Spec, which went down near Kauai?

A: In the spring of 1846, a large order for opium was placed from San Francisco by an underworld group, to runners in Singapore, China. The opium was loaded aboard the schooner Spec in Singapore and she set sail, headed southeast. She sailed for the Hawaiian Islands, which were then independent, and docked at Honolulu on the island of Oahu. The evening after her arrival the transaction was completed and the pure opium was secretly off-loaded and transferred to another ship for the journey on to San Francisco. At the same time a shallow-draft boat pulled alongside carrying a chest of gold coins. Hefting the chest onto the Spec, the sailors locked it securely in the captain's cabin.

The next morning the Spec set sail. She made it as far west as the island of Kauai before a storm broke. Desperate for shelter, the captain sailed the ship into the Kaulakahi Channel, between the islands of Kauai and Niihau. However, the Spec quickly broke up in the twisting water and sank in 700 fathoms, taking her gold to the bottom along with most of the crew.

Two men somehow managed to struggle ashore and made their way back to Honolulu. It is certain that $100,000 in gold was aboard the Spec when she sank, but if the gold was in U.S. $10 coins, as claimed by the two surviving seamen, then the treasure could be worth up to 500 times its face value.

Q: Where would be the best placed to "coin shoot" beaches in Hawaii? Why is so much jewelry lost on the beaches?

A: Almost any beach in Hawaii is worthwhile to search becasue of the large number of tourists that visit there every day. The best time to hunt is right after a severe storm. The reason so much jewelry is lost is because when most people go to Hawaii they are going to take their best jewelry, and are not going to leave it in the hotel room, but are going to wear it. Also, the first thing many people do when they arrive at the beach is to put on suntan lotion. A combination of the lotion and saltwater causes the skin to shrink. Before they know it, they have lost their rings and other valuables in the water. When a piece of jewelry hits the sand it's gone. The sand is so fine that anything dropped on it sinks right in.

Here are the names of several beaches you might like to visit: Waikiki, Ala Mona, Magic Island, Diamond Head, Hanauma Bay, Sandy Beach, Kailua Beach Park, Punaluu and Sunset Beach. All of these sites could prove profitable.

Q: I heard that several ancient graves were found on Hawaii a few years ago. Do you have any information on this?

A: During the 1940's, a burial site was found near the Cinder Cave of lava beds south of the fishing village of Makena below the volcano Haleakala. The graves contained crude stone relics, weapons and tools. More burial sites are believed to be in the area.

Q: Did an English ship ever sink off the Hawaiian coast?

A: Yes, the English priate ship Content sank on the reefs off Palemano Point near the entrance of Kealakekua Bay. It is known that the ship was carrying treasure, but the amount is unknown.

Q: Are there any ghost towns in Hawaii?

A: There are several extinct villages scattered throughout the Hawaiian Islands, but the only known ghost town is Hoopuloa on the southwest coastline of Hawaii.

Q: Is there a burial site of the early kings of the Hawaiian monarchy, and is there a treasure connected with it?

A: It is believed that the Cave of Kings Treasure is hidden somewhere on Ford Island near Oahu. This cache has been searched for several times but there is no report of its having been found.

Q: Was there a large treasure aboard the ship Christopher when she sank on the Maro Reef?

A: When the new regime of Sun Yatsen took over China in 1912, a member of the old Ch'ing Dynasty, Yuan Hsi knew he would have to get his two sons and his immense treasure out of China. Contacting the captain of the Christopher, a four-masted schooner, Yuan made a deal to have his twin sons and several million dollars worth of art treasures moved out of the country.

After terms were reached, the large treasure and two boys were loaded on the Christopher at Shanghi, China, for the trip to the United States. During a storm, the Christopher was forced to try and make it to Hawaii. As they approached the group of islets of western Hawaii the storm increased and swept the ship onto the sumerged shoals of Maro Reef.

The Christopher washed off the shoals and quickly sank in deep water, taking her incredible oriental treasure with her. Ten members of the crew survived and made their way to Laysan Island, where they were later rescued. These men related the experience, exhibiting jade ornaments they had pilfered before the sinking, to prove their story.

The waters off Maro Reef and Laysan Island can be treacherous, at best, and are shark-infested. There is no known record of the wreck or treasure ever having been found.

Q: Do you know of any treasures buried in Hawaii?

A: Indeed, there are some treasures in Hawaii:

1. There is the treasure of Alfred Devereaux, a notorious character who had run opium for a

Chinese merchant in Hihei. He is said to have cached more than $100,000 on the tiny island of Kahoolawe before he died under mysterious circumstances.

2. In 1928 a search was made in the eastern section of Honolulu for a quantity of five-sided coins of the old Hawaiian monarchy, said to be worth $25,000 and believed buried in the area.

3. A Hawaiian legend dating back many years tells of a pirate treasure of $5,000,000 in gold and silver coins, buried near Palemano Point by a pirate called Captain Cavendish.

4. Near the entrance of Kealakekua Bay on the Island of Hawaii, is said to rest the unidentified hulk of a sunken treasure galleon.

Q: I would like to know of two lost treasures in Hawaii, one at Oahu and the other near Kealakekua Bay.

A: Here is what I have on these two sites: Six chests of treasure are believed buried at Kaena Point on Oahu, hidden by pirates in 1823 near some walls of fitted stone at the top of a hill.

Inland from Kealakekua Bay, toward the north side of the bay and in the hills or caves not too far inland, a large number of chests and boxes were secreted in 1818, believed to be a hoard of gold, silver, church treasure, coins and jewels hidden by the pirate Turner. This cache, worth several million, is believed to be still buried on the island.

Q: What is the Marin Treasure in Hawaii?

A: Don Francisco de Paula Marin was shanghaied on a ship bound from California to Hawaii, then still known as the Sandwich Islands. Marin stayed in the Islands and eventually prospered through dealing in sandalwood and pearls. There is a legend that a great part of his wealth was hidden in a cave on Ford Island, known as the Cave of Bones. Ford Island lies in the center of Pearl Harbor and belongs to the United States Navy. Probably not a foot of the island remains unchanged by man. What happened to the cave? No one seems to know. Certainly it rests today under some kind of naval installation if it was not completely destroyed during the years since Marin's death in 1837.

IDAHO

Q: I need information on a lost gold ledge or mine in Clark County?

A: Here is one: During the 1870's a prospector found in the Targhee Forest, three to four hours walking time upstream from the mouth of Buffalo Creek, on the right side of the stream, a lost ledge of gold whose ore assayed $40,000 to the ton. A fabulous find. The finder became lost and was never able to relocate the site. All searches since then have failed.

Q: Do you have a treasure location near Idaho Falls?

A: A lone bandit is supposed to have secreted, in a cave among the lava beds near the old stage road, 250 pounds of gold bullion that he had obtained by holding up a stagecoach a few miles southeast form Big Southern Butte near Blackfoot. He was killed before he could retrieve the gold.

Q: Do you have the story of a ledge of gold quartz that was found by a man named Swimm?

A: A prospector named Swimm discovered gold ore somewhere on the Salmon River. While prospecting, he happened upon a place where a storm had toppled a huge tree. Beneath its roots was exposed a ledge of quartz honeycombed with gold that assayed $18,000 to the ton. Swimm staked his claim and had it recorded at Challis, but winter came before he could return to his mine.

By spring everyone had heard of his fabulous strike, so when he started out toward his claim, he was followed by an army of gold seekers. After a while, he stopped and announced that he would go no farther unless he was left alone. The hangers-on agreed to let him go in peace. He then proceeded down the Salmon River.

After several days, when Swimm did not return, the crowd set out to look for him. They found tracks of his horse leading into the river, but there were none coming out. Months later, the horse's bones were discovered. Swimm's gear appeared one day in a log jam, but he was never seen again, nor was his fabulous ledge of gold ever found.

Q: Would you give me a treasure site in Bonneville County?

A: Here are two: In 1930, a sheepherder found a streak of odd looking sand in quartz, near Rupert. A sample was assayed and found to contain platinum worth $175.00 to the ton. The sheepherder was never able to relocate the site.

Outlaw Jim Looney robbed the Boise-Kelton stagecoach of $90,000 in 1876, and it is believed he buried this money in the area of City of Rocks, near Almo, before he was captured. It is rumored that there are other bandit caches buried in this area. Local research could pay off on these.

Q: Is there anywhere in Idaho that I can search for semi-precious stones?

A: In the early 1900's, a pocket of rich gold ore was discovered near the banks of Goose Creek in Adams County, Idaho. The initial operation ran a long shaft into the mountain, but nothing of any value appeared.

The mining operation, however, was not wholly futile. It was during the search for the gold that a few yards of gravel was tested for value and three diamonds were found. The largest was a third of a carat and of excellent quality.

During recent years, many beautiful gems have been taken from this location. The diggings have also turned up aquamarine, ruby, amethyst, topaz, garnet and other semi-precious stones.

Q: Can you tell me the story behind the treasure supposed to be buried near the Shoshone Ice Field in Idaho?

A: During the placer days of the Boise Basin, two robbers who preyed heavily on miners in the area decided to take their loot and get out while the getting was good. They had reached a point on the road then known as the Cottonwoods, on Big Woods River in Lincoln County, near the Shoshone Ice Fields, where they were overtaken by a posse. When their horses were shot out from under them, they took to the lava fields afoot. Some distance away, they stopped and hurriedly erected a barricade, but to no avail. They were surrounded and both were killed. Their loot, estimated at $75,000, was not found on their bodies, and it is supposed that it was hidden somewhere between the point where they fled on foot and their makeshift rock fort. So far as is known, the money was never found.

Q: What is the Lost Bluebucket Treasure in Idaho?

A: The Lost Bluebucket Treasure is a story not too well known. In the pioneer days of Idaho County, Idaho, a group of men operated a mine on Dry Diggins (correct spelling) Ridge in the extreme southwestern part of the county. They were attacked by Indians and hurriedly placed their accumulation of gold in a blue bucket, buried it and fled. None lived to recover the gold, but before dying, one of the miners told the story to his young son. Many years later, as an old man, the son made several trips into the area in an effort to find the gold, but without success.

Q: I have heard of a cache of stolen gold bars in Lemhi County, do you have any information on this?

A: During the gold rush in Lemhi County, a small smelter was set up in the town of Hahn. One workman, while mining limestone to be used in the smelter, uncovered several gold bars which had evidently been stolen. Assuming that if he reported the find, he would have to give up the bars or share them, he covered them up again, intending to return later and keep the whole treasure for himself.

Winter set in, however, and the entire area was covered with snow. The following spring, the smelter ceased operations, and the workmen moved away. The man returned, but was unable to find the gold bars again. He came back numerous times to search for his gold, but was never able to locate it.

Q: Did you ever hear of the Root Hog Divide Treasure and can you tell me something about it?

A: In the late 1870's, gold bars were regularly shipped from the Custer mine in Custer County, Idaho. One of these shipments was intercepted by a lone highwayman on Root Hog Divide, a few miles east of the Big Butte Stage Station in Butte County. He was tracked northward up Little Lost River but was not overtaken, although he was later surprised in a gambling place in Salmon City. He had $5,000 of the loot on his person and readily agreed to take officers to the remainder, which he said he had buried in the lava beds near the spot where he had taken it.

Upon arriving at the scene, he cleverly escaped and was never seen again. Some 30 years later, a man from New Mexico arrived with a map on which was marked the location of a cave near the old stage road on Root Hog Divide. He claimed the map had been given to him by the robber, who was afraid to return. But the man left without finding the gold bars which are presumed to still be there.

Q: Has mercury ever been found and mined in Idaho?

A: An overlooked treasure is a lost quicksilver mine near Warren, Idaho. During the gold rush days there was an urgent need for quicksilver to be used in mining operations in the area. This requirement was met by a group of Chinese who sold the miners large amounts of quicksilver from a secret source on Ruby Mountain south of Warren.

The Chinese mined the cinnabar and melted the quicksilver in rock ovens. They then filled large metal flasks with about 70 pounds of the silvery liquid, and packed the heavy loads over the mountains to Warren.

This operation went on from 1862 until sometime in the 1880's. To keep the secret of their mine from the white men, the Chinese would carry the slag away from their ovens and deposit it beside the trails on Ruby Mountain.

It is believed that this lost mine is about halfway up Ruby Mountain, on the southwest side. At today's prices this mine could be a valuable find.

Q: Can you give me some idea of the general location of the Lost Squawman Gold Mine?

A: The only Lost Squawman Mine I know of in Idaho is supposedly located in heavily wooded mountains about 25 miles northeast of the town of Shoup, in northern Lemhi County. The mine was found by a young Nez Perce Indian and his squaw. On their way back from the ledge to their cabin, he was attacked by a bear and later died of his wounds. The squaw sold the sack of ore taken from the ledge for $4,000, but all she would say about its location was that it was near a small lake where they had built a small shack of poles and boughs. She said that the Great Spirit guarded the mine and she did not want it disturbed.

Q: I have heard of a bandit cache in southern Idaho, and there was supposed to be a map showing the location. Can you help me locate the site and map?

A: Clark County in southern Idaho holds the secret of a large amount of buried gold. The man responsible for burying this fortune of $50,000 was George Ives, an early day desperado and ex-sheriff. George found it more profitable to join the notorious Plummer Gang than to work as a poor but honest sheriff in Boise.

In the summer of 1890, a man applied for work at the hot springs in Clark County. After several months, he told oldtimers that he was unable to find a large pine that used to be near the springs, and asked them for help.

The stranger confided that while he was a guard in a penitentiary, he had been given a map by one of the prisoners. The prisoner, named George Ives, had robbed a stagecoach and, being closely pursued by a posse, had buried the plunder near the springs.

The map showed a dry gulch north of the springs with a pine tree nearby. The gold had been buried at the base of that tree. When the search for the tree proved fruitless, the stranger gathered his map and belongings and was never seen again in that vicinity.

If George Ives' map was correct, the gold is still buried somewhere near Clark County's hot springs.

Q: Have diamonds been found in Idaho?

A: Yes, glacial diamonds have been found in Ada County. The area is called Diamond Basin.

ILLINOIS

Q: I know a steamboat that was carrying a safe filled with money was wrecked on the Illinois River, could you tell me where and if the safe was ever salvaged?

A: The story goes that the incident occurred and resulted in the loss of a full cargo and a safe containing an undetermined amount of gold and silver coins, in 1861. The captain of the steamer that wrecked, John Belt, was the type of man who insisted on finishing what he had started and was on watch when the explosion occurred. He had made several attempts to put his boat into the Coon Creek landing, against a strong offshore wind that was blowing. Right at the entrance to the creek the boilers blew up, wrecking the boat, which sank with the cargo and the ship's safe, which could not be retrieved.

The water in Coon Creek was about 50 feet deep during the steamboat era. Today, the creek bed is dry and one can walk where the steamboat went down. The weight of the safe would not have let it drift very far. Chances are good that the safe is still there at the mouth of Coon Creek.

Q: I have heard that runaway slaves often carried small amounts of money with them. Were there any stops along the Underground Railroad in Illinois?

A: In a large number of instances, when a slave was planning to run away from his owner in the south and get north, they would steal anything of value they could carry to trade for food along the way. It is known that a farmhouse near Sparta served as a stop on the Underground Railroad for runaway slaves during pre-Civil War days. Rumors of gold and silver coins buried near this farmhouse have circulated for years. When the escaping slaves thought they were about to be captured, they would bury what they had stolen from their masters, so that it wouldn't be found on them.

Q: Do you have a location around Centralia, Illinois, that I can search for?

A: Here is a cache that, as far as I can learn, has never been found. For over forty years, James Gregory operated a country store about a mile south of the Hickory Hill Church. His store was the only one in the farming community and carried all necessary supplies. His was a cash-and-carry business. Not trusting banks, he kept all his money at home. Gregory was considered a rich man for his time. Somewhere on his property, he kept plenty of money for buying cattle, supplies and tools. According to his neighbors, Gregory always made a trip to a certain pasture on the farm before leaving to conduct a business transaction or whenever more money was needed than he had on hand. About 1925, Gregory suffered a stroke. He died without regaining consciousness. His wife searched for the hidden money, but no trace of it ever appeared. It is believed there are several thousand dollars still hidden somewhere on the farm.

Q: I have heard rumors that a large treasure was hidden near Fort Chartres on the east bank of the Mississippi River, by a French engineer in the 1720's. Do you have anything on this?

A: Fort Chartres was built in 1720, 18 miles north of Kaskaskia, on the east bank of the Mississippi River. After completion, it was learned in France that the engineer, Sebastian Vauhan had used local labor in the construction and had not paid for it. King Louis XV sumoned Vauhan to France to give an account of the thousands of dollars in gold that had been sent to New Orleans, then up the Mississippi to pay for the building of the fort. Vauhan, knowing he would be beheaded for hiding the gold, committed suicide by taking poison. The gold is believed to be in or near the old fort.

Q: I thought the Cherokee Indians were in North Carolina and Georgia, how is it that I heard of their hidden caches in Illinois?

A: Tales have circulated for years around Ware about the Cherokee Indians' buried caches of gold and jewelry near Dutch Creek. They camped on that creek from January to March of 1839 on their mass trek to Oklahoma. Unable to cross the Mississippi River because of floating ice and harrassed by unfriendly white settlers, the Indians suffered greatly during their forced migration from the lands of their fathers. Out of the 13,000 Indians camped near Dutch Creek, 2,000 died of exposure. It is believed that several families buried their personal jewelry and money they had managed to hide and bring with them from North Carolina and Georgia, at this campsite. The place is east of Ware on the south side of Illinois Route 146, near the Dutch Creek Bridge.

Q: Was there ever a woman doctor in Illinois named Anna Bigsby and did she hide money?

A: Yes, there was a lady doctor in Illinois in the early 1800's, named Anna Bigsby and her hidden treasure in southern Illinois has almost certainly never been found.

Anna was born and reared in Philadelphia. Finishing medical school, she came to Illinois where she married Isaac Hobbs, a farmer, and began to practice medicine (a most unusual occupation for a woman in those days). Her medical practice flourished, and she accumulated a sizeable fortune for the times.

Dr. Anna's first husband died of pneumonia and she married a man named Eson Bigsby. Dr. Anna is believed to have hidden her money in, or near a large cave in Hooven Hollow, to keep her second husband from obtaining the fortune. The cave was a favorite retreat of hers.

The cave, still known as Dr. Anna Bigsby's Cave, is located on Rock Creek in Hooven Hollow, about six miles north of Cave-in-Rock, Illinois, just west of Route 1 in Hardin County.

Q: What is the story of those kegs of gold buried near Bennington, Illinois?

A: In 1907, an aged Indian came to Bennington in southern Illinois and asked a local farmer for help in locating a cache of three kegs of gold his ancestors had buried. This gold was located on a small stream called Sugar Creek, three or four miles east of Bennington in 1907. The area had been an Indian campground until the whites drove the Indians away.

Before leaving, the Indians hurriedly buried their gold in kegs three or four feet deep. They marked the locations, hoping to return for the gold later. According to some crude drawings the Indian possessed, so many paces north of the bridge and so many paces east of Sugar Creek was a large oak tree which had been marked.

The Indian was certain he could find the treasure site again. Agreeing to help the Indian, the farmer went with him to the stream. When they reached the creek, the Indian stopped suddenly. He looked at his drawings with great concern. "This is the palce we start," he said, motioning with his hand toward a big oak in the distance. They paced off the steps to the tree many times and dug many holes, but found no trace of the gold.

The old Indian soon left and was never heard from again, but those buried kegs of Indian gold are almost certainly still there.

Q: Is there a story of buried treasure on the old Hartwell Ranch in Greene County, Illinois?

A: There is a story of treasure connected with a large stone house known as the Hartwell Ranch in Walkerville Township, which has been deserted for years. The original owner of the house was named Azariah Sweetin. At one time he was considered the richest man in the county. Sweetin was extensively engaged in cattle raising and accumulated a small fortune during the Civil War by selling beef to the United States Government.

Distrusting banks, he kept all his money hidden on his farm. Soon after the Civil War, he fell from a horse and was severely injured. He recovered, but his memory was gone, so he was never able to tell his family where he had buried his money. Several searches were made, but no report of the finding of the money was ever filed. The farm was sold, August 16, 1895, for $125.000. Today, it is overgrown with weeds. Very few people know of the fortune in gold coins believed to be hidden in or near this old home.

Q: Did the writer John M. Hoffman hide any money in Illinois?

A: John M. Hoffman is believed to have cached a large fortune of gold and silver coins and jewels in or near his house in the Chicago suburb of his residence before his death in 1926. It was known that he distrusted banks and carried $5,000 on his person at times when he was earning big money. $35 was found during a search of his house after his death, but nothing else was ever reported found.

Q: Is there a story of a Frenchman burying a cache of gold coins on the Illinois River?

A: A Frenchman by the name of Tonty buried a cache of gold coins worth $100,000 in the immediate vicinity of Starved Rock, located on the Illinois River about halfway between La Salle and Ottawa in Ottawa County. The gold was buried during the days of the French and Indian Wars.

Q: Do you have any information about a treasure at John Hill's Fort in Clinton County, Illinois?

A: John Hill's Fort, a stockade erected for protection from the Indians, was located on a site about six blocks south of the present courthouse in Carlyle, Clinton County, Illinois. Nothing remains of it today. The fort was manned by a man known only as Young, among the early settlers at the time. When Young was killed by Indians, his mother claimed he had buried $5,000 in gold at a spot 50 yards south of the fort.

Q: Did the Mormons hide any money when they were forced out of Illinois?

A: In 1846, when the Mormons left Nauvoo, Illinois, on their trek to Utah, they are believed to have buried a large quantity of gold beneath one of their buildings. The people of Nauvoo fiercely resented the Mormons and their religion, and accused them of counterfeiting and literally drove them from their homes. It is highly probable that the Elders of the Church buried their treasury under one of their buildings in the hope of returning later to retrieve it. Public opinion against the Mormons, however, made it unwise for any of them to come back. Research in the old city records and a town plat could reveal something of this treasure.

INDIANA

Q: I have heard of a keg of silver coins being buried in Indiana by Indians. Do you have any information on this?

A: About 1775, during a raid, a band of roving Indianas took a keg of silver coins. They buried the keg on the banks of a creek which later came to be called Silver Creek. This cache was supposed to be five miles upstream from the mouth of the creek, and early settlers tried to find the coins. General George Rogers Clark believed the story, and his first cabin overlooked the Ohio River near the mouth of Silver Creek.

Navigators on the Ohio River, during the 1840's—1870's, used to remark, "Yonder range of hills is supposed to be rich in silver ore which may be found in the banks of the creek as well."

Many have searched for both the silver ore and the keg of coins, but no find has been reported.

Q: I need the story of an Indian Cave in southern Indiana that was later used by outlaws. Can you help me?

A: A cave known locally as "Little Goss" was named for one Hugh Goss, its first owner. Little Goss is near Greenville, about three miles off Highway 150 on route 335. The cave has two entrances and three levels. From a lookout point above the lower entrance one man could hold off any army, so the spot was a perfect place for outlaws. Tradition has it that the Reno gang of train robbers used the cave as a hiding place. The gang is believed to have hidden money from robberies in or around the cave.

Indians also lived in Little Goss. Several Indian mounds are in the vicinity, and numerous native artifacts have been found near the cave.

No one can decipher the symbols chiseled on a large rock at one of the entrances to the cave. Nobody knows whether the horseshoe, star, footprint, left hand print, arrow, and circle were carved there by Indians or outlaws, but it is quite probable that they were directions to hidden treasure. The cave and land around it are now owned by Edmond Drabek who does not permit anyone to examine the places of interest on his property without permission.

Q: I read about a man hiding his money near Central, Indiana, then was killed during World War I.

A: A cache of gold and silver coins buried by a farmer prior to World War I is believed to be between Central and Gildas, in Harrison County. The man went into the service and was killed. No coins have ever been found on his place.

Q: Is there a lost cannon somewhere around Fort Recovery, on the Wabash River?

A: After the defeat of General St. Clare in 1791, the Indians captured a small cannon which they were supposed to have buried below Fort Recovery on the left side of the Wabash River in what is now Jay County, Indiana. It is apparently still there.

Q: Did Indians ever show a white man the location of silver ore in Indiana?

A: Prior to the last Indian War in Indiana, 1810-1812, an uneasy peace existed between the white man and the red man. About 1807, Absolom Fields lived in the vicinity of McBride's Bluff, in what is now Martin County. He was friendly with a band of Indians living near Indian Creek, a tributary of the White River.

One night he was awakened by two Indians and told, "No light. You come, we no hurt you. We take you and show you something."

The Indians blindfolded him, turned him around several times, led him some distance, then took him aboard a boat. Since the stream was low and the boat could be paddled either direction, Fields never knew whether they went up or down stream. The Indians landed the boat and conducted him a short distance along a trail and into a large cavern where they removed his blindfold. There were several Indians present, including squaws and children.

Some kind of metal and the ore from which it came from was shown to him, and the Indians said it was silver. Several small bars were in a pile. They were about six inches long, two inches wide, half an inch thick and had been formed with a crude flaring mold. Fields was given three of the bars then blindfolded again and taken back to his cabin. After that incident, he spent countless hours trying to retrace the route to the hidden cave.

Years later on a trip down river to New Orleans by flatboat, he met one of the Indians who had lived near McBride's Bluff. The Indian remarked, "If white man only knew it, he could shoe horses as cheaply with silver as with iron."

Fields asked the Indian where the silver might be found. All the Indian would say was, "You stand on Big Bluffs, look away to south over big bottom. Maybe it that way. Maybe not. Don't forget to look down under you. Maybe down there. Maybe not. White man never finds. He heap too big fool—digs till he most finds it and quits. Paleface never find."

Symbols were chiseled on a large rock directly below the highest point in the Bluffs to indicate where the silver was hidden. There was a half moon, a star, and a crawling snake with its head pointed toward the treasure cave. Fields kept the silver bars. One of them was in the possession of a descendant until a few years ago. The cave of precious metal still awaits some paleface who is not "heap too big fool."

Q: Is it true a cache of silver coins was hidden in Franklin County, Indiana?

A: The "Atlas of Franklin County" in 1882 reported, "A peddler from New York squatted on Silver Creek. He was known to have a large number of silver coins. He started for the White River country on a trading trip but never returned to his home." It is believed that he secreted the coins before he left.

Q: Did any of the prohibition gangsters hide any money in Indiana?

A: In 1921, George "Dutch" Anderson and Gerald Chapman robbed a mail truck in New York of $1,424,129. Only $27,000 of that was in cash. Not wanting to sell all the securities at a loss for 40 cents on the dollar, the two bandits went to Muncie where they converted only $100,000 worth of them into cash.

On the way back to New York, they were caught and given 25 years each in the penitentiary at Atlanta. Chapman escaped but was apprehended two days later. Anderson escaped, went to a farm outside Muncie and killed the owners, Ben House and his wife, then burned the house over their bodies. He was killed in Michigan a short time later. Anderson was hanged April 5, 1926.

Nothing has been learned of the almost $900,000 left in securities from the robbery. It is almost certain they were buried along with some of the cash near the House farm. Chapman and Anderson were both city men, so they would not have gone far from the farm house. The money is probably still where they hid it.

Q: Has silver ever been found in Indiana?

A: Scientists believe that the Wyandotte Caves in the Harrison-Crawford State Forest on Highway 62 were used by Indians up to 1500 A.D. In the Senate Chambers of Big Wyandotte Cave, an area of approximately 1,000 cubic feet, Indians mined some kind of unknown mineral before the white man came. Stories of these Indian mines have been told in Crawford County since the days of the earliest pioneers.

About 1900, the Wyandotte Caves were on land owned by a man named Rothrock. Three counterfeiters used the caves without his prior knowledge. Learning by chance of their nefarious activities, Rothrock took several men with him one night and surprised the counterfeiters. A gun fight followed in which one of the gang was killed and another was captured. The third

36

man ran back into the cave with part of the counterfeit coins and was never seen again. Money molds, a small smelter, and a quantity of silver ore was found, but the captured outlaw would not tell where they had obtained the ore. The source of the silver has never been found. There are several other counties in Indiana where silver has been found.

Q: I know John Dillinger's father owned a farm in Indiana. Did his gangster son bury any money there, or anywhere in Indiana?

A: John Dillinger is believed to have buried two caches in Indiana. One was on his father's ten-acre produce farm near Mooresville. He always timed his arrival at the farm late at night. On one occasion Dillinger told his friend, Evelyn Frechette, that he had buried money in a suitcase wrapped in an oilcloth.

John is also supposed to have made occasional visits to a friend of his who owned a farm near Cedar Lake, in Lake County. It is believed that he buried the money from an Indianapolis bank robbery on that farm. After several robberies, he made trips south of Chicago alone and always at night, carrying money.

It has been assumed that on these occasions he visited his father at Mooresville and hid the currency, but this farm has been searched repeatedly by government agents and local people, and nothing has been reported found. It is highly possible that Dillinger only let everyone think he went to his father's farm. Since only about $25,000 of the reported $1,000,000 that Dillinger took in different robberies has ever been recovered, it might be worth while to explore the land around Cedar Lake.

Q: Where can I pan for gold in Owen County?

A: In 1876, State Geologist Collet wrote, "Gold dust has been found with magnetite along the streams of Fish, Lick and Rattlesnake Creeks." Glacial gold can also be found in Brown, Cass, Clark, Dearborn, Franklin, Jackson, Jefferson, Jennings, Montgomery and Morgan Counties.

Q: What is the story of the $100,000 cache of gold coins buried in northeastern Indiana?

A: Until his death in the early 1900's, George Downing owned a farm near York. $100,000 in gold is believed to be buried on that farm. Downing accumulated quite a fortune through farming and cattle buying. His brother Bill went west and became a member of the Sam Bass gang of outlaws. Bill visited his brother's farm several times in the 1880's and told United States Deputy Marshal William Breckenridge that he had money buried on the farm in Indiana. On one occasion, George Downing was tortured almost to death by two men trying to make him reveal the location of the buried gold, but Downing did not tell them. Several people have searched for this money, and one small cache was found. But the $100,000 in gold is believed to be still buried somewhere on the farm.

Q: What information do you have on a French gold cache near Tremont?

A: In 1780, a group of French-Canadians led by Jean Baptiste Hamlin raided Ft. St. Joseph, near present-day Niles, Mich. They seized fifty bales of valuable furs and an undetermined amount of gold, but were followed by soldiers and overtaken near the present site of Tremont.

The report of Major Arent de Peyster stated, "The furs were recovered, four fugitives killed, seven taken prisoner. Of the gold we learned nothing."

The soldiers continued to talk, and Major Peyster had them shot. This is almost certainly an overlooked cache.

IOWA

Q: Has gold ever been found in Iowa?

A: Yes, there have been three miniature gold rushes in Iowa—in 1853, 1857 and 1877. In 1853, as John Ellsworth, a farmer, was working his fields one spring day, he found a small quantity of gold. Within a few months an estimated 700 to 1,200 people were camped about his farm looking for gold.

Residents of Eldora, just north of the Ellsworth farm, tried to explain that the amount of gold found was very small and wasn't really worth the effort of prospecting. But the fortune hunters didn't believe them and kept looking.

The excitement finally died down, only to be revived again in 1857 by O.M. Holcombe, who claimed he found gold while prospecting along the Iowa River. But again gold in very small amounts was all that was found.

In 1877, the fever developed again as specks of gold were seen seven miles upstream from Eldora on the black sand banks of the Iowa River. What possibly is glacial gold can certainly be found in the area today if one wants to search for it.

Q: Are there any treasure locations in Iowa?

A: Yes, here are several sites but you will have to do your own local research on them:

A short time before he was killed in a car wreck, a gambler buried 15,000 in winnings near a pumping station south of Waterloo.

Near Sabula, on the Elk River, $40,000 is supposed to be buried. A horse thief cached this, was later caught and hanged.

About three miles north of Dexter is where the Bonnie and Clyde gang had a hideout overlooking the Raccoon River. They are supposed to have buried money and jewelry near their camp. There are several local stores still being told of this hidden cache.

Another site is near Wapello, where it is believed several caches are hidden, put there by returning California gold miners.

Q: There is supposed to be Indian gold hidden in the Fairfield area of Jefferson County. Do you have any information on this?

A: According to the story, this is what happened: Three Indians buried a portion of early 1800 treaty money, consisting of gold coins, in the Fairfield area. The three were killed in a tribal war and the site was never found. Clues to the location were found in the old Bonnifield log cabin in 1828. The cache is believed buried near the cabin, but has not been found.

Q: Is there a treasure ship in Iowa? How could this be possible?

A: It depends on what one calls treasure. But there are two sunken ships believed to be on the Iowa side of the Missouri River. These boats were carrying a fortune (at today's prices) in mercury and whiskey. Three flasks of mercury from one of these ships were found in 1954. This find lends credence to the fact that the rest of the mercury is somewhere south of Modale, Iowa.

Q: Could you give me the site of the train robbery in Iowa where bandit loot was buried?

A: $30,000 to $50,000 taken in a train robbery near Buffalo, west of Davenport, is believed buried near a creek that flows into the Mississippi River, not far from the scene of the holdup. Another train robbery occurred near Letts, Iowa. An undetermined amount of money was taken which was never recovered. These two sites are worth further research.

Q: Did river pirates ever operate along the Mississippi River, bordering the state of Iowa?

A: Yes, river pirates at one time operated all along the Mississippi River in Iowa. There are stories of a cave near Bellevue in which money was hidden by these outlaws. Also, $7,000 is believed buried near Sabula, on the Mississippi River, put there by river pirates.

Q: Do you have a treausre site I can check out in Iowa?

A: Here is one that could pay off: In 1830, no less than $80,000 was sent from St. Louis to Colonel Zachary Taylor at Fort McKay, Iowa, to pay the regular soldiers whose presence was necessary in the territory of Iowa because of Black Hawk and his anticipated outbreak. That fortune of gold was buried at Zachary Taylor's command and the men who knew of its whereabouts were killed by the Indians. Colonel Taylor had men digging for the money for several days, but they had no luck in recovering it.

Q: I have heard of buried gold somewhere around Mason City. What do you have on this?

A: There is a story of a buried cache of gold coins along the banks of the Winnebago River northwest of Mason City. The man who buried the gold was Thomas Nelson, a mysterious soldier of fortune who apparently made a great deal of money either prospecting in the Black Hills or taking money from successful prospectors in poker games during the 1880's.

38

In 1884, Nelson came to Cerro Gordo County in Iowa and took a job at the Wheeler ranch, where a fellow ranch hand saw Nelson counting gold coins. He had the money stacked in tall piles, the various denominations in separate stacks, and he later put the gold coins in a heavy leather money belt and buckskin sacks.

Before long, reports of Nelson's gold circulated around the county and Nelson, fearing possible theft, buried the money. He later told Oliver Booth, a friend of his in Grant Township, that he had buried a fortune in gold somewhere on the Winnebago River between the Wheeler ranch and the horseshoe bend area, late at night to avoid detection, and was sure he would remember where the spot was. But the next day when he went back he could not find the spot where the gold was buried, about three feet deep.

For the next 10 years, Nelson spent days walking back and forth in an area between a horseshoe bend and Dexter's Bridge. He continued to search for the gold until 1898, when he left for Alaska apparently to search for a new treasure in gold. He returned in the fall of 1900 and was reported to have been seen walking daily along the river during the summer of 1901.

He told a friend he had given up and that somebody else could have the gold if they could find it, and left the country and died in Alaska in 1924.

The search for Nelson's lost gold was a popular activity for residents of the area in the early years of the Twentieth Century but no one ever found the treasure.

Q: Did you ever hear the story of a wealthy lumberman hiding a pot of gold in Clinton?

A: Hope this helps: A wealthy lumberman stuffed an iron pot full of stocks, bonds and gold coins and buried it near the Mississippi River bank at a place now known as River Front Park in Clinton. This has never been reported found. Perhaps the local library has the story on this cache.

Q: Do you have any information on a treasure site near Eddyville?

A: In 1903, W.W. DeLong, then postmaster of Eddyville, Iowa, received a letter postmarked Pittsburgh, Pennsylvania, and addressed simply to "Postmaster, Eddyville, Iowa." It was signed "Le Barge." DeLong was also the editor of the Eddyville newspaper, and he published the contents of the letter, which revealed an amazing story of buried treasure and murder. This was Le Barge's story:

He and two companions had struck it rich in the gold fields of the Black Hills, and were returning to their homes in Illinois in the early summer of 1878. Each of them carried a gallon jug filled with gold dust and nuggets. One night they made camp at a turn in the trail about a mile north of Eddyville. After supper that evening they settled down to a game of poker. William Gunton was the heavy winner, and Le Barge accused him of cheating. In the fight that resulted, Gunton was stabbed to death. The victim's head was severed and thrown into the campfire, while the headless body was dragged some distance away and buried.

Afraid that if they were apprehended with a large amount of gold in their possession, they would be accused of killing the dead man for his share, they buried the three jugs of gold in three separate locations, using the fresh grave as a center point. The two partners then continued their journey, intending to recover the gold at a later date when there would be less chance of their implication in the crime.

Stating that he was about to die, he asked the postmaster to recover the body of Gunton and give it a decent burial, with the gold to go to the men performing the rite.

Three men, DeLong, Sid Crosson and Arthur Beamer, set out to locate the gold from the letter's description of the place, but finding nothing, they eventually called off the search.

The incident of the buried treasure was all but forgotten until 1920, when a road crew grading the old wagon trail north of Eddyville uncovered a human skull which bore evidence of having been burned. DeLong insisted that the skull had been found in almost the exact location described in LeBarge's letter. This discovery set loose a horde of treasure hunters who scoured a wide area around the popularly accepted treasure site, a wooded pasture north of Eddyville's cemetery. Nothing is known to have been found.

Q: What treasure cache is said to be buried near Guttenberg?

A: About 1842, an army payroll train, enroute from Fort Crawford, Wisconsin, to Fort

39

Atkinson, Iowa, was held up and robbed by a band of Indians. According to an old Indian who claimed to have been a member of the band, the money was hidden in a cave on Miners Creek near Guttenberg. The fact that no record of this incident appears in the U.S. Archives in Washington has led some people to assume that the army was too embarrassed to report it. In any event, this has never, as far as I can learn, been found.

Q: Has the Thomas Kelly cache in Iowa ever been found?

A: When Tom Kelly died in 1867, a hunt began for his "lost treasure chest" that still goes on today. No report of this cache being found can be learned. Research suggests there is money still buried somewhere on the bluff that bears his name, overlooking the Mississippi River at Dubuque, Iowa.

An extremely miserly man, Kelly left a personal estate valued at $66.93, plus assorted tools, 60 tons of lead ore that sold for $6,360, and 30 acres of lead-rich bluff land. He had no bank accounts and no cash was found hidden in his small one-room cabin.

The dying miser wouldn't reveal where his fortune was hidden. Instead, he taunted his relatives, telling them to look for it. Only $13,400 was found, leaving $86,000 buried somewhere on the land that still bears his name.

Records at the clerk's office in the Dubuque Courthouse and newspaper files at the public library tell the story of Kelly and his treasure.

Q: Are people still searching for the Ives brothers money in Cedar County?

A: People will always search for buried treasure, but the money hidden by the Ives brothers is apparently still there. Here is the story breifly:

The Ives brothers, well-to-do farmers living near Sunbury in Cedar County in the 1930's, buried their accumulated wealth on their farm. Relatives found $200,000 in large size currency and stocks, but it is known they had acquired a large amount of new (at that time) small paper money (1935) and none of this was ever found.

KANSAS

Q: I need locations of buried treasure in Kansas. Can you help me?

A: Here are two locations you might want to check over. The first one is in Clark County. "Dutch" Henry was a lone operator in the business of stealing cattle and horses in the 1870's. To many he was considered a sort of Robin Hood, robbing only the prosperous and sharing with the poor. When captured by the sheriff of Ford County and sentenced to the penitentiary, he is said to have left a sizeable fortune buried near his cabin at the entrance to Horse Thief Canyon, about twelve miles north of Ashland. When "The Dutchman" escaped from prison, it is believed he tried to recover his treasure but failed. When he was recaptured near Trinidad, Colorado, he had no money with him.

Another location is in Douglas County. In 1862 or 1863, an army paymaster was robbed of $195,000 in gold and silver coins while on his way from Lawrence to Denver. The two robbers were trailed and killed by soldiers. When a witness to the robbery and the burial of the loot refused to tell where it was, he was arrested and served six months in jail. Twice after his release, the witness attempted to recover the loot but was frightened away both times. Before he died sometime later, he told only that the money was buried somewhere between Lawrence and the Wakarusa Creek to the south, and that is was in an oak box between two sycamore trees.

Q: I would like to know about the Morgan Brothers' treasure in Kansas.

A: The story tells that Alexander and Chester Morgan were wealthy wheat farmers and dealers in livestock about 1895. Distrustful of banks and checks, they dealt only in cash. Their safety deposit box was in the ground.

Several men hated them because of their skinflint trading tendencies; supposedly, they were not above cheating widows and orphans. One night several unidentified men shot the brothers dead and set fire to their house, attempting to conceal the crime.

Though many searchers have looked, no money was found on the premises. People who knew the Morgan's well, said they had $100,000 to $150,000 cached where they could get at it readily. Though this is possible, it isn't confirmed. The Morgan's old farm is near Liberal, in Seward County, near the Oklahoma border.

Q: Did you ever hear the story of a hidden treasure in north central Kansas, concerning a man named Edward Moffett?

A: Edward Moffett was a small town banker in Woodruff, Kansas. Right after World War I, he sold a farm for $18,000, which money he buried in the cellar of his home in Woodruff. Another $300 was hidden in a ventilator of another house he owned. Just before he died, he wrote his lawyer, telling where the money was hidden. His lawyer found the $300 but not the $18,000. Check old records at Woodruff to learn where Moffett's home was in the early 1920's.

Q: I need information on a treasure buried a few miles west of Dodge City.

A: I obtained the following newspaper clipping (photocopy) from Thomas Penfield, now deceased, several years ago. I assume this is the site you are interested in. This quote comes from the New York Times, May 19, 1929.

"The latest in treasure hunting devices has been taken to Dodge City. It is an electric needle by which E.T. Mechlin of Moline, Illinois, hopes to find 42 bags, each containing 1000 Mexican silver pesos, buried four miles west of Dodge City in 1853.

The story is that a Mexican train of 120 wagons and 82 men on their way to Independence, Missouri, over the Santa Fe Trail with a load of silver, was attacked by Indians. The savages were repulsed and then began a five-day siege which ended with the massacre of all but one of the Mexicans. The Indians burned the wagons and left the money. The survivor buried the silver in the mounds which may still be seen west of Dodge City and went back to Mexico."

I cannot learn if this treasure was found or not, but you could do local research and probably find out.

Q: Do you have any information on a group of prospectors that buried a large amount of gold dust in Nemaha County during the 1850's?

A: Here is what I have on the burial of $85,000 in gold dust near Seneca, Kansas: In 1854, a party of prospectors returning from the California gold fields, camped on the South Fork of the Nemaha River, about two miles north of Seneca. Before going into the little town of Richmond to buy supplies, two of the group buried $85,000 in gold. In town, the men became involved in a saloon brawl and one was killed. The other fled without picking up the two buckskins of gold and never returned. Many years later, his sons made an effort to locate the gold, but failed. So far as is known, the treasure is still there. The town of Richmond is no longer in existence, and it should not be confused with the present town of Richmond in Franklin County.

Q: I have heard that there are a lot of ghost towns in Kansas, where are they?

A: If you mean ghost towns with the remains of a few buildings still standing, such as there are in the west, you won't find many in Kansas. But no state in the country is richer in the number of completely "lost" towns than Kansas. Literally hundreds of communities were started in Kansas during its period of settlement. True, some of these consisted of only a few log structures, but others lived long enough to acquire a population of a few hundred people.

Some of these towns were abandoned because their locations were not desirable. In some cases the residents simply tore down their buildings and moved to a new site to be near a railroad. Some were absorbed by larger towns. Crop failures, fires, and grasshopper plagues caused the abandonment of others. These towns simply vanished from the maps. Based on studies made by the Kansas Historical Society, it appears that there are some 700 "lost" towns in Kansas. In my opinion, some concentrated on-the-spot research would reveal the site of many of these which could be profitable to a treasure hunter.

Q: Do you have any information on the Bender family that robbed and killed several travelers in Montgomery County, during the 1870's?

A: The Bender Mounds, low-lying hills, are located eleven miles west of Parsons, almost on the Labette-Montgomery County line. Here, in the early 1870's, William Bender with his wife, son and daughter operated a small trading post. Later several travelers on the Independence to Osage Mission trail mysteriously disappeared in the vicinity of the Bender place, and an investigation revealed that the Benders had left the country. Later several bodies were found buried in the orchard. It is believed that the Benders robbed and killed their victims, and that they left $90,000 in gold coins buried someplace around the old building. It is said that the four Benders were trailed and killed by Colonel A.M. York, brother of their last victim.

Q: I have heard of a cache of gold coins in Edwards County, hidden in the 1850's. Can you help me on this one?

A: I assume this is the site you mean: In the 1850's a party of miners returning east from the California gold fields camped on the present site of Offerle. Before they settled down for the night, they buried $50,000 in gold coins along a nearby creek. At dawn an Indian attack scattered the party and all were killed except an eight-year-old girl. About 30 years later, she returned from the east to search for the gold, but eventually gave up. The habit of burying valuables while camped at night is told in many a pioneer diary, and this probably accounts for the prevalence of this type of treasure story along the old trails of the west.

Q: What treasure is supposed to be in Big Basin, Clark County?

A: Big Basin lies 20 miles west of Ashland and is almost astraddle the Clark-Meade county line. In this scientifically interesting area is said to be a break in the earth's curst caused by underground streams. Old-timers insist there is a maze of tunnels underneath, and that there is not only gold in the hills of Big Basin, but there is an unexplained treasure of $200,000 in gold coins hidden someplace in the tunnels.

Q: Do you have anything on Coronado's treasure in Kansas?

A: Coronado's expedition is believed by some historians to have forded the Arkansas River about four miles east of Dodge City. There is a legend that the Spanish were warned by scouts that they were being trailed by Indians. Fearing an attack, the expedition's treasure of an estimated $3,000,000 was buried near the ford and the soldiers continued on. Not returning that way, the treasure was never recovered. Although no treasure has ever been found here, a silver mounted stirrup, believed to be of Spanish make, was picked up, giving credence to the story.

Q: Are there any caches of money in the Republican River Valley?

A: Yes, there are supposed to be several treasure caches of money and liquor hidden around a huge liquor operation on a farm a few miles south of Republic, in the Republican River Valley.

Q: Has gold ever been found in Kansas?

A: In the area of Wichita there is a lost Spanish gold mine, somewhere in the nearby mountains.

Gold has been found in several places on the Arkansas River, believed to have been washed down from its source in the Colorado gold country.

Gold has also been found on several tributaries of the Arkansas River.

Q: What is the story of the Thomas Daly treasure?

A: There are several stories (still being told) of treasures that were buried by Ellis businessmen in different places around Ellis. These different caches have never been found. Thomas Daly was one of these businessmen, and he is supposed to have accumulated a fortune which he buried somewhere around his mercantile store.

KENTUCKY

Q: Could you give me several general locations of gold or silver mines that were believed to have been worked from 1720 to 1780 in Kentucky?

A: Here are three you can check out:

About 1775, a group of men were exploring what is now Lewis County, Kentucky, when Indians attacked them, killing several and taking a man named McCormick prisoner. At the head of Kinney or Kinnicinick Creek, he was tied to a tree and the Indians prepared to burn him alive. There were several French missionaries at the Indians' camp and the French persuaded the Indians to spare McCormick's life. Later the Frenchmen learned that the Indians knew the location of a rich silver vein near their camp. With the help of the Indians, the Frenchmen built a smelter and opened a mine. For two or three years they worked the silver mine, but the

Indians went on the warpath during the Revolutionary War, and the Frenchmen had to leave. The mine was closed, and the silver bars were hidden close to the smelter. The mine, or mines, are believed to be on Quicks Run Creek or Kinney Creek. The richest ore is supposed to be on Laurel Fork.

The directions for finding a silver mine on the South Fork of the Cumberland River, in southeastern Kentucky, are: starting place is Little Indian Rockhouse on Laurel Creek, about two miles east of Stearns, Kentucky. Travel in a westerly direction for one day. If on the right trail, you should find a rattlesnake carved on a large rock, a small pond with a rock and tree in the center, along a curved path or trail.

There is also supposed to be an Indian gold mine on the South Fork of the Cumberland River. Gold ore was discovered on the property of George Patton, near Mt. Pisgah, several years ago, but I can find no mention of the gold having been mined. This was in McCreary County.

Q: Do you know of any treasure in Greenup County?

A: Here is a location that I obtained from an old newspaper clipping: About 1900, two raccoon hunters took shelter in a cave during a severe rainstorm, somewhere on a tributary of the Little Sandy River. While looking around the cave they found peices of gold and silver ore and several Indian artifacts. After several hours, when the storm had let up, they decided to leave. Since it was still raining and dark they became lost, reaching home a few hours later. Neither man could ever locate the cave again. The specimens were tested and found to be high grade gold and silver ore. Because of the Indian artifacts found with the gold and silver, it is believed this treasure was stolen and hidden by the Indians. This stream is now thought to be Raccoon Creek, south of Greenup, Kentucky.

Q: My wife and I spend our vacations in trying to locate pioneer forts in Kentucky. Could you tell us the county that has the largest number of those sites?

A: The largest number were located in Lincoln County, but remember this was when Kentucky had only seven counties. Lincoln County has since been broken up into several different counties. Try to obtain a map of 1793, it shows these seven areas.

Lincoln County covered the southeastern section of the state. There were 20 forts or stations built from about 1780 to 1790. They were: Can Run, Carpenters, Casey, Crab Orchard, Craigs, Fork of Dicks River, Gilivers Lick, Knob Lick, Logans, McKinneys, Montgomery's, Pettits, Whitleys, Worthingtons, Clarks, Daviess, English's, McCormicks, Tuckers and Barrett's. By using a modern topographical map, these sites can be located. Check with the Filson Club, 118 East Breckenrige, Louisville, Kentucky. These people have all Kentucky records from its beginning.

Q: Do you have any information on the John (Jack) Neal treasure?

A: About 1900, a wealthy land owner named John "Jack" Neal is believed to have buried at least $7,000 in gold near Hueysville, Kentucky. I have a letter from Mr. Alfonse Patton, telling me his grandfather knew Neal very well. Neal told Paton's grandfather shortly before he died that he hid the money. It is thought that Neal buried it somewhere close to Hueysville in an apple orchard on his farm.

Q: I have heard of a cache of Civil War coins in eastern Kentucky. Can you help me on this location?

A: This incident happened in 1864: Different patrols of the Confederate Army were looking throughout Kentucky for anyone sympathetic to the North. Pete Akeman was at home near Barwick, Kentucky. He had been, or was at that time, in the Union Army. The Rebel men learned where he was and went to capture him. Akeman, in trying to escape, ran up a long hill back of where he was living, made it to the top of the hill and temporarily escaped from the soldiers.

Under or near a large flat rock on top of the ridge, he buried $800 in silver that his family knew he was carrying, during his flight. Pete was captured the next day, taken to the head of Millers Branch, about three miles from where he lived, tied to a tree and burned alive. It was learned after the war was over that he did not have any of the money on him when he was captured.

It is believed that Akeman never told where the money was buried, because, a few years later, some of his relatives found $9.50 in silver and one $2.50 gold piece (a quarter eagle). The money was found near the only large flat rock on the ridge. All of the coins dated to before 1864. It is believed Akeman dropped the silver change and the gold coin in his haste to escape, or while burying the money. The rest of the eight hundred dollars is still there.

Q: Do you have any information on the treasure at Allegan Hall, in Lexington?

A: Colonel John Campbell, a Revolutionary War officer, was given or bought, a tract of land on the site of where Allegan Hall now stands. He built a log cabin and lived in it until his death. William Pettit later obtained the land, tore down the original log cabin and built the present house near where the cabin stood, during the late 1830's or early 1840's. With the coming of the Civil War, Pettit converted all his cash (he was apparently a wealthy man for the time) into gold coins. He died before he could recover the buried coins.

The coins were buried on the farm and, although many have searched for this treasure, it has never been found. Allegan Hall is located on Nicholasville Road, just north of Stone Road, Lexington, Kentucky.

Q: Where is a place called the "Round Bottom" located in Kentucky and what is the story of a buried treasure there?

A: On Quicksand Creek, near Noctor, Kentucky, in Breathitt County, is a large area of flat land called the "Round Bottom" (about 80 acres) almost completely encircled by the creek. During the 1800's, a man named Back owned the land. I was told by one of his sons (about 70 years old now) that his father had buried $5,000 in gold on the farm. Just before he died, Back suffered a stroke and was unable to speak or walk. When asked where he had bruied the money, he managed to point to a line of cedar trees back of the house. The trees are still there but the family has never found the money.

Several years later, while rebuilding a walkway back of the house, almost $500 in silver that had belonged to Back's wife was found under the old stones of the original walkway, but the gold is still buried where Mr. Back put it.

Q: Where can I find more information on the John Swift lost silver mine in southeastern Kentucky?

A: An excellent account of this story appears in "The Kentucky" (American River Series) by Thomas D. Clark, published by Farrar and Rinehart, New York, 1942. The files of the Louisville, Kentucky "Courier Journal" contains many articles on this legendary lost silver mine and cache. Lengthy accounts can also be found in the quarterly publications of the Kentucky State Historical Society. In addition to rich silver ore, the mine is said to contain a cache of $273,000 worth of minted silver coins and bars. The location is usually placed on or near Pine Mountain, Bell County, Kentucky.

Q: I am very interested in Indian artifacts and would appreciate any information you have on the area of Maysville.

A: See if you can obtain a copy of H. Glen Cliff's book, "History of Maysville and Mason County." It lists thirty known Indian mounds and other information on Indian settlements or camps on both sides of the Ohio River in your area.

Q: Have you ever heard of the McNitt Treasure in Kentucky? What is it and where is it located?

A: There have been several different versions of this story written. Here, briefly, is what I have:

On what is now the Levi Jackson Wilderness Road State Park, near London, Laurel County, Kentucky, a group of 40 pioneers camped on the Little Laurel River, in 1786. They were attacked by Indians and 26 of the party were killed. Before camping, a treasurer had been chosen, and this man buried a large leather pouch, containing the money and jewelry belonging to the party. He was killed during the attack and this cache was never found. The site is known today as Defeated Camp. Be sure to check with park officials before you look for this treasure.

Q: Do you have a location of buried Civil War gold coins near Richmond?

A: A member of the Rice family of Richmond, Kentucky, told me that near Richmond, on a farm, during the Civil War, a man (I have been unable to learn his name, but he was in the Confederate army) converted all his property except his home into gold coins, told his family he had buried the money in the front yard and would show them the location later. He went into Richmond the same day he buried the money and during a short battle between Union and Confederate soldiers he was killed. The family was never able to find the money.

Q: I need a site where Indian battles took place in Jefferson County, do you have one?

A: Off U.S. HIghway 60, east of Louisville, Kentucky, are the remains of one of the oldest churches in Kentucky. Abraham Lincoln's grandfather was killed by Indians here. It is now Long Run Park and it would be a good place to search for Indian relics, as several battles took place in the area during the 1780's. An article in the "Louisville Times," October 15th, 1965, gives a good description of these battles.

LOUISIANA

Q: Can you tell me anything about the Watson Treasure in Tensas Parish, Louisiana? How much is it worth and has any of it ever been found?

A: In 1854, Captain A.C. Watson built Lakewood, his plantation home, near St. Jospeh, seat of Tensas Parish. Before Watson left to join Robert E. Lee in 1861 with Watson's Battery, which he commanded, he withdrew his entire fortune of $80,000 from the banks. He spent $60,000 of this equipping his regiment, and buried the remaining $20,000 on the grounds of Lakewood. Most of this was recovered when Watson returned from the war, but one jar containing $5,000 could not be found. This is still supposedly buried around Lakewood.

Q: There is reported to be a treausre buried at the site of old Fort Iberville. I can't find this site on any map. Can you tell me where it is?

A: The site of Fort Iberville, indicated on early maps as Old French Settlement or simply as Old Fort, was the first fortification in Louisiana. It can be reached only by boat, usually from Pheonix, in Plaquemines Parish. After the founding of New Orleans, the fort was abandoned and the site was completely lost until rediscovered in 1930. It is said that a treasure of $150,000 was left buried here when the fort was abandoned, and that later efforts to recover it have failed. A few gold coins have been found here in recent years, leading some to believe that the main treasure cache may have been disturbed by high waters.

Q: Can you tell me anything about the Wyndham Creek Lost Mine? Where is it supposed to be located?

A: The story of the Wyndham Creek Lost Mine is frequently heard around DeQuincy, in the long-leaf pine section of Louisiana. When pioneers first arrived in the area they found the local Indians wearing gold ornaments. When the Indians refused to reveal where they secured the gold, it was presumed they had a secret gold mine. A white woman is said to have stumbled upon this mine while lost, but was unable later to retrace her steps. Search for this mine has continued sporadically, and as late as 1900, three men who had sworn they would never give up until they found it were discovered brutally murdered by persons unknown. So far as I can determine, the location of the mine remains in a vague area "around DeQuincy."

Q: What can you tell me about the Old Camp Place Treasure?

A: Old Camp Place is the local name for a house, one of the oldest in the region, located about ten miles west of Monroe, in Quachita Parish, Louisiana. The house was built in 1855 and was once an inn on the Monroe-Shreveport Stage Line on the Old Wire Road. As such, it was the first stop out of Monroe, and horses were changed there. So far as is known, the treasure, supposedly buried there by Civil War refugees, has never been found.

Q: What is the nature of the treasure buried in Breaux Bridge?

A: Early in the 19th century, nine slaves of Breaux Bridge, St. Martin Parish, Louisiana, killed their master Narcisse Thibodeaux, and made off with his hoard of gold. Captured by a posse, the Negroes were set to digging their own graves. When the job was completed, a volley of shots rang out and the slaves toppled into the ditch. One bag of gold was not recovered and it is believed to be buried on the old Thibodeaux plantation.

Q: Have you ever heard the story of two fruit jars full of coins buried near Baskin?

A: In the early 1900's, a man by the name of Evans owned a farm about three miles east of Baskin, Louisiana. A prosperous man, he did not trust banks. His savings—two half-gallon fruit jars filled with ten and twenty dollar gold pieces—was buried somewhere on the farm.

Evans' two teenaged sons saw the coins a few days before they were buried, and one of the boys was present when his father took the two jars and left the house. He was back in less than thirty minutes, which suggests two possibilities: One, that the hole was already dug, and he merely had to deposit the jars and fill it in. Two, that he did not go very far from the house, and buried the jars in a shallow hole.

However, it seems unlikely that he would have left the hole open and then later returned to bury the coins, for fear of being seen. So the latter conclusion seems likely.

Not long after this, the father took sick and sent one of his sons to Baskin for medicine. While the boy was gone, the house burned down. Evans was either burned to death, or killed and the house burned to cover the crime. There were rumors both ways.

Over the years, a few half-hearted attempts have been made at finding the coin-filled fruit jars. But to the best of anyone's knowledge, the golden treasure has never been recovered.

Q: Has Col. Norman Frisbee's hidden fortune been found?

A: I cannot say if it has ever been found, but here is a brief account of Frisbee's treasure:

To save his family fortune, estimated at a value in excess of $1,00,000, from advancing Federal forces during the Civil War, Col. Norman Frisbee buried his treasure, carried on two wagons to a point in the marshland, not far from the present day plantation ruins located just north of Highway 14, about midway between New Light and Newellton. The vast hoard of treasure consits of gold coins and ingots, bullion, jewelry, gold and silver doorknobs, tableware and so on, including a silver bell he once had cast from 200 lbs. of silver dollars.

Q: I have heard of a Voodoo Queen that amassed a fortune that she concealed in some manner. Do you have the story on this?

A: Marie Laveau, a free mulatto, was born in New Orleans about 1798. She was a woman of great beauty, both face and figure. A hairdresser, she went to the homes of the best New Orleans' families, plying her trade. She found among them those who would buy her products when she began to deal in amulets and the powers of black magic. She became an active member of the local voodoo organization in the middle 1820's, and about 1830, she seized control of it by some unknown method.

Distinguished women consulted Marie, now the Voodoo Queen, about their affairs of heart, employed her to find lost objects, and bought from her, potions for the cure of maladies. The son of a wealthy family reputedly ascribed his acquittal of a serious charge to her magical powers. In repayment, he deeded her a little house on St. Ann Street where she lived for years.

Shortly after Marie became Voodoo Queen, she built a house on Lake Ponchartrain, between Bayou St. John and Milneburg. It was called Maison Blanche. She hid away there off and on for long periods, during the course of which she occasionally saw visitors who were willing to pay well for the opportunity. Her secret voodoo rites were held outdoors, never twice at the same place, and usually along Alexander Milne's swamp, where the participants could disappear at the first warning sound of the approach of those unwanted.

Replaced as Voodoo Queen in 1869, Marie spent the remainder of her days in the St. Ann Street cottage, and died there in 1881. It is said that Marie Laveau grew rich in the practice of voodoo and that she left buried or hidden, a fortune estimated as high as $2,000,000. It is generally believed that the treasure was buried near the site of Maison Blanche on Lake Ponchartrain.

Q: Do you have any information on a Spanish treasure in or near Winnfield?

A: Winnfield is located in the red clay hills of north-central Louisiana. The area remained unsettled by white men until about 1840. According to a local story, obtained from several sources, a Spanish treasure of five-mule-loads of gold and silver is hidden in man-made caves dug into the north side of Coochie Brake, about 12 miles southwest of Winnfield.

In the late 1700's, there was a small tribe of Indians living at this spot. A caravan of Spaniards came upon the Indians and, fearful that they would become suspicious of the cargo they were carrying, massacred all but three. These three Indians escaped and headed for Catahoula Parish, wehre the Catahoula Indian tribe lived. Since this tribe was warlike, the Spaniards decided they would split up into two groups—each taking a different route to Natchez, Mississippi, and thence on to the east coast where they would eventually ship their treasure to Spain.

However, in the skirmish with the Indians, several of their mules were killed, thus creating a shortage of animals to carry their heavy cargo which was stored in heavy earthen vases, two to the mule. According to the story, ten vases had to be left behind and were buried on the spot.

Considerable searching has been done for the lost Spanish gold and silver, but geologists of the Louisiana Mineral Board say there is quicksand in the area, about 30 feet underground, so it is possible the earthen vases have moved due to the shifting quicksand. This is a good spot for a deep-seeking metal detctor.

Q: I read of an old French fort in Louisiana where a British prisoner that had escaped from the fort, buried a large treasure. Is the treasure in or near the fort?

A: Here is what I have on this:

U.S. Highway 90 crosses one of the two passes connecting Lake Ponchartrain and Lake Borgne over the Rigolets Bridge. The French built the first fort here and called it Petit Coquilles, the original name of the island upon which it was built. This fort was replaced by another built in 1793, which was superseded by Fort Pike, built by the Americans in 1818. Near Fort Pike, now a State Monument, once stood a military hospital. It is said that a British prisoner being treated in the hospital, and in charge of a payroll of $270,000 in gold coins, made his escape. Then he was recaptured nearby, the gold was missing, and it is supposed that he buried it shortly after leaving the hospital. An extensive search was made for the gold but apparently it was never found.

Q: Has gold ever been found in Louisiana?

A: Yes, gold has been panned in several Louisiana parishes, especially in New Iberia, also on Wyndham Creek in Beauregard Parish.

Q: Could you tell me how many caches were made during the Civil War that are not known as "plantation treasures?"

A: It would be impossible to compile a list of all the caches made during the Civil War. Records, diaries, letters, et cetera, that told of different caches were lost or destroyed, and in several instances the people that buried valuables were killed.

The best way to locate these sites is to visit the area and check newspapers of the period 1861-1865, history and land records. Maybe some oldtimers will still remember stories of buried caches that have been handed down through their family. Try to locate these older poeple and talk to them. Check old court records. These sites can be found but it takes local research to do it.

Q: Is there any truth to the story that a treasure is buried near Linecum?

A: There is a story of buried treasure in Linceum, Grant Parish, Louisiana. According to this tradition, an eastern-bound party of Spaniards carrying a fabulous fortune in gold was attacked by Indians in this vicinity. Although the attack was repulsed, a second attack was expected and the gold was buried. Shortly afterward, the men fought among themselves and all were killed or later died of their wounds. This happened on the old Spanish Trail that ran from Texas to the east coast of Florida.

MAINE

Q: What is known of the Baron Castine Treasure?

A: Baron Castine, a French nobleman and one of King Louis XIV's personal guards, migrated to Canada in the late 1600's. Canada was then a French possession. Castine eventually settled near what is now the town of Castine, on Penobscot Peninsula, Hancock County, Maine.

Through shrewd trading with the area's Indian tribes, Castine accumulated a large amount of money, at the same time earning numerous British enemies through his biting criticism. When British authorities to the south decided to silence their critic, they sent a group of troops to destroy Castine's frontier fort and trading post.

Castine received word of the attack and wisely decided to flee, but left his daughter behind to tend to the trading post. She was instructed to seek shelter with friendly Indians when the British approached. The Baron planned to return for her later and recover his wealth, which he had buried somewhere in the woods nearby.

The british attacked the post and captured Castine's daughter, but found no trace of the money. Castine died in France, before he could return to retrieve his cache.

Q: Could you tell me the different places where Captian William Kidd buried treasure in Maine?

A: The stories of treasure that was supposedly buried by Captain William Kidd are so numerous that it would be a waste of time to try and investigate them all. I will give the sites, near the state of Maine, where Kidd is rumored to have left part of his ill-gotten gains. I make no attempt to estimate the value of each treasure but will give the names of different islands Kidd was supposed to have visited. You will have to do the local research on these different locations.

The islands are: Orrs, Outer Heron, Squirrel, Monhegan, Hollowell, Pittston, Isle of Haute, Twobush, Oak Island, Deer and Bailey.

Q: Is there an island near Maine that is associated with outlaws?

A: One of the few instances of counterfeiting in Maine was done on Ragged Island in Cumberland County. This gang operated for several years until they were finally routed by Federal agents. The island, because of its isolated position, was also a rendezvous for different lawbreakers for several years. This little known location could pay off because it is almost certain that something was hidden by some of these outlaws.

Q: I have heard of a treasure buried by a Portuguese sailor in Maine. Where did this take place?

A: This story of buried treasure concerns Little John's Island. Years ago there was a tavern on the north end of the island, a hangout of sailors, and one of these was a Portuguese who never did any work but always had plenty of gold and silver to spend when he blew in from parts unknown. This went on for years.

Finally the Portuguese man died in some foreign land, but before he died, he gave a shipmate a map of Little John's Island, showing the location of a hidden well. At the bottom of this well, he said, was more gold and silver than half a dozen men could carry. He knew (he said) because he'd helped put it there. This has never been reported found.

Q: Has any treasure ever been found in Maine?

A: These two instances of treasure being found in Maine, lends credence to the fact that there is probably more.

Jewell Island, in Casco Bay, is supposed to be one of the places where Captain Kidd buried treasure. Whether or not Kidd ever visited the island is unknown, but there is a story, backed up by considerable evidence, that a Captain Jonathan Chase found a large treasure on the island, killed a helper and buried him during the recovery. No record of what happened to Chase or the money can be learned.

On Bailey Island, also in Casco Bay, there is a well authenticated story of pirate treasure actually having been found in the 1850's. A farmer named John Wilson was duck hunting on the island, when, in an attempt to retrieve a fallen bird, slipped into a crevasse between two ledges. In his scramble to climb out, he uncovered an iron pot filled with pieces of Spanish gold. He exchanged these for $12,000 in coin of the realm, a comfortable fortune at that time.

Q: Have you ever heard of the hidden money of Anse Hanley on the Allagash River?

A: A story of possible treasure on the Allagash River, which could be worthwhile to check out, is that of Anse Hanley. During the early days of timber cutting, the lumber companies were constantly in trouble with "squatters." These people would carve out a small homestead on company land, then hint to the owners that if they were forced to move, a forest fire might start that would destroy millions of dollars worth of timber. In most cases, the squatters stayed.

One such land parasite was Anse Hanley. Around 1900, Hanley came to Fort Kent accompanied by his wife and two children. After obtaining supplies he moved up the Allagash River in Arrostook County, where he "squatted." During the next few years Hanley engaged in making whiskey for sale to the loggers.

It was said of his home-made product, "If a man can drink it and come back for more, he will live forever." Hanley also sold farm products and engaged in smuggling whiskey, guns and cigarettes from Canada, which he sold to American sportsmen and hunters. When Hanley died, he left a rumored $60,000, some of which was hidden before his death. Local research could help on this.

Q: Can gold be found in Maine?

A: Although the search for gold in Maine is little known, gold has been found in eleven places within the state. The State Geology Deaprtment says that no state-wide survey for gold has ever been made but the potential for gold is there. The largest number of discoveries have been made on Swift River and its tributaries. In several instances $300 to $500 worth of placer gold has been found along this river. You do not need a permit to search as a casual mineral collector for recreational purposes on state owned land, but permission should be obtained to search private property.

There is little doubt that gold can be found in Maine, but you will find the terrain very rugged and the recovery is hard work. When one sees that first tiny flake in his pan he is reminded of the words of David B. Whartan's book, "The Alaska Gold Rush," "Feel your pulse quicken and the electric tingling along the surface of your skin and know what it (gold prospecting) is all about."

Q: Did illegal salvagers ever operate along the coast of Maine and could you give me one location?

A: Cliff Island was once the home of a tough, old salvager called Captain Keiff, who lived alone in a log hut. His favorite way to wreck ships was to tie a lantern to his horse's neck, then ride up and down the shoreline. Ships at sea would be misguided by this light and be wrecked on the reefs and ledges that surrounded the island. Keiff would kill any survivors of the wrecks then salvage the cargo. In those days (while it wasn't encouraged, illegal salvaging was condoned) no questions were asked when someone sold salvaged goods.

Keiff is supposed to have made a fortune from his nefarious occupation. There is a place on the island still known as Keiffs Gardens. Local stories tell that somewhere on the island a large part of Keiff's money is still buried. This is quite possible since he had no family and lived alone with very few ways to spend money, as the wrecked ships supplied him with most of his needs.

Q: Where can I go "rock hounding" in Maine?

A: This information can be helpful to the Maine rock hound interested in searching. In Maine are found ores of most metals, as well as useful nonmetallic minerals such as quartz, feldspar, mica, graphite, and the gem stones such as tourmalines, beryl, amethyst, garnet and topaz. At least one mineral, beryllium, has been found nowhere outside Maine, and this state has yielded the finest emerald beryl ever found in the U.S. In mineral production Maine stands about midway among the states, the average annual yield being valued at about $6,000,000. One-third of the state is still unexplored in respect to mineral resources, and only limited areas have received adequate investigation.

Other metals, platinum and iridium are reported, although the possibility of obtaining them for commercial use is not yet clear. Gold is present in small quantities in a number of places. Silver is found in most of the lead and zinc localities, and the copper ore at Bluehill. That there are considerable bodies of lead and zinc of definite value has been known since they were first mined in 1860. Some pure silver has been mined at Sullivan and elsewhere.

The locations of different mineral sites can probably be obtained from the State Geology Department at Augusta, Maine.

Q: Was there a pirate named Timothy Barret in Maine, and where is he supposed to have buried his treasure?

A: Timothy Barret is generally thought to have been a pirate, but only because he had an unknown source of wealth. In the early 18th century he lived in the town of Liberty, Maine, located in George's Stream in Waldo County. Barrett apparently didn't like Liberty, because he moved across the stream and dug a cave in which he lived, raising vegetables in a garden built on a raft of logs. Because he had a seemingly inexhaustible supply of money, people speculated that he had been a pirate. After his death, a kettle containing French coins was dug up near his cave, and it has always been presumed that his main cache was buried nearby.

Q: Could you give me the story, briefly, of the two pirates, Bellamy and Williams and their treasure cache?

A: This is probably the largest pirate hoard ever hidden in the United States and at today's prices, this treasure is estimated to be worth several million dollars. In 1716-1717, at a spot (unknown today) near the mouth of the Machias River, Bellamy and Wiliams had their crews build a fort and underground chambers to hide the vast amount of loot they had accumulated in their high seas robberies. Bellamy, Williams and several of their crew were drowned when their ship wrecked in the shoals of Cape Cod. The rest of the priates were captured and hanged at Eastham, Mass. Somewhere near the mouth of the Machias River is a subterranean vault that holds the most fantastic pirate hoard known today.

MARYLAND

Q: Do you have any information on the ship Indies Ballard, which sank off the Maryland coast with $130,000 on board?

A: The Indies Ballard was a triple-masted sloop which sank in 1792 off the northern stretch of Maryland state's Assateague Island. With her sank $130,000 in gold intended to indirectly fuel the thriving slave trade in America. Despite two known searches, the ship and her treasure have never been found and they remain a tempting lure for treasure seekers even after almost 190 years. This is a very good site for a diver.

Q: What is the story of the Lost Rattlesnake Hill Silver Mine, sometimes called Herr Ahrwud's Silver Mine?

A: According to the story, Ahrwud was a silversmith in the late 1700's. An Indian showed him a secret silver mine on Rattlesnake Hill in Carroll County, and Ahrwud mined the silver for about ten years, then foolishly revealed the secret. As punishment, he and his daughter were tortured and killed by Indians. Supposedly, the Indians started a landslide to conceal the mine tunnel and the bodies.

During the late 1800's, several shafts were dug in the Rattlesnake Hill area, but the Indians' silver vein was never relocated.

Today, Rattlesnake Hill is covered with weeds and brush. No cave or mine shaft can be seen. It is east of Union Mills, Maryland.

Q: I have heard that the pirate Charles Wilson operated along the Maryland and Virginia coast in the 1740's and that he left directions to his buried treasure with his brother. Do you have anything on this?

A: Wilson's hideout was at Woody Knoll in Worchester County, Maryland. The directions were in the form of a letter Wilson wrote to his brother, George, in 1750. I quote: "There are three creeks lying 100 paces or more north of the second inlet about Chincoteague Island, which is at the southward end of the peninsula. At the head of the third creek to the northward is a bluff facing the Atlantic Ocean with three cedar trees growing on it, each about 1 and 1/3 yards apart. Between the trees, I buried in ten iron-bound chests, bars of silver, gold, diamonds and jewels to the sum of 200,000 pounds sterling. Go to Woody Knoll secretly and remove the treasure." As far as is known, the treasure is still there.

Q: Has gold ever been found in Maryland?

A: Maryland had its gold discovery days in the mid 1800's. Near Sandy Springs in Montgomery County, gold was discovered in 1849. The War Between the States slowed down gold prospecting in the South, but in 1861, a soldier camping near the Great Falls of the Potomac, found gold while washing a pan. Rich specimens were obtained in Montgomery County, and later in Carroll County. The gold occurred in association with pyrite. The first mine in the Maryland gold belt was opened in 1867 near Great Falls—placers in this region were active until 1937.

Q: There is said to be a treasure buried at Cellar House in Maryland. Where is Cellar House and what is the nature of the treasure?

A: Cellar House is located along U.S. 113 about halfway between Snow Hill and Berlin, Worcester County, Maryland. Its name comes from the story that an underground passage runs from the cellar of the old house to the Pocomoke River, and emerges under a bluff where a grassy mound is said to mark the former entrance. The story goes that pirates and river thieves brought their loot to the house for storage until it could be disposed of.

Another version is that kidnapped slaves were brought here and held captive until they could be transported south and sold. It is said that when the priates were cleaned out of the area, they fled Cellar House in too great a hurry to recover the treasures they had concealed there.

Q: Where is the Patty Cannon treasure located?

A: The exact location of the Patty Cannon treasure is still being disputed. The site is so close to the state lines of Maryland and Delaware that no one can definitely pinpoint its location. This location is claimed by treasure hunters in both states.

Q: What is the treasure story connected with the Perry Hall Plantation?

A: Burying the family treasure was an annual event for William Perry II, lord of Perry Hall Plantation and wealthy Talbot County senator. Each year before journeying to the Maryland State Legislature in Annapolis, Senator Perry, with the help of a trusted manservant, banked his gold, silver and family valuables somewhere on the fertile grounds of his 350-acre Miles River estate.

The fact that the senator chose to protect his family valuables by burying them wasn't unusual, as there was no commercial bank of the day convenient to protect these valuables during his annual leave of absence from Perry Hall.

It was in 1799, two short months after his arrival in Annapolis, that the senator suffered a fatal attack of apoplexy. As was his custom, or perhaps his precaution, Perry took the servant who had helped bury the treasure with him on all such trips to the state capitol. On the servant's return trip home, after the senator's death, he was in a fatal carriage accident. He died without ever speaking. Thus the only other person that knew the location of the buried hoard took the secret to his grave.

The Perry land, and what many believe to be a great legacy, is located a few miles west of Easton on Maryland Route 33, off St. Michaels Road.

Q: Did a British ship, loaded with valuables, sink off the coast of Maryland in 1812?

A: Yes, there has been a story told for almost 170 years that an unidentified British frigate sank off Tigham Point in 1812, in Eastern Bay. It is said, the ship carried a large amount of plunder stolen from Washingtron, D.C. in 1812.

Q: What is the treasure that is supposed to be buried near Braddock?

A: On U.S. Highway 40, between Braddock and Braddock Heights, stands an old house which was an early 19th century inn known as Hagan's Tavern. In 1830, according to a local story, a guest of the tavern buried a chest of jewels on a nearby mountainside. Two years later he returned to the tavern, and while attempting to recover the jewels he was fatally injured. Just before he died, he confessed that the jewels had been stolen in France. The tavern owner dug futiley for the treasure, which is supposed to still be there.

It could prove worthwhile to use a detector in this area. Relics from the Civil War and the French and Indian War may be found. Confederate cavalry were camped here in September of 1862, when they were captured by Union forces. General Braddock's troops were also in the region during the French and Indian War.

Q: Do you know of any Maryland treasure sites other than the Jean Champlaigne (or Juan de Champlain) treasure near Baltimore and those on Assateague Island?

Q: Maryland has a wealth of treasure sites, particularly in and around Chesapeake Bay. For a starter, there are two authenticated treasures buried by Captain William Kidd. Incidentally, it is debatable whether he was actually a pirate or not.

Kidd knew that orders were dispatched from London for his arrest. He suspected that merchants in New York and London, (big wheels who backed his privateering as a legitimate enterprise), planned to do away with him and seize all the loot. Before surrendering to authorities in Boston on July 6, 1694, he sailed up and down the eastern coast hiding much of his treasure. He was subsequently tried and executed in London.

One of the spots where Kidd stashed treasure was at Druid Hill Park near Baltimore. He buried a sea chest filled with gold and jewels there. A second cache is on the south side of Gibson Island, north of Sandy Point in Chesapeake Bay. It consists of chests containing an undetermined amount of gold, silver and jewels.

The pirate Blackbeard (Edward Teach) also favored this island. While his cutthroat crew caroused in Baltimore Town, he had four men dig a deep hole and bury four chests of treasure on the east point of Gibson Island. Blackbeard then ran his bloody sword through each of the four pirates and went back to Baltimore Town. This was a few weeks before he was killed off the coast of South Carolina.

Q: Have you ever heard of a Quaker treasure near Baldwin?

A: This is not a buried or hidden treasure, but it certainly would pay to check it out. This item appeared in the Boston Herald for November 9, 1906: "Calvin S. Harlam, an eccentric Quaker was struck by the Harrisburg and Baltimore Express as he crossed the tracks near Baldwin. Thousands of dollars were scattered along the tracks for a mile, before the accident was discovered."

The article does not say, but, Harlam was almost certainly driving a wagon to have been carrying this amount of money. Since there were no metal detectors in those days, all of the coins couldn't have been found.

Q: I am free to travel and would like very much to have several locations of buried treasure in Maryland that I could check out. Any help will be appreciated.

A: Here are several locations you might like to research: There is supposed to be a chest of gold coins and jewels on a mountain near Frederick.

In the Watts Creek area of Talbot County, loot worth over $200,000 is believed buried.

In Caroline County, there is a cache of gold coins known as the Poor House Treasure.

There is a house in northwest Baltimore called the Mansion House, and the story goes that $65,000 to $75,000 is hidden either in the house or in the immediate vicinity.

MASSACHUSETTS

Q: Was there ever such a thing as "beach priates" and did they operate in Massachusetts?

A: Yes, "beach pirates" operated along the entire Atlantic coast in colonial times. Monomoy Island, on the southeast corner of Cape Cod, near Chatham, in the late 1700's and early 1800's, was the scene of numerous ship wrecks caused by "beach pirates." These men would put up false buoy lights and lure ships close in to shore where they would wreck, then the pirates would plunder them. This ten mile sandbar should be a good place to search for coins and other items lost by these wreckers.

Q: Can yuou tell me about how much money and valuables are on the ship Andrea Doria that went down off Cape Cod in 1956?

A: According to the Andrea Doria's papers, its safe-deposit boxes contain over $750,000 in money and jewels. In the purser's safe there is $250,000 in American and Italian money. However, this is but a small portion of the salvage value of the ship. If the liner can be raised and salvaged, her worth is estimated at between $10,000,000 and $20,000,000. In 1970, it was announced that the Reynolds Metal Company was considering the possibility of participating in an attempted salvage operation.

Q: Do you know anything about the Thomas Smith treasure in Maynard?

A: During a severe storm in the early days of Maynard, several strangers came to the home of Thomas Smith, one of the early settlers and were housed in a barn. The fact that they paid generously for everything received from the Smiths, including tools for digging, led to the belief they were pirates. Later, they were observed carrying several heavy bags from the barn into the woods, returning without them. They then disappeared, never to be seen again. Sometime later, Smith received a letter in which the writer told him he was about to be hanged, and that if Smith would come to see him, he would be well rewarded. Smith disdained the invitation, and it is said that he missed the opportunity to be told where the treasure was buried.

The site of the Smith house in Maynard is now completely lost, but it was established in 1880 that it stood near the house of A.S. Thompson. If you can locate the site of that house, you could be fairly close to a treasure that almost certainly exists.

Q: What do you have on a treasure buried on Hog Island in Boston Harbor?

A: This treasure story dates back to colonial times. During those days, John Breed, an Englishman, came to Boston to forget his grief over the loss of his young bride. He settled on Hog Island (also known as Susanna Island) in Boston Bay, where he employed an Indian to guard an entrance to a cave. This aroused suspicions that the cave was stored with wealth. When Reed died in 1846, relatives searched the island and found $5,000 in silver hidden in the cave, but failed to find what they believed to be the greater part of his fortune.

Q: Can you give me any information about a treasure ship wrecked near Siasconset, Mass.?

A: There is an old Indian tradition relating that sometime before the settlement of Nantucket Island by whites, a French ship having on board a large quantity of specie, came ashore on the east end of the island in a storm, and was driven up into what was called the "Gulch," a short distance to the west of Siasconset. After getting the treasure ashore and burying it, the survivors had to cut their way through the heavily forested area to reach the Indian settlements.

It is believed they were all killed, as no record of the sailors returning for the treasure can be learned.

Q: I would like information on the Bellamy treasure in Massachusetts.

A: The location of the vast fortune stolen by Samuel Bellamy and his pirates is not known exactly, but one of three theories as to what happened to the money, valued today at $500,000, could be accurate.

Bellamy's first seizure was the Widhaw, a 28-gun British ship, which he used in his activities. There are three versions as to what happened to the Widhaw's treasure cargo. One theory suggests that it was left buried near the fort in Maine, since Bellamy had obviously wanted to locate there. A second version says the treasure was on the Widhaw when it sank, and in support of this theory more than 500 coins of the period have been found on the beaches near Eastham, or near the Wellfleet Light Station. Still another theory suggests that the treasure was divided with some of it left at Machias and some on the vessel.

Q: What is the story of a buried cache of coins on Martha's Vineyard?

A: The 20-mile-long island is rich in history, including the following story of treasure which some enterprising treasure hunter might find:

Up and down the New England coast, Vineyard Haven Harbor on the Island is known as a good port of refuge in a storm. The British were aware of this, and perhaps for this reason the island fell victim to a raid in 1778, led by an English officer named Gray.

The island had no fighting force, so it wasn't unusual for the islanders to feel apprehension for both life and property. Mentioned in the island's history is the incident of an elderly woman who, living alone, hurried to gather up her valuables and money at the first sight of the British men-of-war. She buried all of these near her home.

The woman survived Gray's raid and indeed the entire Revolutionary War. Perhaps her age, or the turmoil of the situation she was facing, explains her inability to remember just where she had buried her money and valuables. But to her dismay, she had hidden the cache so well that she could never find it.

A map of Revolutionary War vintage could be the first step in locating the site once known as Beck's Pond, and possibly a cache that is now nearly two hundred years old.

Q: What is the story of several pirate chests of money believed to be buried on Cape Cod?

A: In 1831, a fisherman named Arthur Doane found a fortune in Spanish gold on Cape Cod. He kept his treasure secret for forty-nine years, and then, on his deathbed, told a friend.

But his friend did not recover all the treasure. Most of it is still buried somewhere in the silvery sand of Cape Cod, not far from the old Chatham Light, where a few scattered gold coins have been found.

In 1831, Arthur Doane had seen pirates bury several chests of treasure near Chatham. Digging the chests up, Doane reburied the money. He then made a deal to sell a few coins at a time to a friend. This transaction went on for 49 years.

When Doane became ill in 1880, he told his friend where the other chests were buried. But a storm (as fate would have it) came up the night Doane died and his friend could not locate the remaining chests. Many have searched for this buried treasure, but its location has never been found.

Q: Is there any hidden treasure around Boston?

A: I found this information in my files, I hope you can use it: A large treasure cache is believed buried in one of the cellars of Dogtown, a ghost town located in a large wooded area on Cape Ann, 40 miles north of Boston, between Gloucester and Rockport. The last resident died in 1830 and thousands of colonial relics and coins have already been found in the area.

Q: Any information you can give me about the Daddy Frye's Hill Treasure in Massachusetts will be appreciated.

A: East of the Center, off Charles Street in Methuen, is Daddy Frye's Hill, topped by the towers of Tenny Castle and the battlement walls of an estate. During the 19th century, the brothers Mark and Nathaniel Gorrill lived on Daddy Frye's Hill. THey courted and were rejected by the same girl, after which they became hermits, never speaking to each other, though they continued to live on Daddy Frye's Hill near the castle. When they died, no money came to light, although they were known to be well off. This led to speculation that they left treasure buried in the area.

Q: I am new at treasure hunting and need information on any locations you have in northwestern Massachusetts, around North Adams or in Berkshire County.

A: Here are three locations. Local people around Pittsfield or Greenfield might be able to help you:

On Greylock Mountain is supposed to be a treasure buried years ago, by a hermit, that has not been reported found.

Near Turner Falls, Captain Kidd is believed to have buried a sea chest full of gold coins and jewels before his capture. This location is on the Connecticut River.

A well known treasure is that of the English General Burgoyne, in Berkshire County. After their defeat at Saratoga in 1777, the British were retreating and somewhere near Dalton they buried the proceeds of several months of looting, in the form of jewelry, gold and silver coins. They were never able to retrieve this, according to local stories.

Q: I heard a story of a cave in Franklin County where objects that predated Columbus were found. I checked on this but no one seems to have heard about it. Can you help me?

A: This little known location is indeed unique and would be well worth the time to search for. I wrote the postmaster at Greenfield several years ago concerning this cave. Like you, I received no help. I then contacted the "Boston Herald" newspaper. All I could obtain in the way of information was a letter that had been printed in 1853.

The story goes that several surveyors were working near Nestor Gap in Franklin County when they were caught in a storm. In seeking shelter they found a cave. Inside were ancient weapons, tools and three large jars of silver, brass and iron coins with no markings or image. There were also several scrolls written in a language none of them understood. The men involved in this find were named Charles G. Proctor, Samuel Emerson and a Captain Edwards. Several coins and a scroll were sent to Harvard Unviersity. But try as I might, I have been uanble to trace this discovery any further. This could be the archealogical find of the century if some interested person wants to investigate it.

Indian rock symbols.

Pistol found by author in barn.

Wheel money, 300 B.C., by author.

Indian mound in Kentucky.

Old tools and relics may be found in barns.

MICHIGAN

Q: Have diamonds ever been found in Michigan?

A: Yes, around Dowagiac in Cass County, is a very good area to search for glacial diamonds. Several have been found within the last few years.

Q: Is there a buried treasure near Benton Lake?

A: Here is what I have on this location: In 1874, Michigan's biggest industry was logging. In August of that year, a gang of desperados laid in wait for the stagecoach carrying $74,000 in gold to a large lumber camp in the area. The robbery came off as planned and the thieves made good their escape.

The bandits, knowing that the lumberjacks would soon be on their trail, decided to bury the gold until news of the robbery had died down. They selected a site between two tree stumps on the north shore of Benton Lake. There they put the money into an old cast-iron stove, dug a deep hole, and buried the whole thing.

Historians say the gold is still in the iron stove, waiting from someone to find it. Experts estimate the value of the gold cache to be almost a half-million dollars today.

The general location is easy enough to find but there are some difficulties involved. Benton Lake is still there on the left side of Highway 37, driving north, and the lake is also south of Baldwin, west of the hamlet of Brohman. The problems are largely due to the time lapse. The two stumps are no doubt rotted away, and the shoreline of the lake may have changed.

Q: I have heard of an Indian cache of coins in the vicinity of the Platte River. Can you provide me with information on this site?

A: This came from the magazine "Inside Michigan" for Juy 1953. "In the early lakeside position where they thought the Menominees with whom they had trouble would be most likely to attack. This was in the northern part of Benzie County, at the mouth of the Platte River.

By spring the Menominees had not come across Lake Michigan from what is now Wisconsin to fight, so the Chippewas decided to cross the lake in canoes and take the Menominees by surprise.

Before they embarked, however, the chief took all the money the tribe owned (two copper kettles full), carried it alone over the brow of a nearby hill, and buried it in a spot that only he knew.

The Chippewa warriors then launched their flotilla of canoes and crossed to the Wisconsin side of Lake Michigan. In Green Bay, however, a sudden storm capsized their frail craft, and all of the warriors drowned."

This is an authentic story that could very well pay someone to investigate.

Q: Do you have anything on the Nicholas Biddle Treasure?

A: In 1823, Nicholas Biddle, president of an eastern banking concern, induced a group of investors to build cities along good harbors in Michigan. One of the planned cities was Port Sheldon, in Ottawa County. The plan was to create a city the size of Chicago, at a cost of $200,000,000. A railroad spur was started to the town, and a large hotel, with gambling halls was finished. But the project went bankrupt in 1837.

In 1839, a mob of investors planned a raid on the hotel to collect their money from Biddle. He learned of the plan and is said to have buried a quarter of a million dollars in a well near the hotel. The raid did not materialize, but Biddle was afraid to touch the buried money and reportedly died without revealing its hiding place. I have investigated this location thoroughly and can find no record of this cache having been found.

Q: How much money did John Smally, Michigan's worst outlaw, accumulate during his crime career?

A: Michigan's most noted train robber was John Smalley, known as the "Whiskered Train Robber." Most of his train holdups and other crimes were committed outside the state, away from his home in Clare County, Michigan.

It wasn't until after his death, at the hands of a sheriff's posse, that his true identity was learned. It is not known how many robberies Smalley and different members of his gang committed during a several year period, but it is believed to have been considerable.

Smalley was visiting his girlfriend, Cora Brown, in McBain, Missaukee County, when the house was surrounded by a posse on the night of August 25, 1895. When asked to surrender, Smalley refused. After his girlfriend and her mother fled out a rear door, the posse began shooting into the cabin. Smalley was hit several times and died with a gun in each hand. He was buried in the McBain Cemetery.

The question has been asked many times, where was the estimated $1,000,000 that Smalley accumulated during the several years of robberies. I believe local research could pay off on this one.

Q: What is the story, briefly, on the Great Chicago Fire loot and where was it hidden?

A: Shortly after the Chicago holocaust, a part of the vast plunder taken during the three-day tragedy was brought in boxes to Leelanau County in a small schooner and buried by a group of five men. In 1871, that part of Michigan was sparsely settled, and the region offered an ideal spot for such an undertaking.

It is a recorded fact that during the great Chicago Fire, October 8-10, 1871, looters made away with an estimated five to twenty million dollars worth of goods and valuables. It is believed by most authorities that most of the stolen property was taken away by boat rather than overland, and if the repeated stories are true, none of the Chicago treasure has ever been admitted found and should still be there. Part of the loot is believed buried on Leelanau County's peninsula near Northport.

Q: Where can I prospect for gold in Michigan?

A: Gold has been found in 68 of the counties in Michigan. For those interested in searching, some of the best areas are: near Allegan in Allegan County; on the Antrim River in Charlevois County; on the Boyne River in Emmett County; near the town of Walton and on the Rapid River in Kalkaska County; on the Little Sable and Manistee Rivers in Manistee County; near Howard City and Greenville in Montcalm County; on the Muskegon River in Newaygo County; near the town of Whitehall and on the White River in Oceana County; near Grand Haven in Ottawa County; near the town of Burr Oak and Marcellus in St. Joseph County; near West Summitt in Wexford County; on Ada Creek in Kent County; on the Maple River in Ionia County; in the area of Birmingham in Oakland County; around Iron Mountain in Dickenson County; and near Harrisville in Alcona County. It could pay to pan any stream in these counties.

Q: What information do you have on the Silver Jack Driscoll lost gold and silver mine?

A: Silver Jack Driscoll was a cagey old prospector of L'Anse in the year 1894. A well-known lumberjack and brawler, he had left Seney in 1883 to follow the timber west and ended up in L'Anse, then a boisterous lumber town. Between his departure from Seney and his arrival at L'Anse, Silver Jack drove logs on the Yellow Dog River north of Ishpeming. It was during this period that he found his legendary gold and silver deposits.

Sivler Jack would set out on foot periodically from L'Anse toward the Huron Mountains to the north of the Yellow Dog River. After an absence of several weeks, he would return with his packs heavily laden with both gold and silver nuggets.

Plying him with drink or following him into the hills, the townspeople constantly tried to pry his secret from him, but no one ever learned the location of his mine. The secret died with Silver Jack. Since his death in 1895, many people have searched for the lost bonanza, but nobody has found it.

Q: I need all the help I can get on "King Ben's" treasure.

A: Benjamin Purnell, better known as "King Ben," is said to have accumulated several million dollars while running the House of David. Every member of the cult of the House of David had to sign over all his possessions to the leader, King Benjamin Purnell, to use as he saw fit. It is known that one family alone handed over $100,000 to the King when they joined the sect.

Everyone led a simple life and was content to work and live in the community, but the King's troubles began in 1910 when charges of immorality were brought against him concerning a number of young girls. The King hid out in the secret rooms of his mansion, but he was eventually captured. He died in 1927 though, without being punished.

After his death, his wife Mary told of seeing large bales of money, and jewelry by the bag full, in different parts of the mansion. She and members of the House of David could not find the $10,000,000 they knew the King had in his possession. Nor could they trace any of the jewelry. For years they searched the house and grounds for the riches King Ben had taken from them. As far as I can learn, none of these were found.

Q: Do you have the story on a mystery ship in Lake MIchigan that was carrying over $30,000,000 in gold?

A: This is all I have on the mystery ship: One of the most persistent rumors of sunken treasure is that of the Poverty Island wreck of an unidentified vessel which sank off Escanaba carrying a load of $4,500,000 in gold bullion. If Lake Michigan does hold this ship, it has the richest treasure of the Great Lakes. If legend is true, this nameless vessel was sailing from or to Escanaba. Its gold was being transported in five chests sent by a foreign power to help finance the outcome of the Civil War—in whose favor nobody knows.

One theory is that the gold came from England by way of Canada and was to be shipped across Lake Michigan, taken by land to the Mississippi River, then sent south to aid the Confederate cause.

The opposition learned of the cargo and attacked the ship. Hoping to recover the gold later, its guards chained the chests together and dumped them overboard. No one has yet been able to identify the gold-laden ship, though it has been referred to on several of the Great Lake shipwreck lists. The missing cargo could be worth as much as $35 to $40 million today.

Q: Could you give me a treasure location on Hermit Island that is not too well known?

A: In 1868, Frederick Prentice started stone quarries on Bass, Stockton and Hermit Islands. Like Hermit, Bass and Stockton were among the Apostle group of islands. By 1890, Prentice's fortune had grown to several hundred thousand dollars. He built a house near the quarry on Hermit Island, but when he brought his bride to live on the island she refused to stay. Prentice lived alone in the house until his death, and very litle of his wealth was found. Since he had no money in banks, it is believed he had buried it near his home.

Q: Is there a story of buried treasure in the area where Fort Michilimackinac stood?

A: Fort Michilimackinac was built by the French about 1715, in what is now Emmet County, Michigan. British troops captured the fort in 1761. On June 2, 1763, during Pontiac's uprising, Chippewa Indians overran the fort. They killed most of the British soldiers and held the fort for over a year. During the battle, the British soldiers are supposed to have buried, inside the fort, the large amount of gold and silver they had accumulated in back pay. This fort was abandoned after 1781 and soon reverted to wilderness. As far as can be learned, the gold and silver was never recovered.

MINNESOTA

Q: Has gold ever been found in Minnesota?

A: The North Star State is the site of very little gold mining activity. Much the same as in Indiana, the small amounts of gold found are the results of glacial drift brought down with gravel from the north. Two areas have shown some pannable gold, Spring Valley in Fillmore County and near Jordan, southwest of Minneapolis.

Q: Do you have any sites of old military forts in Minnesota that I can search around?

A: Here are three but you will have to obtain permission to search:

Fort Ridgley: Established in 1853 in Renville County, 3/4 mile north of the Minnesota River at the mouth of the Rock River, about 20 miles above New Ulm. The fort was abandoned in 1867 and is now in a state park south of State 19 and east of State 4.

Fort Ripley: Established in 1849 on Crow County as Fort Gaines, an outpost against the Sioux, on the west bank of the Mississippi. It is located seven miles above the mouth of Crow Wing and opposite the mouth of the Nokay. The military reservation was on the east bank but the post was on the west. It was abandoned in 1877. The location is off State 371, near the present town of Fort Ripley.

Fort Snelling: Built in 1819 and served for years as a frontier post. The only major action that took place in the area was during the Sioux uprising of 1862. The fort was finally closed in 1946.

Q: Are there any ghost towns in Minnesota?

A: Yes, there are several ghost and near-ghost towns that should be of interest to you. They are: Buchanan, Concord, Forestville, Frontenac, High Forest, Itasca, La Prairie, Landon, Lathrop, and Mantarville. You will have to write the Minnesota Historical Society, 690 Cedar Street, St. Paul, Minnesota 44101, to find where they are located.

Q: Did the Jesse James' gang hide any money near Pipestone?

A: There is a legend of a James' gang treasure buried near Pipestone. Unlike most of the James' gang loot stories, this one could be true.

After the First National Bank fiasco in Northfield on September 7, 1876, the story became current that Jesse James, Bill Chadwell and Charlie Pitts had been recognized while staying at a farm two miles south, owned by a man related to Chadwell. They were supposedly inspecting a getaway route. The story is that Jesse, knowing that the robbery would be attempted in a few days, buried a huge sum of money on the farm intending to pick it up later. The money was from the Otterville, Missouri, train robbery and his share of a stagecoach robbery in Texas.

When lawmen questioned the farmer, he admitted Chadwell stayed there with two friends. Rumors piled upon rumors until they caused the farmer to leave that part of Minnesota.

Some historians place the value of the money buried, from $25,000 to $100,000, and one has said the best guess would be about $50,000.

Q: What gem can I find in Minnesota?

A: Often mistaken for agate, the gem, thomsonite is handsome and valuable. Look for it along the shores of Lake Superior in northern Minnesota.

Q: Are there any lost gold mines or other metals' mines in Minnesota?

A: There are reports of several lost mines, most having to do with placer gold. Indians mined gold or found it in placers in the early 1800's.

There were rumors of a big Indian strike in 1878 which caused Walter and Perry Mize, middle-aged first cousins and bachelors of Minneapolis, to go north into the region of Red Lake. Traders told them they had bought gold from the Chippewa Indians but did not know its source. They supposed it came from the Red River Valley.

The cousins were told by a French-Indian half-breed that in earlier years he had found gold in the area where Two Rivers entered the Red River. They panned the creeks until, about two miles north of Two Rivers in a little unnamed stream, they struck placer gold. They returned to Minneapolis that fall with about $25,000, so the story goes.

In southern Minnesota, most streams entering the Minnesota River from Mankato to Ortonville have produced placer gold. Geologists think it was deposited by glacial drift which is often 100 feet in depth.

The first settlers in central Minnesota found a peculiar ore in six different places, southwest of Cuyuna Range, and east of the Mississippi River. They thought it was iron and carried it home. Eventually, geologists identified it as amosite and crocidolite of the amphibole group of asbestos ore, and the most valuable, called "blue asbestos" commercially. Since about 1910, the locations have been lost.

Pipestone, in Pipestone County, produces the best quality of catlinite found on the North American continent. It has grown valuable in recent years and has been found in other locations in Minnesota, but most of them have been forgotten.

Q: Has any treasure ever been found in Minnesota?

A: There are several stories of treasure having been found along the Red River near the town of St. Vincent and on the Minnesota side of the river opposite Pembina, North Dakota. More is believed to be in this vicinity.

Q: I need the story of the treasure believed to be buried near the site of an old soldiers' home in Minneapolis?

A: It was during the early days of the Civil War, around 1861 or 1862, that a "considerable treasure" consisting mainly of gold was buried by a Minnesota settler either on or near the grounds of the present Minnesota Old Soldiers' Home. Because of the widespread economic disturbance at that time, he no doubt considered it the safest way of hanging onto his fortune.

At any rate, the man went to the trouble of secreting his wealth somewhere on the west bank of the Mississippi River near what is now the southern city limits of the city of Minneapolis, then to all appearances, proceeded to forget about it for many years. In a deathbed statement to a friend, the old settler revealed the story of his buried treasure, but apparently was not too certain of its exact location.

Following his death, the friend made several unsuccessful attempts to find the treasure. Failing to locate it, he finally shared the secret with still another friend. After further investigating the story, the second treasure seeker asked permission to dig at the spot where he believed the gold to be located, since by this time, the property had come into the possession of the state. He was refused. Permission to do any searching will have to be obtained from the state.

Q: I read somewhere that bandit treasure had been found near La Seur. Do you know about this?

A: There are several stories of hidden treasure around La Seur but the one you mention concerned an outlaw named Rheinhart, who was lynched for murder in 1858. In May of 1906, a large amount of money was found in the trunk of an old tree near La Seur, believed to have been put there by Rheinhart, almost fifty years before.

Q: I need help on locations in, or near Lake City?

A: Lake City, on the Mississippi River, holds secrets to several treasure caches, hidden by bootleggers during the prohibition days and by wealthy farmers and businessmen. Check local library files, they could help—also newspapers.

Q: I have heard of the Charles Ney treasure, but where in Minnesota is the general location?

A: Charles Ney operated a brewery for many years in Henderson until prohibition went into effect. Soon afterward, he died. It is known that Ney amassed a considerable fortune, but it was not found in banks or in his home. In 1924, the brewery was razed. Two years later, a shaft was sunk 30 feet in an effort to locate the underground vault where the money was believed to have been stashed. The vault was not found.

Q: Could you give me a brief story of the Barker-Karpis gang's locations of currency?

A: The Barker-Karpis gang received ransom of $200,000 in five and ten dollar bills for the release of Edward George Bremer in 1934. Fred Barker and two other members of the gang picked up the money on the outskirts of Rochester and set out driving 19 miles southeast toward Chatfield.

Fred had orders from Ma Barker to split the money and cache half of it. During the night, on a gravel road, which today is Highway 12, Fred had the car stopped. He got out alone with the steel box wrapped in a canvas tarp, carrying a shovel. The other gangsters did not know where he buried the box on a farmer's fence line.

Piecemeal, less than $100,000 showed up in various places. Fred and Ma Barker were killed in a gun battle with officers at their Florida hideout. In addition to the Bremer ransom money, lawmen claim that other loot amounting to another $100,000 and possibly as much as $250,000, is buried in the same place or nearby.

Q: Do you have any treasure locations in south-central Minnesota?

A: Here are two in Sibley County: $40,000 is believed to be near Green Isle. This was hidden by two brothers named Curran.

In the area of Henderson, gold coins worth over $10,000 are supposed to be buried in a grove of trees. Check the library at Mankato, perhaps they will have more information on these locations.

Q: Are there any treasures hidden around Rochester?

A: Numerous stories relate to the burying of vast sums by prosperous doctors and businessmen at Rochester and occasional discoveries have verified some of these stories. This is a good area for local research.

MISSISSIPPI

Q: What is the story on the Captain Dane Treasure?

A: Captain Dane was Master of the Ship, Nightingale, which plied between the Gulf ports of Central and South America during the early 19th century. On what proved to be his last trip, he took on board at Montevideo, a rich, elderly Portuguese and his young Spanish bride, who was wealthy in her own right.

Captain Dane, making love to the young bride, obtained her promise to desert her elderly groom upon arriving in the United States. When the husband became suspicious of his bride and the captain, Dane knifed him to death. The bride then suffered remorse and threatened to reveal the murder.

When the Nightingale dropped anchor near Pass Christian, Captain Dane loaded all the money and jewels on board, into a chest, selected four sailors and abandoned the ship, after locking the passengers and remaining crew members below decks. Before leaving, he set fire to the vessel, and everyone on the Nightingale, including the young Spanish bride, perished.

Dane afterward bought a plantation and settled down with his treasure, but as yellow fever swept the coast, the last of his four men to die told the story of the Nightingale.

Learning that officers were arriving to question him, the captain hanged himself from an oak tree. He left no clues as to where he had buried his treasure of about $200,000 in money and jewels.

Q: Did a Union army paymaster hide a cache in Mississippi during the Civil War?

A: Here is all I have on this: During a Civil War battle, a Union army paymaster buried $8,000 in gold within sight of the Holly Spring Railroad station, only to die at the hands of Confederate soldiers before he could recover it.

Q: I have heard of a treasure hidden by a pioneer named Gore in Calhoun County. Do you have anything on this?

A: It is a matter of record, that the town of Calhoun City was settled on part of a 640-acre tract of land, that pioneer T.P. Gore had purchased from an Indian named Ish-ta-hath-la. Tradition says that Gore obtained the entire section for a handful of brightly colored beads and a few quarts of whiskey. Migrating here from Oklahoma, Gore settled himself in a large plantation house, living a life of ease in which horse racing and cock fighting played an important part. Sometime prior to his death, Gore buried a great part of the gold he had amassed on his plantation. He died without revealing its hiding place. Hopeful treasure hunters still search near the site of the old house, but so far as is known, no treasure has ever been found.

Q: Is there a buried treasure near the town of Doddsville?

A: The town of Doddsville is located on US 49W. Rumors have existed here for many years of a treasure buried in the area in seven fruit jars. No one seems to know the name of the person burying the treasure, but his habits were apparently common knowledge. He traveled extensively, and always when he returned home from a business trip, he made a secret trip into the woods, presumably to hide his wealth. One day, his wife missed some fruit jars and two gallons of alcohol. She assumed that her husband had used them to store his accumulation of coins, and that he had poured the alcohol in to prevent thier rust and corrosion.

Q: Do you have any information on a buried cache of coins near Little Rock, Mississippi?

A: This cache, believed to be $7,200 in coins, is almost certainly still where it was hidden. And since this happened during the 1930's, there are people, including members of the family, still living, that can remember this incident. This is one instance where permission has to be obtained before searching.

In 1929, when the stock market crashed, Zackary (Zack) Goforth lost most of his life savings. Goforth owned 640 acres which were tended each year, and was considered one of the more wealthy men of the area. After losing his money, Zack just worked harder to accumulate another fortune. It took time, but in a few years he had again become one of the more affluent men in his community.

This time Zack did not trust banks. His family knew that somewhere on the farm he had hidden several fruit jars full of coins. Sickness struck suddenly and Zack tried vainly to tell his family where he had hidden his small fortune, estimated to be over $7,000, but he died without revealing its location.

Indirect proof of the cache came in 1936, when two boys, fishing in a creek on the farm, found a small iron pot with $800 in gold coins inside. This is believed to be one of the first caches Goforth made, since gold had been called in by the government early in the 1930's. It is almost certain that somewhere on the Goforth farm near Little Rock, Mississippi, there is over $7,000 waiting for some lucky treasure hunter.

Q: Are there any sunken treasures in the Mississippi River?

A: Several ships known to have been carrying (what we call) treasure have gone down in the Mississippi, but whether they are still under water, or now under land because of the river's constant changing of its course, is not known. River pilots in the 1880's estimated that 5,000 river steamers had already been lost because of accidents between St. Louis and Cairo alone.

Q: What is the story of buried gold on Percy Creek, in Wilkinson County?

A: Percy Creek, in Wilkinson County, is a long, twisting, overgrown stream but somewhere along the creek's banks there could very well be buried a fortune in 200 year old coins.

In the early 1780's, a ship sailed into the Mississippi River and later stopped at the mouth of Buffalo Bayou. On board was a man that gave his name only as Charles Percy. He had in his possession a Spanish grant for a large tract of land north of Ft. Adams. Unloading farm equipment and a large number of slaves from the ship, Percy started immediately to build a home which he called Northumberland Place.

He must have been quite wealthy because Percy was made an alcalde, or judge, by the Spanish authorities. Records show that Percy registered his land grant and married a French woman.

A few years after Percy's arrival, a ship docked at Buffalo Bayou and an English woman and her son visited Northumberland Place. After a few minutes conversation with the woman, Percy walked down to the creek, tied a large iron kettle around his neck and drowned himself.

The lady was very interested in Percy's money and landholdings. All the slaves and Percy's wife would tell her, was that he had hidden his money (believed to be gold coins) in three ship's casks that had been waterproofed with tar and that they did not know where the casks were. The woman and her son returned to England after searching unsuccessfully for the coins.

Charles Percy's mysterious actions and death, the English lady's visit, and what happened to Percy's fortune were almost forgotten until a few years ago, when a story came out that two moonshiners had found one of the casks in a hollow tree stump while gathering wood for the still's cooker. The coins were made in an odd shape (probably eight-sided) and the two superstitious brothers thought the money was spooked, or haunted. They covered up the stump, quit moonshining and never went back to the place.

The creek is still there, following the same course it did when Charles Percy came there and the events concerning his fortune occurred. If the one cache was found (even if it was not left), there should be two others nearby. Some of the older residents living in or around old Fort Adams could probably help an interested treasure hunter to get on the right track of this hidden fortune.

Q: What is the treasure story connected with a man named Pluger in Adams County?

A: During the height of the flatboating days on the Mississippi River, many schemes were created to relieve flatboatmen of their cargoes. A Natchez character named Pluger, better known as Colonel Plug, was said to have accumulated a considerable fortune through a clever ruse he devised. Sneaking aboard a flatboat, Plug would conceal himself until the craft swung downstream. He would then suttle the boat by boring holes in its bottom. When the craft began to founder, his accomplices would row out in skiffs, supposedly to rescue the crew but actually to murder them. Only Colonel Plug would be saved. One day, Plug miscalculated the time between scuttling and rescue, and he was drowned. It is said that he left a considerable fortune buried someplace in Natchez-Under-the-Hill and that it was never found.

Q: I have heard of a treasure being buried during the Civil War at Vicksburg, by a man named Pickett. Do you have any information on this?

A: During the Civil War, Vicksburg was called the "Gibraltar of the Confederacy." Both the North and South recognized its strategic importance. In the hands of the Confederates, it severed the nation, and the North determined that it must be taken at any cost. As hostilities opened, many residents fled to the caves in the hillsides, burying their wealth which htey knew would be seized by Union soldiers if found. For various reasons, numerous of these buried treasures were never recovered. A typical example is a treausre buried in a Vicksburg hillside by the wealthy Pickett family. Only the father and son knew where the valuables had been placed. Both were killed in the seige of Vicksburg, and the surviving members of the family were never able to locate the treasure.

Q: I have heard of a place called the Devil's Punchbowl in Mississippi. What is the story of treasure there?

A: The area near Natchez, Mississippi, known as the Devil's Punchbowl, should be of interest to treasure hunters, because of the large number of hidden treasure stories connected with this (several acres) circular indentation, believed to have been made by a meteor thousands of years ago.

The Punchbowl's position made it a natural spot for all kinds of outlaws. Legends tell that pirates from the Gulf of Mexico came this far north, up the Mississippi River, to hide loot. River and land pirates, plus numerous other outlaws reportedly used it. Some of the outlaws from the robber infested Natchez Trace came here to hide out and supposedly hide some of their ill-gotten gains.

There is no question that some of these caches were removed by their depositors, but since this type of person lived a violent life, the odds are good that a large number of them were never retrieved. By spending a little time in local research, the Devil's Punchbowl should be a reward-ing palce for interested treasure hunters.

Q: Is there an Indian cache of gold coins buried on the Bogue Chitto River?

A: Yes, it is rumored that a large amount of gold coins, which had been received from the United States government in payment for land, were buried by the Choctaw Indians at the foot of the first hill past the river, north of Bogue Chitto in Lincoln County.

MISSOURI

Q: Is there a cache of Civil War gold in Bates County?

A: Sometime during the Civil War, a band of guerrillas supposedly robbed a bank and looted a small unnamed town in the vicinity of Adrian, Missouri. The raiders, with $90,000 in gold, were pursued by a party of Union soldiers. They halted only long enough to bury the three buckskin bags of gold they had obtained, at the base of a large tree. This spot is believed to have been about eight miles west of Adrian.

The raiders then fled west into Kansas. The Union soldiers were about to overtake them when Jayhawkers caught and killed the guerrillas. One of the dying bandits told of burying the gold by the tree. He died, however, before he could give the exact location. It is said that this treasure has never been found. The burial site is usually placed on or near White Oak Hill.

Q: Did the Spaniards ever mine silver in Missouri?

A: Over two hundred years ago, seven Spaniards, who were working a silver mine, after crudely smelting and stamping it, secreted their vast wealth in a cave about a mile from the smelters. After a while, they began fighting among themselves, and finally there was only one survivor, Pedro Diego.

Diego realized that he could not carry on the operations alone so he took into partnership two Irishmen named Higgins and McCabe. Diego disappeared not too long after the formation of the partnership; the Irishmen heavily loaded with silver, arrived in Boston several years later.

They boasted that 2,000 men could not carry the silver from whence their current wealth had come. The Irishmen, however, did not return to the Ozarks, preferring to live a life of ease in Boston.

Years later, in 1873, a Vermont farmer, Watson Johnson, sold his land and bought from one of Higgins' descendants the meager details of the mysterious mine and cave. Johnson located the mine but was found dead at the mouth of it the day after he entered it. No one has ever located the treasure cave, supposedly a mile or so away. This is believed to be about eighteen miles south of Galena, Missouri.

Q: I need a location of bandit loot around Liberty, Missouri. Can you supply me with any information?

A: Early on the morning of February 14, 1866, twelve men quietly entered the town of Liberty by different routes, and slowly gathered in the town square. While nine or ten of the men patrolled the street in front of the Clay County Savings Association Bank, two men entered the bank. They held pistols at the head of Mr. Bird, the cashier, and his son, forcing them to hand over $72,000 in specie and currency.

As the bandits rode off, Bird shouted to George Wymore, a 12-year-old student on his way to school, that the bank had been robbed. When the boy took up the cry, he was immediately shot. A posse attempted to follow the robbers but lost their trail on the wooded slopes to the north of town. The loot was never recovered. Clay County residents long believed that Cole Younger and the James boys were involved in the robbery. Pinkerton detectives, however, made a detailed record of the James gang robberies and never credited this crime to them.

One of the bandits who sped out of Liberty ahead of the rest is believed to have carried the loot. Before meeting his companions at a prearranged rendezvous, he is said to have buried the money, planning to recover it for himself at a later date. It is said that when he was overtaken by the gang and could not account for the loot, he was killed, and the treasure was not recovered.

Q: Did Mark Twain (Samuel Clemens) ever search for treasure near Hannibal, and what is the story on this?

A: Hannibal is best known as the home town of Mark Twain (Samuel Clemens). The Clemens' family moved to Hannibal from Florida, Missouri, in 1839, when Samuel was still a boy. It was here that Twin experienced the adventures in the cave that he later wrote about in "Tom Sawyer." The cave (now known as Mark Twain Cave) is located about two miles south of Hannibal and is privately owned, but is open to the public for an admission charge. It was originally known as Sims Cave after Jack Sims, who found it in 1819. It was later claled Big Salt-peter Cave and then McDowell's Cave, the name by which young Sam Clemens knew it.

In the 1840's, an eccentric St. Louis physician, E.D. McDowell, placed the corpse of a 14-year old girl—said by some to have been his daughter—in a glass and copper cylinder which he filled with alcohol and suspended from a rail, bridging a narrow passage in the cave. McDowell claimed that this was an experiment to see if the limestone cave would "petrify" the cadaver, but it is said that his real purpose was to create a tourist attraction.

Many tales of a treasure buried in the cave originated during the gold rush of 1849. Clemens himself spent many hours searching for treasure in the cave, probably having heard the legend that returning Forty-Niners had buried gold there.

Q: What information do you have on $20,000 in silver coins and $15,000 in gold coins hidden near Ozark Springs?

A: This amount is believed to be buried at Ozark Springs in southwest Howell County, in a long trench near the mouth of a large animal den on the northwest edge of a sink hole. The outlaws were captured and shot by Confederate troops, except one man, a Union deserter Hanford Groce, who was spared only to be recaptured by Union forces a few days later when they surprised the Confederates. In 1911, as he lay on his deathbed in Kansay City, Groce told the story of hiding this loot.

Q: Could you give me a location of Spanish treasure in or near Polk County?

A: Noble Hill is located on State 13, about 13 miles north of Springfield, and almost on the Polk-Green County line. There has long been a story known locally of a Spanish treasure buried in this area but details are scant. From 1940 until 1946, a man named Mullen owned 80 acres at tl. top of Noble Hill. When he had the land surveyed, the surveyors from Springfield found two graves on the land. In the brush-covered area they uncovered piles of stones obviously not placed there by nature, and some flat ston˙ with strange marks chiseled on them.

Bill Mullen, son of the farmer, was 10 years old at the time. He remembers the surveyors and his father wondering who would be foolish enough to pile rocks up like that and chisel marks on them. It was not until many years later that people realized these marked rocks might indicate the site of the legendary treasure. All efforts to locate the rocks since then have failed.

Q: I need a treasure location that has happened within the last fifty years.

A: In 1928, a Kansas City Southern passenger train was held up between Joplin and Webb City. Three bandits made off with a strongbox containing an undisclosed amount of money. One of the three outlaws was later captured and revealed that the treasure box, too heavy to carry in their flight, was buried just south of Webb City. Before the treasure could be recovered, the two participating bandits were killed in another attempted robbery. The surviving bandit became ill and died in prison before he could lead authorities to the buried strongbox.

Q: Do you have a bonafide Civil War location of gold in Missouri?

A: No site is bonafide until it is found but here is a good one you can check out. $30,000 is Civil War treasure, mostly gold coins, is believed secreted about 20 miles south of West Plains at a spot very close to the route taken by Confederate Col. Parker and his troops when they were raiding Federal troops in Missouri. The site is close to the Missouri-Arkansas border, west of Spring River.

Q: Did Jesse James hide any money in Missouri? How many caches did his gang make?

A: Stories tell of caches in these different places: Jesse James is said to ahve buried $100,000 in gold coins at Gads Hill in Wayne County. He is also said to have cached $100,000 in loot in a cave in the vicinity of Gainesville, in Ozark County.

The outlaw Cole Younger, along with Jesse James, buried a cache of gold and silver coins in the area of Alba, in Jasper County. It is also believed that Jesse may have hidden some of his loot near the old town site of Orongo, north of Webb City.

Q: What is the treasure story connected with Possum Lodge east of Waynesville?

A: Possum Lodge is a long established fishing camp on the Gasconade River east of Waynesville and almost on the Phelps County line. Near the camp is an old ford used by pioneers. Several legends are connected with the site. One story tells of a wealthy easterner returning from the California gold fields where he had struck it rich. It is said that he fell ill while camped at the ford and buried $60,000 worth of gold in the nearby hills, intending to recover it when his health improved. He died instead and the treasure was never recovered.

Q: What do you have on the Lock Treasure?

A: In the 1840's, a man named John (or Jonas) Lock is supposed to have amassed quite a fortune from his various enterprises which included a tavern, a farm and a racetrack. After his death, his assets amounted to only $7,000 so it is believed he hid a small fortune near his farm in Barry County.

Q: Was the Greenlease kidnap ransom money ever recovered?

A: Bobby Greenlease, a six year-old son of a wealthy St. Louis, Missouri family, was kidnapped on September 28, 1952. A ransom of $600,000, consisting of 20,000 $20 bills and $200,000 in $10 bills, was paid. Forty-three days later, the kidnappers, Bonnie Heady and Carl Hall were taken into custody. They led authorities to the grave of the boy, whom they had slain. So far as is known, slightly less than $300,000 of the ransom money was ever located. It is generally believed that the remainder was buried in two garbage cans along the Meremac River bottom in St. Louis.

MONTANA

Q: I have heard of several bags of gold that were scattered and lost by miners in 1806 or 1807, in Beaverhead County, Montana. I need information on this.

A: The first discovery of gold in Montana is generally accredited to Deer Lodge County, but some students of Montana history believe that distinction belongs to Beaverhead County. In

1862, when gold was discovered on Pioneer Creek in Beaverhead County, evidence was found of a much earlier mining activity. This evidence supports the long-standing legend that five gold seekers came to Pioneer Creek sometime in 1806 or 1807. These prospectors had heard of gold in the area from a hunter with the Lewis and Clark expedition. the hunter is supposed to have learned of the gold from a friendly Indian. Accompanied by a few of this friendly tribe, the prospectors located gold on Pioneer Creek near what later became the mining camp of Pioneer. The Indians warned the prospectors that they were in hostile Indian country and would be killed if they were discovered. When the prospectors insisted on staying and mining the rich placers, the Indians left them.

After mining all the gold they could pack on their ten horses, the prospectors started out of the territory. Somewhere near the site of the Big Hole Battlefield National Monument, they were attacked by the hostile tribes. The heavily-laden horses stampeded, scattering their sacks of gold in the forest, and four fo the miners were killed. The fifth managed to hide in the bushes until the savages left the scene, and although badly wounded, he managed to reach the camp of some friendly Indians.

Before he died, he said the attacking Indians had left the sacks of gold where they fell from the horses. The friendly Indians made a careful search for the sacks when they buried the four slain miners, but they found no trace of the scattered gold. The mystery of its disappearance still remains.

Q: Did a hermit named Knoles bury any money near Dillon?

A: After making a fortune in mining on Grasshopper Creek during the great gold boom at Bannack, Joseph K. Knoles returned to Dillon in Beaverhad County. In 1872, he became a sort of hermit, living in a crude cabin at the edge of town. One day he had a friend write to his sister, daughter and son-in-law, asking that they come see him. He confided to the friend that he knew he could not live long, and wanted to tell his family where his fortune was buried.

By the time Knole's relatives arrived, he was dead. They searched his cabin and the land around it, but found nothing. It is presumed that his treasure is still hidden. Some people believe that Knoles may have buried it at one of the camps where he had previously lived. Others contend that he would have taken his fortune to Dillon when he moved there.

Q: Has silver ever been found in Montana? If so, where and when?

A: Neihart was once the hub of all the surrounding mining towns. It had a population of 4,000. Today, the population is only about 150. Rich silver deposits were found near there in the Little Belt Mountains in 1881. Some of the lodes yielded as much as 500 ounces to the ton.

Among the many prospectors attracted to Neihart in its boom days was August Smedberg. One day during a snowstorm, Smedberg was traveling along Jefferson Creek at the base of Yogo Baldy. He stopped to rest beside a large tree that had blown down. In the hole where the roots of the tree had been torn out, he picked up a sample of ore which he gave to an assayer in Neihart. He left town immediately and stayed away for several weeks. When he returned, he found that the assayer's test on his ore showed some gold and an amazing 2,600 ounces of silver to the ton.

When he returned to Jefferson Creek to stake his claim, he could not find the fallen tree. He searched alone for months for his lost silver lode. Finally he told his secret to a friend, and the two searched together for almost twenty years.

One day Smedberg disappeared from Neihart. Sometime later, his body was found beside Jefferson Creek. He had tied a stick of dynamite around his neck and ignited it. To date, no one has found his great lode of silver.

Q: Did the outlaw Henry Plummer bury any money in Mineral County? If so, near what town?

A: Mullan Road, never more that a crude trail, was a 642 mile stretch of heavily traveled pioneer road between Fort Benton, Montana, and Walla Walla, Washington. Local legend says that Montana's outlaw-sheriff, Henry Plummer buried $150,000 along this old road in north-western Mineral County, probably somewhere in the vicinity of Haugan. U.S. Highway 10 runs approximately along the old road between Farrison, Powell County, and Lookout Pass on the Idaho Line.

Q: What is the Madison John treasure near Rainy Lake?

A: Rainy Lake is one of the smallest of the Clearwater Lakes in the east central section of Missoula County. It is an area dotted with campgrounds and summer homes. Sometime in 1864, members of the Henry Plummer gang of outlaws are supposed to have buried $100,000 in gold along the shores of Rainy Lake.

Q: Have diamonds ever been found in Montana?

A: In 1883, a miner named Ed Mason picked up a 3¼-carat diamond in a sluice box on his gold claim at Ophir Gulch. The weight and value of the stone was verified by a New York jeweler upon Mason's subsequent visit to the east. Before his death, Mason told of a sackful of diamonds he had found and buried near his cabin in Ophir Gulch. No one knows now exactly where that cabin stood.

Ophir Gulch is about halfway between the two small towns of Garrison and Elliston. Glacial diamonds have also been found on Nelson Hill in Glacier County. The possibilities of more being in the area are very good.

Q: Is there a lost gold mine in Lewis and Clark County?

A: About 1886, a man named Oldendorf worked a secret mine, making his headquarters in Augusta and later in Gilman. He made frequent trips into the mountains to the west, sometimes being gone for several weeks. Upon his return from one of these trips, Oldendorf went to Great Falls where he shipped 1,200 pounds of almost pure gold. On another occasion he shipped 1,000 pounds from Gilman. While waiting to receive his check in payment for the Gilman shipment, he suddenly announced that he was leaving to go to his mine, and would return later for his mail. He was never seen or heard of again, nor has his fabulously rich mine ever been found.

Q: Has the gold taken from the ship Far West ever been found and what is the story?

A: $375,000 in gold bars were removed from the riverboat, Far West, and buried less than a half mile above the Yellowstone River's junction with the Big Horn River, about 500 yards inland at the foot of the nearest hill. When the party returned to recover the hoard, rains had caused a landslide which hindered all efforts to recover the gold. It's supposedly still there, at the base of the slope facing away from the river, on the far side of the hill.

Q: Is there a lost Indian gold mine near Landusky?

A: The trading post of Fort Browning existed on its fur trade with the friendly Gros Ventre Indians. When the hostile Sioux increased their attacks on the Gros Ventre, the flow of furs to Fort Browning practically ceased. To remedy this situation and replenish their trading stock, the personnel of Fort Browning invited all of the Gros Ventre in the area to a Thanksgiving Day feast in 1868. The Indians arrived at the post in large numbers, including an old man known only as Neepee.

Particular attention was paid to Neepee, because it was believed that he knew of a rich gold deposit in the Little Rockies, a small range of mountains on the Blaine-Phillips County line north of Landusky. After the feast, Neepee showed his appreciation by presenting the commander of the post with a bag filled with gold dust and nuggets. When the white men tried to find out the source of the gold, the Indian would only say that death was the tribal penalty for revealing the secret to any white men.

A white man named Joseph Huntus, commonly called "Buckskin Joe", is reported to have learned of the mine's location, but was killed by the Indians when he went to search for it. His body was found by a party of trappers near the approaches to the Little Rockies.

Neepee died in 1876 and the secret of his gold deposit died with him. Gold was later discovered in the Little Rockies, but not in the quantities described by Neepee, nor was it like the samples the old Indian displayed at Fort Browning.

Q: Was there a miner (that buried a cache of gold) named "Beastly Butler" in Highland City during the 1870's?

A: The discovery of gold on Fish Creek produced the boom town of Highland City which once outstripped Butte in population. Among the thousands attracted to the area was a man known only as Butler. Butler was called "Beastly Butler" because of his untidy appearance and his filthy cabin.

In a camp known for its wild spending and scandalous living, Butler was conspicuous for his quiet behavior and frugality. Instead of throwing his money away on women and whiskey, he placed his daily accumulation of gold in the empty tin cans in which he had purchased goods. He is said to have cached them near his one-room cabin on his claim.

One day Butler's mine caved in and crushed him to death. His few close friends said he had at times boasted of a hundred or more cans of hidden gold. He had declared that when his mine was exhausted, he would dig up all the gold and return to the east. Immediately after his burial, prospectors made a search for his cans of gold but found none of them. Perhaps they are still there amid the ruins of Highland City, now a complete ghost town south of Butte.

Q: What do you have on the Albert Briggs lost rich ledge of gold and silver?

A: Freighter Albert Briggs' greenhorn helper who was later killed, found a rich ledge somewhere in the Alaska Basin area of southwestern Montana. The samples assayed at 2,000 ounces of silver and $20,000 gold per ton. It took Briggs several years to find this spot, but when he did he would not go back to it again for fear of the cutthroats who might jump his claim. He died without revealing the lcoation or realizing any benefits from this rich ledge.

Q: Can you tell me anything about the $80,000 which the "Wild Bunch" buried near Malta?

A: In 1901, Kid Curry and members of his "Wild Bunch" held up a Great Northern passenger train at Exeter Siding, just west of Malta, Montana. They obtained $80,000 in currency, but when it was found the bank notes were unsigned, they were cached nearby. It was the intention of the robbers to recover the bills at a later date, forge the necessary signatures and place them in circulation. But the Kid soon ended up in prison, the gang scattered and the unsigned notes are presumably where they were buried near old Exeter Siding.

Q: What is the "Chinee Grade" and what is the treasure story connected with it?

A: Going from Beartown to Garnet, the road reaches a summit that was known as "Chinee Grade." The Chinese miners were not always welcome, and their lot was usually a hard one in the mining camps. A group of Chinese had accumulated a considerable amount of gold which they stored in a five-pound baking tin. Being forced to leave the area quite suddenly, they cached their five pounds of gold near the foot of "Chinee Grade." They were afraid to return for the gold because of the white men.

NEBRASKA

Q: Do you have any information on an army surveying party that was killed by Indians in 1869? Did they bury any gold?

A: In the summer of 1869, a 12-man surveying party drove its wagons out the gates of Fort Kearney and headed for the desolate Republican River country in southwest Nebraska. Among them they carried over $3,000 in gold.

Later Pawnee Killer, an Indian chief, revealed that the surveyors had attacked a band of his warriors and were killed. The surveyors were near a range of hills south of the mouth of Red Willow Creek when they spotted the small band of Indians. They cached their gold, dug in and opened fire on the surprised Indians.

In the first round, three Indians were slain. Then over 100 others, hearing the gunfire, came riding up. Greatly outnumbered now, the surveyors made a dash for a timber stand on nearby Beaver Creek. There, they were all killed.

The army later pinpointed the party's last stand as being on Beaver Creek in Red Willow County, but thought the gold had been buried a short distance away, near the place the surveyors first spotted the Indians. None of the gold, the surveyors' wagons or their equipment were ever found.

Q: Could you give me the names of two pioneer or army forts in Nebraska and several ghost towns?

A: Fort John was established in 1850 in Scottsbluff County, nine miles southwest of Gering, off State 92 in Helvas Canyon. Used by the American Fur Company, the fort was visited by Father Desmet and Prince Paul of Wurtenburg.

Fort McPherson was established in 1863 in Lincoln County on the South Platte River, about two miles west of Cottonwood Springs and eight miles above the confluence of the North and South Platte Rivers. Intended to guard travelers, the fort was also the scene of a lavish hunting expedition attended by General Custer, General Sheridan, Buffalo Bill and the grand Duke Alexis of Russia. The fort was abandoned in 1880. The site is one-half mile east of a National Cemetery on State 107.

These five ghost towns are in eastern Nebraska: Omadi, Desota, Manosha, Pleasant Hill and Wyoming.

Q: I have heard of gold buried at Point of Rocks, Nebraska, but have never been able to find any details. Can you help me?

A: There are two Point of Rocks in western Nebraska. The one with the treasure story is located in Box Butte County, about 18 miles west of Alliance. This was a favorite camping place for freighters and wagon trains on the old Deadwood-Sidney Trail. When a wagon carrying an undisclosed amount of gold from the Black Hills to the railhead at Sidney camped here one night in the 1880's, a member of the three-man crew stole the gold and buried it nearby. The theft not being discovered, the man continued on with the wagon the following morning, intending to return later to recover the loot. Before the wagon reached Sidney, however, the theft of the gold was discovered and the suspected man was killed in the argument that ensued. So far as is known, the stolen gold has never been recovered.

Q: Was there a large sum of gold money buried at Fort Kearney?

A: In December of 1866, while Fort Kearney was under siege by the Sioux Indians, after the Fetterman command massacre, a howling snowstorm accompanied by below-zero weather hit the fort. Col. Carrington feared the Sioux would gain entrance to the fort by climbing over the walls with the aid of snowdrifts. He issued orders for the few women and children to gather in the powder magazine where they would be blown up before falling into the hands of the savage Sioux. He also instructed his paymaster to bury an unknown sum of gold contained in two chests.

A soldier named Portuguese Philips made a long ride under cover of the storm to Fort Laramie, Wyoming, for help. Fort Kearney was reinforced before the Sioux decided to attack.

The paymaster dug up one chest, but for some unknown reason did not retrieve the second. It is believed that the soldiers burying it were killed by Sioux snipers.

Q: What is the story on the cache of coins at Mud Springs?

A: In 1865, the Sioux ran rampant over Colorado and Nebraska, attacking wagon trains and stage stations, killing and burning them with abandon.

Only five civilians and nine soldiers were available to defend the stage station at Mud Springs, when it was attacked by scores of Indians. Reinforcements came from Camp Mitchell and Fort Laramie, driving off the Indians, but not in time to save the station attendant who had buried the station's money at the first sign of trouble. No one else knew where he had cached the coins. It is believed that the coins, hidden over 100 years ago, are still there at the site of the old Mud Springs Station, north of Dalton and west of U.S. 385.

Q: Did Buffalo Bill (William Cody) ever hide any money in Nebraska that was never recovered?

A: Yes, one night Cody was reported to have hidden between $17,000 and $20,000 in $20 gold pieces on his ranch. As the story goes, Cody came home to his ranch late one night about half loaded and one of the hired hands watched him unload a heavy chest from the buckboard wagon. Cody walked several paces, then stopped, turned around and slowly made his way back to the wagon and placed the chest onto the wagon once more. He looked in all directions as if to make sure he was alone. Finally, he climbed up on the wagon and drove somewhere out in the pasture.

About 45 minutes later Cody returned without the chest. He was still staggering around a little and he had black dirt all over his body. He could never find it thereafter.

Q: What is the story on the lost Mormon gold near Wood River?

A: In 1946, a farmer named Gust Anderson uncovered more than $100,000 in gold while plowing one of his fields near Wood River. It was later learned that this was part of the treasure buried by the Mormons as they moved west nearly a hundred years ago.

Anderson was the kind of Midwesterner who distrusted banks and was reported to have buried his Mormon gold on one of the many islands in the Platte River near Wood River. Anderson died in 1950. He had no family and according to the story, never told anyone where he had buried the gold.

Q: Do you have any information on a blacksmith's cache of coins near Peru?

A: In 1855, a hard working blacksmith came to the tiny settlement of Peru, in southeast Nebraska. Before many months passed he was able to put a few gold coins in the bank. In this instance the "bank" was the ground. The cache, variously estimated at $1,000 to $2,000, is still there.

If blacksmith Al Medley's trove seems small, remember that those glittering coins would fetch many times their face value today. A good palce to start, is in the area around the old blacksmith shop and store. Also, you should check the river bank near where he operated his ferry. Wherever the cache is, it has eluded searchers for over a century and it is well worth hunting.

Q: I have heard of a buffalo hunter's cache in Chase County. Do you have any information on this?

A: A buffalo hunter named McGuire sold a load of hides at Fort Kearney. After purchasing supplies he had $800 left. Leaving the fort, McGuire returned to his campsite.

Shortly after he reached his camp, two men rode in. They knew he had the money and had followed him from the fort. The old hunter offered them food, and while they ate, he walked to the spring to get water.

As he bent over the pool, he was clubbed from behind and killed. They searched the campsite without finding McGuire's money, then took his team, wagon and supplies and left.

The murderers were caught near Naigler and a fight ensued. One was killed and the other was sent to the penitentiary. The msising money is now lost somewhere near the old campground. The cache of old coins would be worth a lot more at today's prices.

Q: Did pioneer families bury their money when camping at night? Do you have any locations of such caches?

A: Yes, burying money was a common practice while camping at night among pioneers when traveling. Here are two sites: When camping at night, pioneers frequently buried their money under their wagon or nearby. Sometimes they were killed before their cache was reclaimed, and at other times they simply couldn't find it the next morning and had to move on with the train or become the prey of Indians. One wagon train family is said to have buried their money near Nebraska City and had to leave the following morning without recovering it.

Ash Hollow is located across the North Platte River, just south of Lewellen. Westbound Oregon Trail travelers usually camped there overnight before making the river crossing, and they were frequently attacked by Indians. Many travelers buried their wealth at night for safekeeping, and two Oregon-bound families, following this practice, buried their money there and were killed by Indians before recovering it. It is believed to be still there.

Q: What do you have on the Bennett and Abernathy cache near Alexandria?

A: In 1867, two wealthy ranchers named Bennett and Abernathy retreated to a cave near Alexandria when attacked by Indians. They were smoked out and killed. Their large amount of gold is said to be buried in another cave nearby. In 1908, a bag of 58 gold coins, believed to have been part of the cache, was found, but the rest remains lost. Some investigation in Alexandria might reveal the exact location of the cave.

Q: Where is Dobeytown, and what is the story of a hidden treasure worth $60,000 being there?

A: At Dobeytown was a scab town that spring up around Fort Kearney and was a hangout for hundred of desperados. It is the hiding place of $60,000 that was buried by a crooked gambler named Dud Wilson, who was killed in 1851, when he would not reveal the hiding palce to his abductors.

70

Old barns shouldn't be overlooked.

Old house sites are good.

Indian rock symbols.

A rock symbol.

Type of Indian cave used long ago.

Author examining rock carvings.

NEVADA

Q: I heard somewhere that diamonds have been found in Nevada. I am very interested in this story. Can you tell me where, when and what type of strata they were found in?

A: One day in 1872, a gold prospector known only as Lawrence arrived at the old O.D. Gass Ranch, now the site of Las Vegas. He left the following morning and traveled in a southeasterly direction toward the Colorado River.

In the volcanic formations characteristic of this country, Lawrence's attention was drawn to a seam of blue "mud" which ran at right angles to the surrounding formation. He carried away a few samples of the substance which he later panned out and recovered a handful of "rocks" or "crystals."

After carrying the rocks with him for some time, Lawrence asked a jeweler in Los Angeles if they were worth anything. Indeed they were, the jeweler informed him. They were diamonds from one to three and one-half carats in weight!

Under the impression that he could return to the seam of blue mud at any time, Lawrence is said to have given the diamonds to friends. But when he went back to wash out more diamonds, the blue seam had vanished. He was never able to locate it again.

Q: What do you have on the Lost Skillet mine?

A: The Lost Skillet mine near Searchlight was discovered by a mining engineer looking for a suitable campsite. He came upon some shallow diggings, investigated and found nothing. But near the excavation he dug out a half-buried skillet filled with fabulously rich gold ore. Examining a nearby ledge, he saw the same type of ore as that in the skillet. After thoroughly exploring the neighborhood, he concluded that he had stumbled upon a valuable find which had been previously worked. He gathered a generous supply of samples, covered the exposed ore, carefully marking the spot, and left. Sometime later, he outfitted himself and started out to work his new find. But when he returned to the place he thought contained the ledge of gold, he was unable to find a single marker. He spent years searching in the region then gave up. The Lost Skillet Mine is still lost.

Q: I have heard that most of the known minerals have been found in Nevada, what about platinum?

A: When the owners of the Boss Mine, a copper mine near Goodsprings (in Clark County), were notified that a yellow-gray substance in their copper was platinum, worth $70 to $90 per refined ounce, it raised an important question. Was there also platinum in the mine dump? A test was made which showed the same values as the sample. Immediate steps were taken to recover the fortune which had been cast aside. It is said that a single carload of this dump material yielded $135,000.

The vicinity around Goodsprings was thoroughly explored. No other platinum, however, was found. The Boss Mine was methodically investigated and worked, but it showed no further trace of platinum. Mining experts decided that one huge pocket had been struck and its supply exhausted.

Some geologists suggest that the platinum in the Boss Mine was only a part of a huge deposit formed centuries ago and that the mother lode is still concealed somewhere in the area.

Q: Do you have a story of two brothers that buried a cache of silver coins in Clark County?

A: I assume this is the site you want information on: In 1877, two unnamed brothers accompanied by a mule skinner drove a wagon from Utah with supplies for the Mormons remaining in the area. They also brought two chests containing $20,000 in minted silver to invest in the Colorado Mining Company. At Mountain Springs, the three men were attacked by Indians. One brother was killed, and the other two men, both wounded, were left for dead. Some days later, the two survivors were found near death from loss of blood and exposure. Taken to the Colorado Mining Company camp, they were placed in the care of the cook, a Paiute Indian woman. The brother told the woman that just before the attack, he and the mule skinner had taken the two chests of silver coins from the wagon and hidden them behind a large rock. After the attack, when they had regained sufficient strength, they had dug a shallow hole and buried the chests.

The two men died a few days after confiding their secret to the Indian woman. She immediately made a search of the battle site and found the charred remains of the brothers' wagon. Alone and concealing her movements, she dug around the largest rocks in the vicinity but failed to locate the two chests of coins. After revealing the information to others, she was aided in her search, but no treasure is known to have been found.

Q: What is the story of "Old Allegheny" in Elko County? Is this a person or mine?

A: The now deserted mining camp of Allegheny was named for an old Indian fighter, George Washington Mardis, better known as "Old Allegheny." "Old Allegeny" prospected in this section of northeastern Nevada, grew rich, bought a ranch, and settled down to raising horses.

One day in the 1880's, he left Charleston to Elko to deposit $40,000 in gold dust and coins. Near the headwaters of the Bruneau River, south of Charleston, he was murdered by a lone highwayman.

Some friends came upon his still warm body and captured the murderer. The highwayman had no gold and denied that the dead man had any. Since no gold was to be found, only two assumptions could account for the absence of the $40,000 known to have been in "Allegheny's" possession when he left Charleston. Either the murderer had had time to bury the gold before he was caught, or "Old Allegheny," suspicious of the approaching rider, had hurriedly buried it before the murderer overtook him. So far as is known the gold has never been found.

Q: Do you have any information on the Henry Knight cave of gold?

A: About 1880, Henry Knight prospected the Painted Hills, a small range near Sand Springs, and located a minor vein of gold. Tracing this vein, he came to a place that looked promising and sank a shaft. At about 50 feet, he broke into an opening that turned out to be a cave, the walls of which were lined with free gold. As he dug in the walls, more gold appeared. He did not take the time to investigate the full extent of his find.

Working hard to prepare some of the ore to be taken out, he suddenly began to feel ill and emerged from the cave for a breath of fresh air. When the illness persisted, he left the gold and went to Sand Springs to see a doctor.

Knight never recovered, and although he told the doctor about the cave, he gave only vague directions as to its location, so no one has ever been able to find it.

Q: I need information on a train robbery in Washoe County.

A: On November 4, 1870, five men robbed an east bound Central-Pacific Railroad passenger train near the small station of Verdi, about eight miles from Reno. A confederate had telegraphed the bandits form San Francisco that the train's express car would be carrying $60,000 in gold coins. It was a Wells Fargo shipment consigned to Reno. For his part in the crime, the informant was to receive $2,895, which was to be buried at a certain spot for recovery at a later date.

The robbery succeeded, the strongbox was seized, taken into the timber, broken open, and the informant's fee counted out. The rest of the gold was divided into five parts. As agreed, the informant's $2,895 was buried near an abandoned mine tunnel overlooking the railroad at the scene of the crime. Then the bandits fled in separate directions, each hiding his share of the loot as he saw fit.

When Wells Fargo agents captured the outlaws, they all received prison sentences after revealing where their caches were hidden. All of these were recovered, but none of the robbers lived to reclaim the $2,895 buried near the little station at Verdi, and Wells Fargo agents never have been able to find it.

Q: Can you give me any information on a Chinese party of miners that were killed in Nevada by Indians? Also, what happened to the gold the Chinese were carrying?

A: Sometime in the 1860's, a small Chinese wagon train made camp at the southern tip of Pyramid Lake. The Orientals had come from California, where they had successfully worked claims left by other miners. Aware that impatient whites seldom removed all the gold from a mine, the Chinese frequently gleaned considerable wealth from abandoned claims. The Chinese who had camped at Lake Pyramid had prospered in this manner and had accumulated two chests of gold coins which were being transported in one of their three wagons. They were now headed for the mining camp of Tuscarora where they would work over more claims left by others.

Early on the morning of their first day in camp, a band of Paiute Indians attacked the Chinese miners and kiled them all. The Indians removed the food and clothing from the wagons, but scorning the two chests of gold coins, they carried the chests to the base of a cliff along the lake and buried them.

This story was told in 1923 by an old Indian who said he had participated in the massacre as a boy. Although many searches have been made at the southern tip of Pyramid Lake, no gold has been found. Since the water of the lake has gradually receded, it is believed that the treasure now lies farther from the shore.

Q: What is the Disaster Peak Treasure and in what part of Nevada is it believed located?

A: In Humbolt County, and here is the story I have: During the gold rush days, a wagon train was returning east from California. Its members had been successful in the California mines and their wagons carried quite a lot of gold. On the journey, they met an Indian who was in need and gave him food and clothing. Out of gratitude, the redman attached himself to the party, as a kind of self-appointed advance guard and scout. In this country where a friendly Indian was rare, his services were welcome.

Riding ahead one day in his chosen position, the Indian met some tribesmen who were on the warpath. Unable to turn them back by persuasion, he eluded them and raced back to warn the white men, whom he found camped at the base of a mountain peak, in the northern part of what is now Humboldt County.

When the travelers heard the Indian's warning, they quickly unloaded their gold and buried it on the slope of the peak and prepared to defend themselves against the impeding attack. At dawn the following day, they were overwhelmed by screaming redskins. All the members of the wagon train were killed, their wagons rifled and burned.

It is said that a man named Thompson, the first surveyor in that part of the country, found the remains of the wagons years later and named the cliff, Disaster Peak. The Disaster Peak Treasure has never been found.

Q: I would like to search for bandit loot in western Nevada. Do you have a location I can check out?

A: Try this one: Robbers held up a stage and were hotly pursued by the posse to the canyon, just behind the ghost town of Columbus, where they were trapped. The posse killed them shortly thereafter, but the loot was not found and is presumed to be buried in the nearby rocks. This location is east of Basalt.

Q: Has gold been found recently in Nevada?

A: Yes, several mines have opened up since 1965. In the U.S. Geological Circular 560, which covered Nevada, it states small amounts of gold were detected in 27 samples out of 81 taken. The samples were taken in Western Churchill County. The hot spot for samples seemed to be on the southern part of Fireball Ridge which is in the northwest part of the county. There are several other areas in Nevada, namely in Lander, Eureka, White Pine and Elck Counties, where gold is being found today.

Q: What is the story of a robbery where one bandit was killed and the other put in jail within sight of hwere the gold was hidden?

A: This is an odd question, but here is the answer: Following a stage holdup, the bandits hid $60,000 in gold bullion. Two of the bandits were killed in the ensuing gunfight while the third was captured and sent to the Nevada State Prison where, it is said, he could see the burial site from his cell window. The robbery took place just out of Empire, northeast of Carson City. When he was finally released, the prisoner was watched so closely, he never had a chance to retrieve his cache.

Q: I read somewhere of a river pirate caching a large amount of silver. Do you have the story on this?

A: A lone pirate robbed the steamer Gila of its cargo of silver bars in 1880. The priate had to shoot his horse when it broke a leg days later and it is assumed the loot was buried near a spot around Crossman's Spring. One silver bar was found here in the early 1900's. More silver could be in the area.

NEW HAMPSHIRE

Q: Is it true that gold has been found in New Hampshire? If so, where are the best places to search?

A: Gold was first discovered in New Hampshire, in the 1830's and after 1900, the recovery of gold became a minor New Hampshire industry. Most of the streams originating in the White Mountains, particularly the tributaries of the Lost River and the Pemigewasset River, carried flake gold and BB-shot sized nuggets. No one has ever been able to trace it to the mother lode.

However, gold panning is part of the summer fun to some resident prospectors. The most likely spot will be in the Indian stream area and the contributory branches north of Pittsburgh, New Hampshire. Grafton County has also been the site of some commercial gold production.

Q: I have heard that a fortune in rubies went down with the ship Nottingham in December 1710. Is this true?

A: According to British Naval records, the Nottingham sank near Boon Island, just north of the Isles of Shoals, in December 1710. The rubies in her safe were worth $1,500,000 at that time, a fortune today.

Q: I know this sounds like historical fiction, but I have heard that one of Marie Antoinette's necklaces is hidden in New Hampshire. Is this true, if so, it would be worth a fortune today.

A: Somewhere on the banks of a small pond in New Hampshire, may be buried a fabulous diamond necklace that once belonged to Marie Antoinette, Queen of France. Just prior to the French Revolution, Marie Antoinette commissioned the best jewelers in the land to create an exquisite diamond necklace. Records show the necklace "cost six million pounds."

As the revolution became imminent, the necklace was sent to Canada, then a haven for exiled Frenchmen. There is no written account of what happened to it after that, only a legend.

In the late 1700's, a Frenchman, with an Indian companion, came down from Canada to settle near Nashua, New Hampshire. The two men built a hut beside a wood road that led to Pennichuck Pond.

At intervals, the Indian made trips back to Canada. While he was gone, the Frenchman kept to himself, only leaving the house for vital necessities, or for a solitary walk along the banks of Pennichuck Pond. Both men were extremely close-mouthed and took no one into their confidence.

While the Indian was away on one of his periodic trips to Canada, the old Frenchman died in his sleep. Upon returning to find his master and long time friend dead, the Indian seemed very grieved. He stayed at the house only a few days, then left and was not seen in Nashua again for many years.

When he did return, many former residents had moved away and only a few knew him. He went about inquiring as to the whereabouts of a string of "wampum" that sparkled in the sunlight. He told the townspeople that the Frenchman had been its caretaker, and that the two of them buried it somewhere on the shore of Pennichuck Pond. But he could not now remember the exact spot and had been unable to locate it.

The string of sparkling wampum that may well have been Marie Antoinette's lost diamond necklace never was found, and may still be buried somewhere on the banks of small, quiet Pennichuck Pond.

Q: Did counterfeiters ever operate in New Hampshire?

A: Yes, in the 1840's, a group of counterfeiters made fake coins near Hillsborough, close to what was called the Lottery Bridge. It is believed that the bogus counterfeit plates and a cache of good coins are hidden in a cave near the bridge.

Q: I need information on treasure buried by the pirates, Gordon and Blackbeard, on Star and White Islands off the New Hampshire coast.

A: Captain Sandy Gordon, with his own ship and crew, and with a working agreement with the infamous pirate, Blackbeard, was a highly successful plunderer. After one of his many piratical expeditions off the English coast, he set forth in his vessel—which was laden to the gunwales with treasure—to rendezvous with his partner, Blackbeard, in the Isle of Shoals. He arrived some weeks ahead of Blackbeard.

A division of the Flying Scot's extensive treasure was decided upon, and the day following the pirates' arrival in the Isle of Shoals, the division was made on Star Island. The crews separated into many different, cooperative groups and a number of individual treasure burials were made.

Captain Gordon took his share of the booty to neighboring White Island and buried it. When Blackbeard and his crew at last arrived, there was more dividing and burying of treasure.

Several weeks after Blackbeard left, a vessel was sighted, and believing it to be a rich merchant ship, Gordon and his men set after it with the Flying Scot. However, it turned out to be a heavily armed British man-of-war, which made short work of the pirate crew. The Flying Scot was sunk, and those pirates who weren't drowned or killed were hanged from the man-of-war's yardarm. There is no indication that the treasure, believed to be on Star or White Island, has ever been found.

Q: I know there are dozens of stories of pirate caches along New Hampshires coast, but has any pirate loot ever been found?

A: Yes, a cache of four silver bars was found on Smuttynose Island in 1880. Remember this was before metal detectors were invented, so it could pay to spend a vacation there with a good deep-seeking instrument.

Q: I know pirate treasure is supposed to be buried all along the eastern coast of America, but I would like several near New Hampshire.

A: Captain Kidd is believed to have buried loot in these places: Near Colebrook in Coos County; in the area of Weare, Hillsboro County; Rye Pond, close to Antrim; and near Portsmouth. Blackbeard is thought to have hidden treasure somewhere near the Isle of Shoals on Smuttynose, Landover, White and Star Islands.

The pirate John Quelch is supposed to have buried over nine pounds of gold and 190 pounds of silver on the west side of Appledore Island. Almost all historical societies and libraries along the coast of New Hampshire have records and accounts of pirate treasure.

Q: Have coins been found washed up from shipwrecks along the coast of New Hampshire?

A: Yes, old coins have been found on the beach near Colebrook in Coos County and in the sands of Duck Island.

Q: Has lead ever been found in New Hampshire? I have heard of a lost lead mine, but do not know the facts concerning it.

A: A vein of lead is thought to be on the eastern slopes of Mt. Sunapee near Newbury. The ore was used by the Indians in the early 1700's to make bullets for thier guns. One white man saw the mine in the 1750's as a captive during the French and Indian War. After escaping he returned to the area to search for the mine, but was uanble to find it.

Legend has it that another lead mine of almost 100% pure metal exists somewhere in the vicinity of Ossipee Range near Wolfeboro or Mirrow Lake in Carroll County. This was lost in the 1740's.

Q: What is the Mother Worchester Cache in New Hampshire?

A: I have very little information on this site in my files, but the Mother Worcheser cache of gold coins is believed hidden, or buried in a cave near Compton in Grafton County. Perhaps the historical society at Lebanon can help you. Here is their address: Lebanon Historical Society, 1 Campbell Street, Lebanon, New Hampshire 13766.

Q: What is the story on Governor Wentworth's cache?

A: When the American Revolution moved across the colonies, those public officials who were loyal to the British often found themselves tarred and feathered before they were run out of town. New Hampshire Governor John Wentworth, decided that he had better "get while the getting was good." So it was that he took his wife and servants, along with seven chests of his belongings, and headed post haste toward Canada.

It didn't take Wentworth long to realize all that weight was slowing them down too much. It was a painful decision, but he decided to cache the seven chests along the way. After all, he could always come back and get them after the colonists were beaten and the British had everything under control again.

One of the chests was reported to have been filled with $25,000 in coins and the other six with silverware and silver service for his table. So far as is known, the treasure has never been recovered. It is still cached in the vicinity of Durham, New Hampshire.

Q: What is the story of a silver statue of the Madonna lost in New Hampshire? Please explain how and when this happened.

A: The loss of a silver statue of the Madonna in the White Hills of New England in the 1750's is quite a mystery. The monetary worth of the silver statue is not particularly great, as treasures go, but it has extremely high intrinsic value.

The story of the silver Madonna began in the days of the French and Indian War, when the border conflict between the French Canadians and the British colonists was at its highest pitch. Raids by the French and their Indian allies against small settlements in New York and New England had aroused the ire of Lord Jeffrey Amherst, commander of the British forces at Fort Ticonderoga and Crown Point. Determined to put a halt to these border attacks, he summoned Major Rogers with orders to field an expedition of his famous rangers against the Indian village of St. Francis in Quebec, a well known jumping-off place for raids against the Colonies.

Rogers' band of 200 picked men first rowed by whaleboats to the northern end of Lake Champlain, moving only under cover of darkness to successfully evade patrolling French vessels. Finally, Major Rogers called a halt one evening 22 days out of Crown Point. Their destination, the Indian village of St. francis was only a few miles distant. After the battle a group of rangers rushed into the chapel, stripping the altar of its gold chalice, two heavy gold candlesticks, a cross and a large silver statue of the virgin.

Rogers ordered his men to march southward for home. They had been on the trail only a short time when the rear guard reported that a strong force of French and Indians were coming at them. Many of the stragglers were caught and killed immediatley by their pursuers.

The group carrying the silver statue of the Madonna made its way past Lake Memphramagog to the Connecticut River. They were pursued so closely that they had no opportunity to stop and hunt for food. By the time they gained the banks of the Connecticut, the group was reduced to four.

One of the four, professing to know something of this wilderness country, led the little band through the Great Notch of the White Hills. Here they crawled into the meager shelter of some overhanging rocks on a precipice near the Isreal River. One of the Rangers suddenly seized the silver Madonna nd hurled it over the edge of the precipice.

Years later, woodsmen in the region of the Isreal River discovered remnants of the lost detachment, but all efforts to locate the silver Madonna were fruitless.

There is sufficient historical documentation to affirm that the silver Madonna was carried by that part of Rogers' band which fled toward the Connecticut River. Also it is certain that the treasure was never found.

Q: Did a Spanish ship ever sink off the coast of New Hampshire?

A: Yes, legend tells of a Spanish galleon running aground on Star Island's eastern shore in 1685. For further information write the New Hampshire Seacoast Regional Development Association, Seacoast Regional Plan, 140 Daniel Street, Box 807, Portsmouth, New Hampshire 03801.

Q: An Indian trader named Cromwell is thought to have buried a treasure near Dunstable. Was this treasure ever found?

A: Some time prior to 1656, John Cromwell, an Indian fur trader, built a post on his 300-acre farm on the west side of the Merrimack River, about two miles above the mouth of Pennichuck Brook, at the place now known as Cromwell Falls. Suspecting that Cromwell was cheating them, the Indians burned his post to the ground. Cromwell had received an advance notice of the attack and buried his wealth and escaped. He left the country and died in England in 1661. As far as is known, he never returned to recover his cache.

NEW JERSEY

Q: Where can I get information about ghost towns in New Jersey?

A: I am certain you can find a copy of Thomas F. Gordon's "Gazetteer of the State of New Jersey and History of New Jersey," published by F. Denton, Trenton, New Jersey, 1834, in the New York City Public Library. Gordon lists many New Jersey towns which no longer exist. Two books by Henry Charlton Beck, "Forgotten Towns of Southern New Jersey," and "More Forgotten Towns of Southern New Jersey" contains information that will aid you.

Here are three you might check: Ong's Hat and Old Half Way were in Burlington County. Topanemus was in Monmouth County. It will take patience and perseverance to find these sites and others in New Jersey, but they will almost surely pay off.

Q: What is the story of Patrick Flynn, the Hermit of Harkers Hollow, who lived in New Jersey? Was all of his money found?

A: It was in mid-April of 1903, that concerned neighbors became worried about Patrick Flynn. He was 82 years old and known as the Hermit of Harker's Hollow. Flynn hadn't been seen for several days around his house, or in the surrounding area of Belvedere, New Jersey. They checked his house and found him dead.

Flynn, a bachelor, had a distrust for banks and it was common knowledge among his neighbors that he hoarded all the money that came into his possession. Seeking to locate his wealth, now that he was dead, a search was made. The search was productive on every hand. "In fact, wherever the men searched, they found money," was the official report. About $3,000 was found by the neighbors.

The neighbors knew Flynn had a sister living in New York and they wired her the news of Flynn's death. After arriving on the scene, and seeing what monies and valuables the neighbors had found, the sister alleged that the money found was only a small part of the wealth of her brother.

Without a waybill, or even an estimate of how much money the old man had buried or hidden, the amount left behind is still unknown. but from all indications, the remaining treasure of the Hermit of Harker's Hollow is well worth a modern treasure hunters quest.

Q: Did Blackbeard the pirate bury any money in Burlington?

A: Yes, the story goes that Blackbeard (Edward Teach) buried a large cache near a large tree on or near a certain lot in Burlington about 1718, described by the local historical society as the Florence Stewart property today. Blackbeard reportedly buried this treasure shortly before he died in a battle with a vessel commanded by Lieutenant Robert Maynard of the English Navy, off the coast of Carolina.

There has been much activity on this property from time to time by Burlington treasure seekers, but no treasure has ever been reported found.

Q: Can you tell me who is supposed to have buried a treasure on Schooleys Mountain?

A: A man named Arthur Barry, about whom very little is known, is said to have buried a considerable fortune on Schooleys Mountain (sometimes known locally as Hackettstown Mountain) while a guest at this health resort. It is believed that Barry's treasure was buried along the grade, up the slope near the old stone huts of the early German settlers. Schooleys Mountain Springs was known to the Indians as a remedy for rheumatism and skin eruptions, and has been famous as a health resort since 1770. This should be a good location for artifact hunting.

Q: Is there a large number of silver bars still unrecovered off Sewaren? I am a professional diver and would like to look into this.

A: Yes, the approximately 1800 silver bars would be well worth checking into by a treasure hunter that is experienced as a diver. Here is the story:

The Mallory Shipping Line brought the silver ingots, consisting of 7,678 silver pigs, each weighing about 100 pounds each, from Mexico for the American Smelting and Refining Company. On the night of September 27, 1905, the silver was being towed on the deck of the barge Harold from Elizabethport to Perth Amboy, New Jersey.

The silver had been loaded secretly at dusk by stevedores. As it turned out, a haphazard job of loading had been done. Sometime during the night, while being towed, the huge cargo of silver shifted and about 400 tons went overboard. The captain of the barge Harold, Peter Moore, was asleep on another barge and did not know that the silver had been lost until the Harold docked the next morning with only 200 ingots of silver lying scattered on her deck.

A contract was given to the Baxter Wrecking company to locate and salvage the lost silver. A crew was selected and then sworn to secrecy. William H. Timans, an experienced salvage operator, was put in charge of the operation. After a few days of dragging Staten Sound, contact was made in an area known as Story's Flat.

Within five days, 3,000 ingots had been retrieved through the use of a mechanical shovel, grappling hooks and divers that brought up the bullion by hand. By October 16th, another 2,500 ingots were retrieved and sent to the smelter.

The wrecking company then abandoned the rest of the silver because of threats made by local water pirates and the insurance company, after paying off, forgot about it. The approximate 1,800 silver ingots that remain in Story's Flat, on the bottom of Staten Sound, off Sewaren, could be worthwhile to search for.

Q: Did illegal salvagers operate in New Jersey?

A: Yes, on Absecon Island, near Atlantic City, land pirates would lure ships into running aground during a storm by tying a lantern around the neck of of a mule and walking the animal back and forth to give the illusion of a ship safe in a harbor. Because of this fact, legends of buried loot abound in the area.

Q: I read that there is a lost spinel mine in New Jersey. What is spinel?

A: A lost site in New Jersey once yielded the largest spinel crystals in the world. One crystal weighed almost 30 pounds, and there could be other fabulous crystals still there.

As the demand for spinel increases, the lost mine becomes more and more valuable. Records show it was worked in the early 1800's, and was located about half a mile south of the old town of Amity in Orange County.

One clue to finding the spot is the fact that less valuable deposits of green, black and brown spinel crystals are found in a broad belt of Franklin Marble that stretches across both Orange and Sussex Counties. The crystals usually occur in raised hummocks of marble.

Spinel is a hard crystalline combination of magnesium oxide and aluminum. It can be almost any color, from clear to bright red or even black. it sometimes reaches gem quality and can be quite valuable.

Q: I know this sounds ridiculous, but I have heard that German Nazis cached money in New Jersey. Is this true?

A: Yes, records show that at Lake Lliff near Andover, Camp Nordland was located. It was a spot for Nazi sympathizers, who according to rumors, stashed large sums of cash away to help finance spy rings operating in the United States.

Q: Would you give me a general description of the islands and beaches, especially Long Beach, where pirates might have buried treasure, their methods of concealment and what known pirates operated along the coast of New Jersey?

A: Many of the Jersey beaches are located on outer islands ranging in length from a few hundred feet to many miles. Legend has it that the vicinity of Long Beach and others was once the stomping grounds for pirates from many ports of the Spanish Main. They sought shelter from the rigors of the open seas in the secluded back bays of the islands.

Contrary to popular opinion, pirates did not bury their treasure in the sand dunes. such locations were too obvious, as other buccaneers might come along and dig it up. Also, the winds shifted and changed the landscape almost daily. Instead, they usually buried their treasure back on the mainland, in the nearby forests, in the vicintiy of a large tree, or rock, that could easily be remembered at a later time when they returned. It is a known fact that the notorious Captain Teach, better known as "Blackbeard," made his headquarters at various times near Long Beach. It is believed by many that he buried large amounts of treasure here before he was killed at Ocracoke, North Carolina, in 1718.

The nearby back bays of Brigantine were a favorite stomping grounds of Captain William Kidd. It was his interest in a farm lass, identified only as Amanda from Ocean County, who lived in the vicinity of Barnegat, which eventually led to his capture. Captain Kid is said to have buried a large share of loot near the mouth of the Mullica river or in the vicinity of Oyster creek just south of Long Beach.

It is also rumored that the pirate John Bacon and his crew buried loot on Long Beach during the 1780's.

Q: Could you give me a brief listing of sunken ships off Long Beach Island?

A: During the 40 years prior to 1878, more than 125 ships are known to have wrecked in the vicinity of Long Beach Island and left their bones on the beach. This stretch of coastline is truely "The Graveyard of the Atlantic." Here are a few of the known wrecks:

The Spainsh frigate Sagunto wrecked on the southeast point of Smuttynose Island in January 1813. Fifteen of her crew survived the wreck and reached the island only to freeze to death. Several silver bars have been found among the rocks in shallow water near the island. These are believed to have come from the unfortunate Sagunto.

The City of Athens, with $300,000 in her strong room, lies off Cape May at the southern tip of New Jersey.

In 1769, the schooner Live Oak went down off Squaw Beach carrying $20,000 in specie for the British troops in America.

A British ship, type unspecified, was bound from Liverpool, England, to New York when she grounded and wrecked on the southern end of Brigantine Shoals. Her cargo was tea and silver plate.

The 1,248 ton wooden steamer Cassandra wrecked on February 1867, while enroute from New Orleans to New York. In 1968, coins were found under her hull that dated from 1804 to 1850. The coins were coated with tar and as the practice of placing coins in tar barrels for concealment was a popular thing during this period, it is believed that more money is still within the wreck.

The Delaware sank in 1898, three miles off Point Pleasant. Her reported cargo, including gold bullion, was $250,000.

There is a wrecked ship off the shore at Ft. Mercer. Local legend says it was a Spanish galleon. The date of sinking and cargo are unknown.

Q: I would greatly appreciate any information you have on the Hendrick Dempster treasure.

A: When Hendrick Dempster died in 1873 on his farm in Homestead, near North Bergen, New Jersey, so little of his reputed wealth came to light that a legend grew up to the effect that he had buried a fabulous fortune in gold deep under a hillside on his farm. In 1923, two teenage boys spent 10 days undermining the hill, until they were discovered by a farmhand and forced to fill in the excavation. Nothing was found.

Q: What is the Furman Dubel treasure?

A: Before his death in the early 1900's, Dubel denied that he had any money. After his death his relatives found $9,000, believed to be a part of his estate which was valued at $500,000. Dubel owned extensive property and had collected rent on these holdings for years. He lived a frugal life and is known to have cached money in numerous places.

This would be an excellent location to research through newspapers of the period in Burlington.

NEW MEXICO

Q: Could you give me a location of buried outlaw loot in New Mexico?

A: There are several stories concerning buried bandit loot in New Mexico. This is one of them:

Prior to 1875, the Star Line Main and Transportation Company began the operation of a stagecoach line on a regular schedule between Prescott, Arizona and Santa Fe, New Mexico. This line was used mainly by the United States Army traffic to and from Forts Wingate and Whipple.

In 1874, Samuel Wharton and another man known only as Tom, held up one of the stage coaches northwest of Santa Fe and escaped with $50,000 in gold coins and bullion (believed to have been an army payroll). They traveled north after stealing three horses from a Navajo Indian herd.

It is believed the two outlaws followed Largo Canyon until they reached the San Juan River, somewhere near Blanco. By this time the two felt no posse could have trailed them this far. As they checked their back trail, they were surprised to see an army patrol of cavalry chasing them.

They started looking for a place to hide the gold before they were overtaken. Finding a rock shaped arch that would serve as a landmark, they buried the gold nearby. (This is thought to be in Slane's or Potter Arroyo.)

A short time later the cavalry caught the two outlaws. They were identified by two Navajo guides as having been the two men that stole the three horses. Tom and Wharton were arrested, tried and sentenced to forty years in the penitentiary.

It wasn't until 35 years later that Wharton turned up in Aztec, New Mexico. His partner, Tom, had died in prison. Wharton spent an entire summer riding around the countryside between Blanco and Aztec, searching for the arch that he and Tom had used as a landmark when they buried the stolen gold. Wharton left in a few months and no record of his finding the arch or gold can be learned.

For anyone interested, the search area is between Aztec and Blanco, New Mexico. Look for an outcropping of sandstone with an arch.

Q: I need information on a lost gold mine in Bernalillo County.

A: The original Isleta Pueblo is on a mesa about 14 miles south of Albuquerque. It is visible just to the south of US 85. The story of the Isleta Pueblo Lost Mine is one of the most persistent tales of the ancient Indian pueblos, but its origin has not been traced.

The legend says that a padre at Isleta once had an exceedingly rich gold mine where Indian workers were employed. Raids by Apaches were frequent, and the padre could offer the miners little protection. Finally, the Indians refused to work and the mine had to be abandoned. Before sealing the mine, the padre decided to make one more trip to bring out some gold he had stored there. He was captured by the Apaches and held as a prisoner until his death. As was their custom, the Apaches erased every trace of the mine.

Q: What is the story of the Lost Swede's gold mine and cache of gold?

A: The story of old mines once worked by Indians in Grant County has been a part of the folklore of that region for many years:

About 1900, a Swedish prospector known only as "Swede" is said to have uncovered traces of one of the mines in the Little Burro Mountains. These traces apparently consisted of tailings and some old tools. but in one instance the Swede found an old shaft from which he took a considerable quantity of gold ore. This ore the Swede packed to a mill in the Gold Hill country and received $14,000 for it. Returning to his dugout near his mine, he buried the money.

Sometime after this, he was in Lordsburg to obtain supplies, but got involved in a saloon brawl and was knifed to death. Although he had talked openly about his source of gold, he had kept its location and his movements a secret.

John Bailey of Lordsburg is supposed to have found evidence of the existence of the Swede's mine but never actually uncovered it. Nor was the Swede's $14,000 ever unearthed.

Q: I have heard of a cave in Lincoln County that is filled with silver bars. Do you have anything on this?

A: Somewhere along the Rio Bonito of south central Lincoln County is a cave reportedly packed with blackened silver ingots. it is said that the treasure was placed there when an expedition transporting it to Mexico was attacked by Indians. Many years later, according to the story, the treasure was discovered by a man named Hawks when he fled into the cave to escape Indians who were pursuing him. After the Indians left the scene, Hawks took out all the bars his mule could carry and concealed the entrance to the cave He sold his silver bars near Albuquerque. He later tried to find the cave again, but was unsuccessful.

Q: Could you tell me the circumstances concerning a lost vein of gold in the Rincon Range in New Mexico?

A: Somewhere in the Rincon Range in the western section of Mora County, a rich vein of gold was said to be uncovered in a crater by a falling meteorite in 1871. An old prospector named John Fazzi claimed to have witnessed the fall of the meteorite and found the vein of gold it exposed in the crater.

Fazzi, according to accounts, staked out a claim to the site, then went into Santa Fe to file it and celebrate his good fortune. He talked too much in a saloon and a band of outlaws forced him to agree to lead them to the crater, but Fazzi stalled and led the men astray. In his attempt to escape from them, he raced his horse, fell off, and broke his leg. The riderless horse, however, kept going, and the outlaws chased it, allowing Fazzi to evade them. He was soon found by a group of friendly riders and taken to a doctor where his broken leg was set. Complications set in, however, and he died of gangrene. Many searches were made for the crater, but it was never found.

Q: I have heard of a plane crash in New Mexico, where there was supposed to be $100,000 on board that was never found. Where did this crash occur?

A: In the huge lava flow at the foot of Mt. Taylor, near the town of Grants, is the site of an airplane wreck, a crash that occurred in 1936. On board was a cache of $100,000 in currency which was being transported from California to New York to further the political ambitions of presidential canidate Alf Landon. It was never reported recovered.

Q: What, briefly, is the story of the Lost Adams Diggings?

A: In the north central part of Valencia County, or in the south central part of McKinley County is a narrow, deep canyon containing a hewn rock vault, under a fireplace. The site originally held a cabin built by Jim Adams in 1874. The vault holds $10,000 in gold nuggets and the canyon has a secret entrance just wide enough for one horse and rider. The streambed located nearby is very rich in gold nuggets.

Q: Is it possible for 200 burro-loads of treasure to be buried? Did the Spanish ever hide this amount? If so, where in New Mexico is the general location?

A: Over 200 burro-loads of Spanish gold and silver church treasure, a hoard of gold bars, statues, ornaments and raw gold and silver, was buried on two knolls overlooking the old mission site within sight of the Gran Quivara National Monument and to the south of Mountainair. The cache, valued at over $120 million, was buried by Padre Francisco Letrado. The mission was established in 1627 and was abandoned in 1679.

Q: Do you have a story of a cache of guns hidden during the 1890's? If found the weapons would be worth a fortune today.

A: Here is what I have: Somewhere in the mountains northeast of Cimarron, New Mexico, in what was called the Cimarron Territory,there is believed to be a cache of several cases of guns, that filled a wagon.

The guns were hidden in a cave (some people think they were buried) while still packed in a protective coating of grease. If this is true, they would still be in good condition today.

The story goes that this cache was made by the Black Jack Ketchum gang during the early 1890s. This gang had a hideout about four miles from Cimarron, and it is highly possible that the guns are hidden near this hideout. This same gang is supposed to have buried $70,000 in gold coins taken in a train robbvery on July 11, 1899, near the same area in Turkey Canyon. It is very likely that somewhere in Turkey Canyon, near Lookout Rock, there is a cache of guns that would be worth a small fortune on today's market.

Q: Is there a lost deposit of turquose in New Mexico?

A: One rich strike of turquoise that was made near Hachita, New Mexico, in the early part of this century is especially puzzling in that its location is documented and turquoise was mined, but even the Bureau of Mines and Resources of New Mexico can only place this mine as "supposedly on a mountain near Hachita, facing east."

In the issue of "Southwestern Mines" for August 5, 1909, G. W. Robinson reported that he had discovered a rich deposit of turquoise near Hachita. He described the pocket as being 36 feet underground and that he had removed 60 pounds of large stones. He shipped this to Jacksonville, Florida, for sale. Robinson left the area without telling anyone the mine's location, and was never seen again.

Several turquoise deposits have been found in the area during the past few years but none that will produce the amount of turquoise that Robinson reported was still in the mine he located. The location of his discovery is still unknown.

Q: Is it true that some time in the 1800's a Catholic priest hid 20 or 30 mule-loads of silver in the Caballo Mountains of New Mexico, and what would the silver be wroth today?

A: The most comonly accepted version of this story is that the treasure, valued at $48,000,000, was buried by the Indian bandit, Pedro Navarez, who is said to have confessed the fact to a priest at the convent of St. Augustine in Mexico City before his execution in 1850. This treasure is said to be buried in a very deep cave in the Caballo Mountains, and the spot is marked by a cross chiseled on a large rock.

NEW YORK

Q: Could you give me at least two locations of buried pirate loot on Long Island, New York?

A: In 1699, Joe Bradish buried $300,000 in gold coins and jewels, which was contained in several boxes and bags, on Montauk Point on Long Island. It was a year's accumulation from his pirate activities and is secreted on the extreme eastern tip of Long Island.

The pirate Charles Gibbs secreted a hoard of treasure in the early 1800's, in the Southampton Beach area of Long Island. One of the many treasure caches by this pirate, it has never been found.

Q: Is there a lost Indian silver mine in New York?

A: There are several lost silver mines in New York and here is one that is almost certainly south of Ellensville, New York, in Ulster County: (Some of the jewelry made of silver taken from this mine is still in existnece, although it is rare.)

The mine was known to the Dutch, and there are several different stories and records as to its location, but they all agree that it is in the Shawangunk Mountains of Ulster County, near or in the 2289 foot high mountain known as "Sam's Point," south of Ellensville.

After Henry Hudson discovered the Hudson River, the Dutch began to colonize what is now New York. Sporadic fighting with the different Indian tribes started almost immediately but it wasn't until about 1660 that real war occurred. It was during this period that most of the Mohawk Indians migrated north into Canada. Before leaving, they sealed the mine entrance and no record of it ever being found is known.

History and a mixture of legend does show that the Mohawks did work a silver mine or vein prior to their migration, and used the jewelry in trade with the Dutch. The silver was pure enough to hammer, by hand, into different objects.

In 1804, three men, John and William Bauch and Casper Bertram, formed a company to mine silver in Schoharie County, New York. Bertram was the only one that knew the location of the ore but he was killed in an accident before mining could start.

In the area of Blue Mountain Lake, in Hamilton County, there are three lost silver mines, the Mt. Golden, the Nippleton and the Lavigne. The Lost Schechtushorst Silver Mine is in Green County, and a lost ledge of silver was worked by a man named Rufus Evans near Accord in Ulster County.

Q: I have heard of a French treasure that is still in the St. Lawrence River in New York. What is the story on this?

A: During the French and Indian War, a large fort was constructed on an Island in the St. Lawrence River by the French, about three-and-one-half miles below where Ogdensburg, New York is today. Most of the French troops in New York were stationed here until 1760, when the British drove the French out and took possession.

Stories of French and British treasure caches being buried on the island have circulated in the area for over 200 years. Recent searches have uncovered many relics but no reported amount of treasure. However, the story that the Marquis de Lewis did, in 1760, bury a large cache of gold on the island before surrendering it to the British was given considerable credence. A man named Pauchet (supposedly a grandson of the Marquis) came to the island with a riverboat pilot named King.

The two men are said to have dug up over 400 pounds of fused metal which was gold, melted when the fort was burned. After breaking the mass apart (they could carry only part of the metal) and putting it into bags, the men started for the American side of the river. About midstream, a storm broke that threatened to sink the small boat. Rather than throw the gold overboard, Pauchet tied several bags around his waist. A short time later the boat capsized and Pauchet drowned. King was able to swim to shore but the gold and Pauchet's body were never recovered.

Q: Can you supply me with information on the cache made by the gangster Dutch Schultz?

A: The notorious 1930's gangster Dutch Schultz is believed to have cached an iron box, 3' x 2' x 1½', that contained a large quantity of $1000 bills, jewelry, gold coins, negotiable bonds, diamonds and other portable wealth worth seven million, shortly before his death. The hoard is thought to be secreted four or five miles south of Phoenecia in a stand of stately pine trees on the bank of Eposus Creek.

Q: What is the story on Moses Follensby and his hidden cache?

A: Moses Follensby came to what is now the extreme north central part of New York, in the Adirondack Mountains, sometime in the mid 1700's, but avoided all contact with everyone. From his speech, Follensby was apparently an Englishman. The few white trappers that visited Follensby's lonely cabin told that he seemed to fear someone was searching for him. He was known to make secret trips north, but to where and for what reason, no one knew.

As more people moved into the area, Follensby withdrew to himself even more. After several years of this secluded life, Follensby died. After his death, papers and documents were found among his possessions that established the fact that Follensby was of noble English birth and quite wealthy. Why he preferred a life of lonely solitude was never learned. Several searches have been made for the supposed $400,000 he concealed, but according to all the available information I can obtain, the money has never been found. Although the cabin site where Follensby lived, and even his grave site, are unknown today, it is known that he lived near the lake that carries his name, Follensby's Pond, a few miles southwest of Tuppers Lake, in Franklin County.

Q: Is there a buried treasure near Pitcher Springs in Chenango County?

A: A traveling medicine man buried two chests of treasure known as the Sulphur Springs Treasure, in Chenango County, between Pitcher and North Pitcher near Sulphur Springs. Gold coins have been found near Pitcher Springs and may be part of this treasure cache.

Q: Did counterfeiters ever operate in New York?

A: Located in New York's Catskill Mountains, Balsam Mountain is part of the sumimt divide between Big Indian and Dry Brook. Its interest to the treasure hunter stems from Lost Clove, a long valley which splits it in two, and is the hiding place of a counterfeiters presumed cache.

About 1856, an educated man named Flint built a log cabin far up the Clove. Flint's seclusion and his desire for secrecy aroused the curiosity of the local citizens, as they were used to knowing everyone's business. But not even his housekeeper, who remained with him for about five years, knew Flint's occupation.

Periodically, Flint disappeared from the Clove for a month or so. When he returned, he always had a plentiful supply of money. Finally, Flint failed to return from one of his periodic trips. While it was believed by many that he was wealthy, no money was found in or about his cabin. About ten years after his disappearance, it was learned that a man named Flint had died in Sing Sing Prison while confined there for counterfeiting U.S. coins. It is believed he may have buried a cache of legitimate coins somewhere around his cabin that has never been found.

Q: Has gold ever been found in New York? If so, where?

A: Yes, gold dust and flakes (believed to be glacial) have been found in Schoharie Creek, near Middleburg. This is one area that needs further checking for a possible deposit of gold.

Q: Do you have any information on the Hanging Tree Treasure near Pawling, New York?

A: A large bag crammed full of gold and silver coins looted during the Revolutionary War period is believed buried in a meadow near the community of Pawling. The rich haul was supposedly cached in the Dutchess County location by a British officer shortly before he was hanged from the limb of the only tree growing in the meadow. No report of this cache having been found can be learned.

Q: What do you have on the Claudius Smith treasure near Goshen?

A: One of the most famous of all Tories (they remained loyal to England during the Revolution) was Claudius Smith, a convicted cattle thief who had managed to escape from jail in Goshen, New York. He organized a band of cutthroats, including his two sons, Richard and James, and looted, murdered and pillaged prominent Orange County Whigs. When they killed an important Colonial officer, Major Strong, a reward was offered for thier capture and they fled to Long Island. Claudius was captured while asleep. Returned to jail in Goshen, he was sentenced and hanged in 1779. His sons and other members of the gang fled to Canada, leaving behind a tremendous amount of hidden booty. In 1804, some of Smith's grandchildren came to Goshen with instructions for locating the loot, but all they found was a cache of rusty muskets.

In 1824, descendants of another member of the gang, Edwin Roblin, appeared in Goshen with a map and written instructions. They also searched and found nothing. The treasure is generally believed to have been buried in the hills around Goshen, or in the Claudius Smith caves, a shelter that once housed the outlaws, near the station in Tuxedo, Orange County.

Q: Where in New York did the Loomis gang operate and did they hide any of what we would call treasure today?

A: From about 1840 to 1897, the tightly-knit family of renegades terrorized and plundered upper New York state, leaving more than $40,000 in gold and silver currency cached at their stronghold in Nine Mile Swamp near Brookfield. This cache has been the object of many searches, but as yet it remains to be found.

Q: Do you have any information on gangster caches made during prohibition in the Catskill Mountains?

A: Yes, there are several stories of caches being made by bootleggers and gangsters during the prohibition era. $2,500,000 in gold ingots, coins and currency is believed hidden near Kingston in the Catskill Mountains. Most of the men hiding these different caches were killed in gang wars or by the police.

NORTH CAROLINA

Q: Where in North Carolina could I go to pan for different gems?

A: Corundum Hill is known the world over. To the serious rockhound it offers a wide variety of gems and minerals. Stones from Corundum Hill are unsurpassed anywhere. It is located seven miles east of Franklin on U.S. 64 and N.C. 28.

Also, about 10 miles north of Franklin near West's Mill, John West stashed a fifty pound bag of rubies, garnet, amethyst, zircon and other gems when he got tired of carrying the gems. The cache is halfway between West's Mill and the bridge at Caler Fork.

Q: How many ships have sunk off Cape Hatteras?

A: There is no way of knowing how many actually sank, because some of them were not recorded, but during the past 300 years, over 2200 ships have gone down in treacherous waters off Cape Hatteras. More than 400 of these shipwrecks carried with them to the bottom, a huge quantity of treasure-laden cargoe too numerous to list individually.

Q: Did the pirate Stede Bonnet bury any loot in North Carolina? If so, what is the general location?

A: Stede Bonnet was a professional soldier in the English King's army, stationed at Bridgetwon, Barbados. After retiring as a major in his middle years, he entered the business of piracy, supposedly to find respite from a shrewish wife. He later formed a brief partnership with Blackbeard, similar to the one enjoyed by Captain Sandy Gordon of New Hampshire legend.

One day in August, 1718, again on his own, Bonnet chose an inlet near the mouth of Cape Fear River to repair his ship, the Royal James, which had been badly battered in piratical forays. It was here that Bonnet is said to have gone ashore with a small company of men and buried three chests of treasure.

But, as the Royal James repairs were being made, the Governor of Carolina, having learned of Bonnet's whereabouts, sent a force against the pirates and, after a battle, captured them. Bonnet was later tried and hanged. His cache of three chests filled with gold and silver coins, buried close to the mouth of the Cape Fear River, near the end of the peninsula, has never been reported found.

Q: I have heard of a Confederate cache of gold coins being buried along some railroad tracks. Where in North Carolina did this take place?

A: Hundreds of iron cooking pots filled with gold coins from the Confederate Treasury, were buried by the Confederates at the close of the Civil War. The caches were made along the Old Southern Railroad right-of-way in the area about 15 miles between McLeansville and Burlington. The caches were made in lots of three on each side of the tracks and within 100 paces of the right-of-way. At least one of these pots was found by a farmer near a small town to the east of Greensboro.

Q: Has silver ever been found in North Carolina, and do you have information on any lost silver mines?

A: Here is the story of a lost silver mine that has been authenticated as closely as possible without actually finding it. This story of the lost silver mine and copper kettle full of silver "wads" predates the Revolutionary War. Thomas Clapum, Pennsylvania prospector, accompanied by a young Negro servant, came to what was in the 1760's, part of Rowan County, North Carolina. They crossed the river at Buffalo Crossing on the Indian Trading Path and prospected around Horse Mountain (so called because of its swaybacked shape), about ten miles away.

In a cove on the west side of the mountain he found a spring and while cleaning it of debris he found several nuggets or "slivers" of silver. He decided to build a cabin and prospect the area. Clapum traced the vein of silver to the mother lode, which was only a few feet under ground.

This section of North Carolina was inhabited by roving hands of Cherokee Indians that were jealous of all white men. In order to avoid interference from them, he built a crude furnace about three-quarters of a mile east of the mine. When the ore was taken from the mine, Clapum and his servant carried it to the furnace and smelted it into bullion. When they had smelted enough silver to load two horses, they decided to leave for Pennsylvania and return later. After concealing all traces of the mine and destroying the furnace, Clapum marked a rock giving directions, in code, to the mine. He then had his servant mark a large poplar tree, under which they had buried a large copper kettle full of "wads" (drops of smelted ore about the size of acorns) of silver. This tree stood on the east bank of what is now Richland Creek, in a straight line, one-half mile from the furnace.

As Clapum and his servant left the area they stopped at the cabin of Peter Elliott, which stood several miles form the furnace and mine. It was to Elliott that Clapum disclosed the secret of his mine, but not its location. He showed Elliott the two horse loads of silver bullion and told of burying the kettle full of silver "wads" under the roots of a large poplar tree, and that he intended to come back later and file a claim on the mine. However, Clapum died before he could return.

Years later, just prior to 1851, a legatee of Clapum's made a trip to the area, accompanied by Clapum's negro servant, now an old man, to search for the mine. They were never able to locate it. This trip and the legend of the silver mine was recorded in the "Evergreen Magazine," published in Asheboro, North Carolina in January of 1851.

Q: What is the story on the treasure of British General Cornwallis in North Carolina?

A: In 1781, Lt. General Cornwallis cached a hoard of plunder he had captured from the colonists, consisting of a large amount of gold and silver, which was contained in kegs and chests, at a point just to the east of Lexington, on the banks of Abbott Creek. The site is a few hundred yards north of the present-day highway bridge on U.S. 64, and was covered over to hide the booty.

Q: Do you have any information on a chest of coins hidden by the crew of a blockade runner in North Carolina during the Civil War?

A: Here are two locations of blockade runner treasures you might like to check out.

The Fanny and Jenny, a Confederate blockade runner, sank off North Carolina in 1864 as she tried to evade Federal warships and reach Wilmington. Reportedly it carried a jeweled gold sword, sent to General Robert E. Lee from English admirers. An undetermined amount of gold, sent to the Confederate government was also believed to be on board. The captain and his purser were drowned in an attempt to retrieve this gold, immediately after the ship sank.

Attracted by the high prices offered to ships' owners and crews by the Confederacy, for bringing in from Bermuda and the West Indies, the much needed supplies to maintain the Confederate army, many foreign ship owners became engaged in running the blockade into a few southern ports held open by the Confederacy.

The Prevensey, an iron steamer, was of English register, built by Charles Langley of Liverpool, England, in late 1863, as a blockade runner for the firm of Stringer, Pembroke and Company of London. The craft was some 500 tons, ironhulled, had side paddle wheels, and was schooner rigged.

Loaded on Confederate account with a cargo consisting of: arms, blankets, shoes, cloth, clothing, lead, bacon and other items, the Prevensey had run off her course to avoid capture by the Federal boat, Quaker City. To lighten her cargo, 30 tons of lead and 20 tons of bacon had been thrown overboard.

In the early morning of June 9, 1863, the supply boat New Bern, out of Fort Macon supply base, returning from supplying Union ships off the mouth of Cape Fear River, spotted the Prevensey, some 45 miles southeast of Fort Mason. Giving chase, the New Bern put a shot across the enemy bow, carrying away the forward davit.

Changing course, the Prevensey headed for the Bogue Banks, striking the beach about six miles west of Fort Macon. There she was blown up after the crew had pulled for shore. One sailor was left on board to set off the charge, and was later found unharmed. One man of the crew of 35 died on the beach before the remaining crew members were captured by Union soldiers.

The crew, knowing they were close to Ft. Macon and would be captured, buried the ship's cash box plus their own money and any personal items they had. Since they were not in either army, and were classed as mercenaries, it isn't likely any of them ever came back after they were released from a Union prison.

Following the close of the Civil War, stories were circulated that the money chest of the Prevensey had been brought ashore and buried opposite the wreck, the place marked by a clump of three large oak trees. The shifting sands would have made it almost useless to search in the 1860's, but with a good metal detector, the chances of finding this cache today are good.

Q: What is the story on the treasure at Pop Castle Inn?

A: Not far from Kittrell at a place called Ruin Creek, there was once a colonial tavern called Pop Castle Inn. It was in operation until about 1860, and was named after a pirate called Captain Pop, who was supposed to have buried his gold near the tavern.

Q: I have heard of a cache of gold coins near Jamestown, do you have the story on this?

A: Five miles from Jamestown on Rich Fork Creek, where the old Brummel Inn was located, there is a story of a satchel of gold being buried somewhere in the nearby woods between two very large trees. It was buried there by a man named Weatherford in 1854, who due to a stroke, became ill and died. Because the innkeeper had been nice to him, he told of burying the gold and wanted the tavern owner to have it as he knew he was dying. The next day Mr. Weatherford was buried in the graveyard behind the tavern, and the inkeeper started his search for the gold bearing stachel. However, he failed to find it, and the gold still has not been reported found.

Q: Is there a treasure site in North Carolina called the Camp Ground Treasure?

A: Camp Ground was the site of the last encampment of General Joseph E. Johnston's Confederate Army, before it surrendered to Union General William Tecumseh Sherman. It is due west of the town of Red Cross, in Randolph County, and is one of the best sites in the South to search for Civil War relics.

Many believed Gen. Johnston's command carried considerable amounts of money, which they buried rather than turn it over to the victorious Yankees. This money was estimated at tens of thousands of dollars. It is almost a certainty that all of these caches were not recovered.

Q: Could you tell me where gold was first discovered in North Carolina and was it found on a large scale?
A: Gold was first discovered in North Carolina, near the Stanley County line, on Highway 27. From 1799 until 1849, North Carolina was the chief gold mining area in the United States. Several gold mines operated during this period. Gold is still being panned in the streams of Stanley County.

Q: Could you give me a treasure location near Greensboro?
A: In 1854, William B. Wentworth buried a satchel of gold in the nearby woods at Brummel's Inn, between two trees. He died during the night and the gold was never recovered. The Inn was located on the stage road between Greensboro and High Point in Guilford County.

Q: Where can I find diamonds in North Carolina?
A: Glacier deposited diamonds are reported likely to be found in the following areas: near Tweety's Mine in Rutherford County; on Kings Mountain in Cleveland County; at Cottage Home in Lincoln County; on the Tood Branch in Mecklenburg County; on the headwaters of Muddy Creek, near Dysortville in McDowell County; near the Brindletown Creek Ford in Burke County and around the Portis mine in Franklin County.

NORTH DAKOTA

Q: What is the story of the lost gold on the Missouri River?
A: The story of $90,000 in gold dust and nuggets that was lost about a half-mile north of the present Northern Pacific Railroad bridge near the mouth of Burnt Creek between Bismarck and Mandon, North Dakota, in Burleigh County, has been written several times with different versions. But this is the best one from a serious and authentic viewpoint. The information comes from several different and reliable sources. Approximately $70,000 was recovered, but the remaining $20,000 has never been reported found.

In the summer of 1863, 24 white people, including a woman, a small girl, and a baby, were killed here by the Sioux, and nearly $90,000 in gold dust was strewn on the banks of the river. The white people had spent the winter mining at Bannock, Montana, and were returning east with thier gold. Stopping at Fort Berthold on their journey down the Missouri, they were warned by the trader, F. Gerard, that it was unsafe to continue until a large group was ready to make the trip through the territory occupied by the hostile Sioux.

The Indians, following the departure of the military forces, had returned to the east side of the river, as game was more plentiful there, and a party was camped on Burnt Creek. The ever-changing Missouri had cut a long sand bar near the creek mouth, forming a narrow, shallow channel between the shore and mid-river. On this bar, an old Sisseton was fishing as the white men's boat floated into sight. In a gesture of friendliness, the old man waved the boat away from the shallow channel, but his motion was mistaken for a signal, and the white men shot him.

Indian women bathing at the river's edge ran screaming to their camp, bringing the warriors. After the leader of the white party had been killed by the Sioux, they swarmed on board and disposed of the others. They found the gold dust, but thinking it was only yellow clay, scattered it on the sands.

It was several days later that Gerard heard of the massacre and sent a party of 10 Mandans, headed by his brother-in-law Whistling Bear, to recover the gold and bury the bodies. They scooped up approximately $70,000 worth in a coffeepot found in the boat, for which Gerard gave a fine horse and a few small presents to Whistling Bear, and a feast for his helpers. The gold that was thought to be hidden in the hull of the boat was never recovered, although several attempts were made by treasure hunters in later years.

Q: Can you tell me of any abandoned mines in Chalky Butte or any other area in North Dakota?

A: There are abandoned mines (or prospect holes) in Chalky Butte, the Turtle Mountains, Fox Hills, Killdeer Mountains and the Pembina Mountains. In the latter there is also a lost placer mine. It is not known whether it is in Pembina or Cavalier County.

Q: I have heard of a Hudson's Bay payroll that was taken during a robbery, but I thought the Hudson's Bay Fur Company was in Canada.

A: I'll explain how the robbery occurred and its subsequent results, causing the cache to be in North Dakota. This story of a $40,000 robbery has the ring of truth because, among others, the Royal Mounted Police of Calgary, Canada, have searched unsuccessfully for this lost cache.

In the late 1870's, a Hudson's Bay paymaster was enroute to pay the employees of the company at their scattered posts in the region of Saskatchewan, Canada. The paymaster was robbed of the $40,000 payroll near Estevan, Canada.

Fleeing south, the robber crossed the border into North Dakota. He was apprehended in the vicinity of Big Butte, a large grassy hill located about seven miles south of Lignite in Burke County, North Dakota, (there is a cave in Big Butte known locally as "Robber's Cave" that has been the reputed hiding palce of the money) but the bandit had already hidden the loot.

The robber died under torture at Portal, where he was taken. All attempts to force him to reveal the hiding place failed. The only clue he left was a rough chart which was found on the tanned side of his fur coat, and was believed to be a map showing the location of the cache. However, if the map ever led anyone to the treasure of Big Butte, the finder has kept it quiet.

The finding of an unearthed stone on Big Butte, bearing the date 1877, lent fresh hope to searchers a few years ago. No one has ever learned if this stone had anything to do with the missing money or not.

Many people have attempted to locate this cache and even the Calgary Mounted Police has sent men to search for it, but it has never been reported found.

Q: What is the story of George Trikk and his buried money?

A: In 1900, a bandit named George Trikk, managed to steal an unknown quantity of gold coins from an express shipment at Fargo. Fleeing southwest, he was finally overtaken and killed near what is now the town of Leonard. It is believed that the coins were hurriedly buried by Trikk just before he died, as none were found by his killers.

Q: Can you tell me the details of the Lost Fisk Treasure?

A: In 1864, an 80-wagon train captained by James L. Fisk, was enroute to the Montana gold fields when it was held up for 14 days by the Hunkpapa Sioux, in Slope County, very near the Montana border.

The expedition, accompanied by a cavalry detachment of 50 men, left Fort Rice in August and encountered no trouble until September 1st, when a wagon overturned in crossing a steep-sided creek. Fisk detailed another wagon and a detachment of eight cavalrymen to remain and right the overturned vehicle. As soon as the main party was out of site over a hill, a band of Sioux—part of the group met by General Sully at the Killdeer Mountains and in the Battle of the Badlands—who were at that time engaged in hunting buffalo, attacked the detachment, killing nine and mortally wounding three.

At least four men are known to have hidden their money at the beginning of the assault. One man buried a reputed $40,000 in gold, which he planned to use to establish a store in Virginia City, but he was among those killed. No account of this gold being found can be learned.

The gold is believed buried approximately 13 miles in an easterly direction from the Fort Dilts Historical Site, a sod foundation of fortifications the troops had established to protect the wagon train from the Indians.

Q: What do you know about a bootlegger's cache near Rock Haven?

A: In 1926, a whiskey runner reportedly buried $10,000 in one hundred dollar bills near a boatyard at Rock Haven, three miles north of Bismarck on the Missouri River.

Q: Do you have any information on a bandit cache, that was dug up by an Indian and then reburied?

A: In the 1880's, an outlaw gang of four men had successfully robbed several banks and trains in Minnesota and the North Dakota Territory. They had managed to make their way to Chalky Butte (one of the highest points in North Dakota), located about six miles south of Amidon, in Slope County.

The bandits decided to bury the money from the robberies, after taking what they would need for expenses. During the process of burying the money they were watched by a Sioux Indian hiding nearby. A few months later, all the bandits were killed. (If any of them ever returned to recover their cache before being killed, they failed to find it because the Indian had beat them to it and reburied it.)

After this, the Indian always had money after he visited Chalky Butte. He continued to obtain money in this manner until he died in 1910. Although he was followed several times, he always managed to elude his pursuers. His cache (it's almost a certainty, that he dug up the bandits gold and reburied it) has never been reported found.

There are oldtimers in the area of Chalky Butte that still tell of this lost cache. With his few needs, it is almost a certainty that the Indian did not spend all the gold.

Q: I have heard of a bank robbery in Dunseith, during the 1890's. Do you have any information on it?

A: The town of Dunseith is situated at the edge of Turtle Mountains. In 1893, the Turtle Mountain Bank of Dunseith was robbed of an undisclosed amount of money. The robber had time to hide his loot in the nearby hills before being overtaken by a posse and promptly killed. Although the bank refused to disclose the amount of the loot, it was sufficient that the Turtle Mountain Bank had to close its doors and was never able to reopen. One source said the amount taken was $150,000.

Q: Could you give me the names and locations of some old army forts in North Dakota?

A: Fort Ransom was established in 1867 in Ransom County. It was located north of State 27 and northwest of Lisbon on the west bank of the Cheyenne River. The fort was abandoned in 1872.

Fort Rice was established in 1864 in Morton County, and the fort is now within a state park.

Fort Seward was established in 1872, in Stutsman County, on the James River, for the protection of the Northern Pacific Railroad.

Old Fort Abercrombie was established in 1858, on the Red River, in what is now Richland County and was abandoned in 1877. It was a point of departure for emigrants embarking on the Minnesota-Montana Road.

Q: Was an army payroll ever lost during a robbery in North Dakota?

A: Yes, according to the story, in the early days of the Dakota Territory, a small party of soldiers left Fort Meade, in the Black Hills of South Dakota, with an army payroll to be delivered to Fort Keogh, Montana. They never arrived at their destination and it was presumed they had been ambushed and killed by Indians. About 1900, three revolvers marked "U.S.", and Army wagon irons, were found near Sunset Butte to the south of Amidon. It was believed that this was the remains of the luckless expedition, and that the payroll had probably been hidden nearby just before the attack. So far as is known, no search has ever revealed it.

Q: Are there any ghost towns in Barnes County?

A: About 17 miles north of Valley City, was a ford on the Cheyenne River, still known as Sibley's Crossing. Wagon trains bound for the Montana gold fields camped here where there was a post office known as Ashtabula.

The small town of Eckelson was once located a mile east of its present location.

Q: Are there any treasures hidden near the old Rock Haven boatyard?

A: Two or three miles north of Bismarck, was the old Rock Haven boatyard. Trappers and freighters often buried their valuables nearby while having their boats repaired. Some never lived through the wild celebrations and their property still lies waiting to be claimed.

OHIO

Q: What is the story of Fort Wapatomica and was any money buried there?

A: The British built Fort Wapatomica at Zanesville in the 1780's. Zanesville was the main town of the Shawnee Indians in Ohio at that time.

George Rogers Clark and Benjamin Logan were raiding Indian towns along the Miami and Mad Rivers. When Captain Caldwell, the British officer in charge of Fort Wapatomica, learned of those raids, he decided to attack Kentucky. At Bryan's Station, near where Lexington, Kentucky, is today, the American pioneers resisted, and Caldwell had to retreat into Ohio. He then prepared to attack Fort Pitt in Pennsylvania and Fort Henry in western Virginia. This was in open defiance to the Treaty of Paris of September 3, 1783, which officially ended the American War of Independence.

Before leaving Fort Wapatomica, the British collected all their valuables and placed them in a large iron kettle which was then buried within the stockade. This hoard consisted of gold coin to pay the British troops, reward money for the Indians collecting American scalps and the personal accumulations of some of the soldiers who had saved their pay.

While Caldwell was attacking Fort Henry—Wheeling, West Virginia—Benjamin Logan and his Kentuckians burned Fort Wapatomica to the ground. Logan knew nothing of the treasure buried inside the fort. Since this treasure has not been publicized, very little searching for it has been done. A marker erected in 1953 at Zanesville, tells the location of Fort Wapatomica, where a possible fortune in gold coins may be buried.

Q: Has silver ever been found in Ohio?

A: Yes, silver and lead were discovered in Adams County in 1900, on Brush Creek near Peebles. Disagreements over mineral rights and a lack of funds prevented the organization of a projected silver mining company.

Q: Is there a place called Tinker's Cave and what is the story of Indians connected with it?

A: After General Anthony Wayne's victory over the Indians in 1795, most of the aborigines moved west. A few renegades remained near Nelsonville, and they stole horses and other property from the settlers. The cave they used for their hiding place was named Tinker's Cave for their leader. The cave is on Route 363 close to Nelsonville. The Indians are believed to have hidden their stolen money in the cave.

Q: Do you have any information on the caches made by the famous Indian fighter, Lewis Wetzel?

A: Lewis Wetzel, famous Indian fighter of the 1780's and 1790's, lived near Fort Henry where Wheeling, West Virginia is today. Wetzel declared a one-man war against the Shawnee Indians. He hated the Indians so much, he cached guns, ammunition, supplies, and a little money in three different places so he could have ready access to them. Two of the caches were in Belmont County. The third was in Fairfield County. In Belmont County, one cache was under a rock shelter at the mouth of a small creek emptying into the Ohio River near Martin's Ferry. The other was near St. Clairsville. His cache in Fairfield County was at Lancaster in a cave near the top of Mt. Pleasant. But Wetzel confided to friends that when he was being trailed by Indians, he forgot where he had hidden his rifles, lead, and powder.

Q: Can you help me learn anything about the Morgantown gang and their hidden loot?

A: From about 1882 to 1885, the Morgantown Gang consisting of Asariah Paulin and his seven sons, each an expert in a specific type of crime, operated around Woodford near East Liverpool. They committed murder, arson, robbery and a host of other crimes. It is believed that most of the proceeds from their infamy were buried on the Ohio River near the two shacks they used for headquarters.

Asariah Paulin was known as the "Old Fox." He was caught in Pennsylvania and returned to Youngstown for trial. Paulin and other members of the gang received long terms in the penitentiary. When they were released, the police kept them under such effective surveillance, they were afraid to try to retrieve their hidden loot.

Q: What is the story of sixteen pack horse loads of loot buried by the French in 1758?

A: About the middle of the 1800's, an elderly man named Lesuer came to the vicinity of Rochester. He had a letter which had been given to him by his father. The letter told the location of sixteen pack-loads of gold, silver and silverplate that had been buried by the French army when they evacuated Fort Duquesne in 1758. The following is a verbatim copy of that letter:

"We, of the French army, were defending Fort Duquesne against the British. When it was learned that the English were attacking in force, a detail of 10 men and 16 pack horses were selected to carry the French army's gold and silver away from the fort. I was chosen for this detail.

Three days and a forenoon later, northwest of west from the fort, while on the Tuscarawas Trail, our advance guard returned to our little column and reported British soldiers advancing on us. The officer in charge of our detail ordered us to stop in our tracks and dig a hole in the ground. He posted a few guards while the rest dug. The gold was unloaded from the horses and placed in the hole. Then the silver was lowered into the hole. On top of this, we shoveled the dirt and covered it with branches.

The British started firing at this time. The digging shovels were put under a log on the hillside. No sooner was this done, than the British were upon us. Eight were killed, only Henry Muselle and myself were spared. The English had not noticed where we hid. We made the following marks on the area before we fled. The gold was buried in the center of a sort of square formed by four springs. About one half mile to the west of the hole where the gold was buried, Muselle jammed a rock into the fork of a tree so that it would stay. 600 steps to the north of the hole, the shovels we hid under a log. As we left by the east, I carved a deer into a tree which I judged to be about one mile east of the hole."

The area referred to in the letter is now the farm of George Robbins, near East Rochester in Columbiana County. The shovels and the rock in the tree have been found, but the gold and silver, if found, has not been reported.

Q: Did General St. Clair bury a payroll near Findlay?

A: In the fall of 1791, on orders from President Washington, General St. Clair left Fort Washington, now Cincinnati, with 2300 men and supplies to insure the white settlements safety from further Indian raids. Indian resistance was stubborn. By the time St. Clair reached the area of the present town of Findlay, he had only 1400 men left. It was here that over 2,000 Indians attacked St. Clair. They killed over 631 American soldiers. When it seemed the army would be completely annihilated, the General is believed to have ordered the payroll money buried somewhere on the battlefield. This was never found because General St. Clair was captured and burned alive at the stake by the Indians.

Q: Is there a lost lead mine in Ohio?

A: Buckchitawa, now known as Sunfish Creek, runs through the small community of Cameron. Legend has it that a rich lead mine is on the creek not too far from the small town. There is documentary proof that the Indians obtained lead for bullets on this creek during the 1780's and 1790's. Martin Wetzel, who was captured by the Indians and escaped, reported that while he was being taken to the Indian village of Wapatomica, the Indians stopped and got lead for bullets on Buckchitawa Creek, near where Clarington is today.

Q: Can you give me information on a man named Bailey, who was a member of John Dillinger's gang?

A: Near Jackson, in Jackson County, in 1936, the F.B.I. arrested a man named Bailey. It is believed he was a member of John Dillinger's gang. Though he took no active part in the gang's bank robberies, it is known that gang members visited his farm on several occasions. Just prior to his arrest, Bailey had purchased a new Ford car in Jackson and paid cash for it, which was unheard of in those days of the Depression. People thought the money came from one of the gang's bank robberies. The old farm where Bailey lived is about eleven miles north of Jackson. It might be a good place to search for the $825,000 John Dillinger hid that has never been found.

Q: What is the treasure story on the Andrew Meyers' House in Canton?

A: History and legend surround the old home of Andrew Meyers. Built in 1816, it is now on the northeast corner of 13th Street and Broad Avenue in Canton. Meyers, was one of Ohio's wealthiest men. His home is almost hidden in ten acres of wooded land, which is conducive to stories of hidden treasure.

One of these stories tells of a strongbox in which Napoleon carried his payrolls. This strongbox is supposed to be somewhere in the house or on the grounds. Another story is proven factual. It reports that a farmer plowed up several gold coins on the premises a few years ago. These tales and others have led to speculation that there are thousands of dollars in gold and silver buried in the old mansion and the ten acres surrounding it.

Q: Can you tell me if any outlaw gangs operated in, or near, East Liverpool?

A: In the 1890's, East Liverpool was a wide open town. It is estimated that gamblers, bootleggers and illegal stills alone brought over $1,000,000 a year into the town. The Dutch Zellner Gang ruled the region during this period, and there are several reported caches hidden by them near both East Liverpool and the neighboring Wellsville. The Cool Street section of Wellsville is a promising place to search for the gang's booty.

Q: I have heard of a huge treasure in Snyder Park. Is this story true?

A: I cannot say for certain if any treasure story is true, but here is what I have on the Snyder Park treasure: It is believed that from three to four million dollars is buried in Snyder Park in Springfield. This money is in gold coins. It was buried in 1890 by John Snyder on land he later granted to the City of Springfield. Snyder later told his family the money was buried near what he called "the abutment." This cache has not been found, because the city officials have kept an eye on the park for years. They would probably reach an agreement with anyone who could find the treasure.

OKLAHOMA

Q: Do you have the three locations where Cherokee Indians buried gold in Oklahoma?

A: There is a legend that a cave, which is located in a narrow valley in the Horseshoe Bend of the Illinois River, has several earthen churns filled with gold bars. This cache was placed in the cave by Cherokee Indians during the middle 1800's.

Prior to the Civil War, four Cherokee Indians placed $50,000 in two nail kegs and buried them on Tahlequah Creek. This was gold coins received from the United States government as land payment. The four Indians that buried the gold were killed during the Civil War and the gold was never found.

There is another treasure believed to be Cherokee, hidden in the area of Wilburton. This consists of three separate locations, near each other, close to a creek bed. This treasure is supposedly from robberies committed by a gang of renegade Cherokee. No part of any of these caches are known to have been found.

Q: What is the story of $10,000 in hidden Liberty Bonds, south of Bartlesville?

A: In October of 1923, a bandit named Albert Spencer, cached $10,000 in Liberty Bonds he had taken in a robbery near Okesa. He was killed on a farm in the Osage Hills a short time later. A shovel was found near his body with fresh dirt on it, indicating that he had buried the bonds shortly before his death, somewhere near where he was killed. This cache has never been reported found.

Q: Did the Jesse James gang ever bury treasure in Oklahoma?

A: Yes, according to old stories still being told in Oklahoma, the James gang buried $200,000 in the vicinity of an old road, probably the historical Western Cattle Trail to Dodge City, near Cache Creek between Fort Sill or Lawton, Comanche County, and the Keechee Hills country to the northeast, between 1867 and 1882.

During their bandit reign, the James Brothers' gang systematically hid much of their loot in a single location, somewhere near Cache Creek in the southwestern part of the State. After the killing of Jesse James, in 1882 and the subsequent death or imprisonment of the remainder of the gang, Frank became a fugitive. At last, he too finally surrendered, although he was never required to stand trial.

It was more than twenty years after the heyday of their crimes before Frank James was able to return to the locality where the outlaws had secreted most of their loot. But since his departure from that part of the country, the land which had once been sparsely settled, was now divided and fenced into homesteads. Frank James was unable to locate the wealth.

Using a small farm which he had purchased in the vicinity of the treasure cache as a base of operations, he rode out each morning for many months in an attempt to recognize the burial site, but without success. There is no information that the vast treasure was ever discovered by anyone else.

Q: What is the treasure of the Indian called Scarface or Blackface?

A: The story goes that during the 1830's, Blackface, sometimes called Scarface, a renegade Seminole and Negro half-breed, and his gang, plundered and robbed homesteader caravans, traders, Mexican pack trains and anyone else they thought might be carrying valuables.

The outlaw band had several hideouts in the heavily timbered hills of eastern Oklahoma. It is known that on one occasion, a party of Mexican traders were traveling from Mexico to St. Louis with several mule loads of gold bullion to trade for goods and supplies. When Blackface learned of this pack train, he and his men set up an ambush near where Ft. Gibson National Cemetery is today.

The renegades killed all the traders, then rounded up the mules and led them to a well hidden cave where the gold was hidden by Blackface and a few trusted members of the gang. A short time later, Blackface was killed in a fight with another outlaw band and the few of his men that weren't killed, fled to other parts of the country and were afraid to return. The story of the hidden cave was known among the Indians living in the area but none knew its location.

A well known story is that one old Cherokee almost certainly found the hidden cave and showed it to a white man. During the early 1920's, this Indian came to the home of a tavern keeper in Tahlequah and told him he was searching for a treasure that his people had talked about for years.

After spending what money he had, the Indian told the innkeeper that he would give him half the treasure if it was found, for one more month's lodging. One evening, when only a few days remained of the agreed month's stay, the Indian found the concealed cave and agreed to take the innkeeper to it.

The next day, after walking a short distance from town with the innkeeper blindfolded, they came to a concealed cave entrance. The Indian removed several stones and with a torch led the way deep into the cave.

The innkeeper saw several large clay jars that were filled with small gold bars. Taking one gold bar, the two left the cave. The Indian again blindfolded the innkeeper and then concealed the cave's entrance.

The next morning when the tavern owner checked on the Indian, he was gone. The innkeeper spent several years searching for the cave. It was later learned that the Cherokee had killed a man and the Indian police were after him. The Tulsa Daily World reported in February, 1936, that several citizens were still trying to locate the Cherokee. This effort was unsuccessful.

Q: Did the Choctaw Indians ever work gold mines in Oklahoma? Where was the general location?

A: Early chronicles record that the Choctaw Indians had at least two gold mines in the Kiamichi Mountains of southeastern Oklahoma. The mines were worked by a white missionary and twelve Choctaws as late as 1884. These mines were all concealed when white men learned that the Choctaw were obtaining gold. All the Indians who knew of the mines are now dead.

Q: Is there a lost silver mine in Oklahoma?

A: Yes, a lost silver mine awaits rediscovery a few miles south of Heavener, somewhere in Round Mountain. It is believed that this mine was worked by the Spanish and that a hoard of silver is still hidden nearby.

Round Mountain, so named for the cap on its top, is about two miles long and runs from east to west. Approximately three-quarters of the way up the north side, a shelf or bench circles part of the mountain. Somewhere along the flat wall of this shelf is where an ancient silver mine is thought to be. This mine has had very little searching done for it, which would make it a good place to check with a metal detector over a weekend, or to spend a vacation.

Q: I have heard of the Dick Estes Cache in Oklahoma. What is it?

A: It was in 1902 that Dick Estes pulled a jewel robbery in Denver, making off with a sizeable haul of $40,000 in jewels, watches and another $20,000 in gold coins. Estes lost no time in getting to Oklahoma Territory, where he had previously eluded the law.

Estes had a mountain hideout up Panther Creek toward the north side of the Wichita Mountains, which seemed to be a regular lair for his unsavory kind. While holed up at his mountain lair, Estes cached his haul of jewels, watches and gold, keeping out only enough money on which to get by. A certain cedar tree, ten paces west of his dugout, was the earthen bank which only Dick Estes had the key to.

Estes was later arrested and spent the rest of his life in the penitentiary. The cache still remains hidden near the old outlaw's hideout.

Q: Can you tell me anything about a train robbery near Kasumi during the 1890's?

A: In 1920, two small boys found a safe under a pile of rocks, north of Kasumi. Not being able to move it they went for help but could never relocate it. It is believed the safe was one that had been taken in a train robbery north of Kasumi some thirty years before, that contained $3,000 in gold coins.

The area where the two boys found the safe is near the junction of Buck Creek and the Ciamiske River.

Q: Did the U.S. army ever lose a payroll in Oklahoma? I have heard of one being buried in the western panhandle of Oklahoma.

A: During the Indian wars of 1868, a contingent of U.S. Cavalry was carrying a payroll of $42,000. During an Indian attack, the payroll was buried somewhere in the panhandle of Oklahoma. Several searches have been made for this cache, but it is still undiscovered.

Q: What is the story of the cave with the iron door in the Wichita Mountains?

A: This legendary cave has been called by several different names and there are different stories as to what is in the cave. One version is that the Spanish put $11,000,000 in gold bars and coins with Indian slave skeletons to guard the gold.

Another story is that outlaws used the cave as a hideout and left thousands of dollars hidden inside. This cave has been seen by two different people but they were unable to relocate it.

Q: What is the story on a half-bushel of coins buried in Oklahoma?

A: Six or seven miles east from U.S 271, on the Holsum Valley Road in Le Fore County, a half-bushel basket full of silver coins may be buried. It is believed to be loot from Hartford, Arkansas, and Heavener, Oklahoma, bank holdups by the Henry Starr gang around 1920, when Starr was quite active in eastern Oklahoma and western Arkansas.

The cache is on private property, and any treasure hunter wanting to try his luck should, of course, first obtain permission.

Q: I have heard of the William Stinnett treasure. What is it and in what part of Oklahoma is it thought to be located?

A: Billy Stinnett accumulated a fortune through trading. After he died, none of it was found. It is believed that Stinnett buried his money on the grounds of his trading post. This location is in the southeast part of Park Hill in Tahlequah. A stone chimney is all that is left of the old post. This was on the old road to the Illinois River.

Q: What is the largest hidden treasure in Oklahoma and has it been found?

A: In 1805, French outlaws who had robbed gold miners in what is now southern New Mexico were on their way to New Orleans where they planned to sail for France with six cart loads of gold bars, each weighing seven pounds. This vast amount was worth over $2,500,000. When the Frenchmen reached what is now Cimarron County, Oklahoma, they learned the U.S. government had completed the Louisiana Purchase, so they could not take their loot to New Orleans. It is believed the Frenchmen buried the gold near Sugar Loaf Peak. A few years ago several location stones were found on the Cyrus Strong ranch near Boise City.

What happened to the Frenchmen is unknown, but the six cart loads of gold is believed to be buried somewhere on the Strong ranch.

OREGON

Q: I have heard of a large amount of money and gold dust that was buried by an army paymaster at Fort Grant. Would you explain the story to me?

A: The Fort Grant paymaster deposited at Phoenix, Oregon, government funds he handled, as well as money and gold dust that miners and cattlemen placed in his care. All the deposits were buried in a large iron kettle, at a secret location near the fort until he could make a trip to the bank.

This practice continued until the paymaster suffered a stroke, leaving him unable to talk. He tried to draw a map showing where the money was buried, but died before completing it.

After his death, the earth all around the fort was prodded with an iron rod. Nothing was found and the fort was abandoned shortly after that. The paymaster's kettle stuffed with coins and gold dust may be hard to find but it would be well worth the effort.

Q: Have diamonds ever been discovered in Oregon?

A: Diamonds have been found in the Coos Bay area of western Oregon.

Q: What information do you have on outlaw loot in Horse Thief Meadows?

A: Horse Thief Meadows was named for an outlaw who had built a cabin near by. In the summer of 1884, a man who called himself Phillips, came to Hood River Valley and hired Dave Cooper to aid him in the search for a cabin, under the floor of which, he declared, there was hidden a cache of $25,000 in gold. He said the money had been taken in a stagecoach robbery near Walla Walla, Washington, a few years before. The search was continued for two years after the cabin in Horse Thief Meadows was found; but if any money was recovered it was never reported.

Q: Can you give me the general location of two lost saddlebags of gold in Douglas County?

A: Somewhere in Oregon's northern Douglas County, there are some missing saddlebags with $14,000 in "gold dust and coins" in their rotted interior.

That is the value placed on the saddlebags' contents in 1856, when a Mr. Abrams, of M. Abrams and Company, lost them in a freak accident. On today's runaway gold market, the contents could be worth ten times as much.

The saddlebags were on a mule Abrams was riding. While separated from the animal momentarily, just south of Calippia Creek, something frightened the mule and it bolted. Later, the mule was found sixteen or seventeen miles away, at a place where he was used to being fed, minus the saddlebags.

The missing saddlebags should be somewhere between Calippos Creek on the north and Deer Creek on the south, where the mule was found without them.

Q: I would like to spend a vacation in Oregon as a rock hound. Where could I obtain a book on the subject?

A: The Travel Information Division, located in Salem, Oregon, will provide a little booklet called "Oregon Rocks, Fossils, Minerals—Where to Find Them." It can also be obtained from the Oregon State Highway Department at Salem. The Oregon Department of Geology and Mineral Industries at Salem or Portland, can refer the rock hound to several maps of gem stone areas as well as some of the old mining areas.

Q: What do you have on a jewelry store robbery in Portland, in 1923?

A: Somewhere near the highway between Scappose and Portland, Oregon, is a cache of $100,000 worth of gems that could be well worth investigating. The exact day and month of the robbery in which the jewelry was taken and the subsequent burying of the loot is unknown, but it was sometime during 1923.

Three men participated in the robbery of a jewelry store in Portland. They were Frank Bud Maxfield and C.R. Williams. The "take" was $100,000 in jewelry. The trio fled north aı the old Columbia River Highway. Knowing they would be pursued, they decided to hide t. gems until later.

While Williams remained with the car, Nash and Maxfied buried the loot in two mason fruit jars alongside the road. They then fled the area. Frank Nash was later killed at the Kansas City Union Station, Kansas City, Missouri, by the F.B.I. during a shootout, in which several men were involved.

Bud Maxfield was also later killed by the F.B.I. C.R. Williams is believed to have lived for a while, but supposedly never recovered the buried jewelry.

This sounds logical, since he was one of the prohibition gangsters and was always on the run. He is known to have visited the area once after the robbery, in search of the gems, but was unable to locate them. Williams is supposed to have told one man, with whom he was friendly, that the cache was on the left-hand side of the highway. The reason Williams could not locate the cache was, he stayed with the car while Nash and Maxfield buried the jewels. After telling his friend this, Williams left and was never seen again.

Q: I have heard of two tin cans of gold that were hidden along the old Seven Devils Road. Can you tell me the story on this?

A: Somewhere along the old Seven Devils Road (originally called the Randolph Trail, approximately Highway 101 today), between Charleston, Oregon and south to the mouth of Whiskey Run Creek, there is believed to be still buried $40,000 in gold dust and nuggets contained in two tin cans. This was hidden by two brothers, Peter and Charles Grorluis, in 1853.

The first discovery of gold on Whiskey Run Creek was made by these brothers in 1850. They were from French Prairie, in the Willamette Valley of northern Oregon. They camped one night at the mouth of the Coquille River. Deciding to prospect the area after noticing banks of black sand along the beaches, the brothers found gold that had been washed out by the action of water. After exploring the beaches, they learned the richest deposits were along the mouth of what was later called Whiskey Run Creek.

For three summers they worked the beaches, returning the 200 miles to their Willamette Valley home during the winters. It wasn't until 1853 that the news of their rich strike leaked out. The rush of miners to the area included two other brothers, "Big Mac" and "Little Mac" McNamara, from Port Orford, about 30 miles to the south. Convincing the Grorluis brothers to sell for $20,000 in gold dust, the McNamara's took over.

After selling their rights to the claim, Charles and Peter figured they had enough gold to last them a lifetime, but the brothers were concerned about being robbed on their way home. Several robberies of miners in the area had taken place since the location of the claim was now well known.

Since so many people knew they were leaving and carrying a fortune, the Grorluis' decided to go part way, then hide most of their gold, and go on home where they had enough gold already taken there during the last three years to make them rich. Packing up, they headed north along the Randolph Trail.

After traveling several miles they stopped and put two tin cans containing $40,000 in gold dust and nuggets into a hole beneath the roots of a large spruce tree, a few yards from the trail. They then made their way safely to French Prairie, and home. The brothers later went to France to visit relatives and then toured Europe. Charles died while in England.

It was twenty years before Peter returned to get the cache of gold. But the Randolph Trail had changed so much because of rain, underbrush and forest fires that he was never able to locate the two tin cans.

Q: What is the story on the Spanish Treasure in the northwest corner of Oregon?

A: About 1679, Spanish survivors of a shipwreck buried a chest of gold and silver somewhere on the slope of Neahkohnie Mountain, near what is now Nehalem, in Tillamook County, Oregon. Here is the story briefly:

The vessel carried a large quantity of beeswax from the Orient, which was intended for use in

'les and religious figures. Along the beach, many tons of this wax was strewn,
n existence today and bears the significant date of 1679.

:ck, local legend tells that four of the some thirty members of the crew left
traveled north, supposedly to the Columbia River region, but nothing else
n. The rest of the crew decided to build homes and stay in the Neahkahnie

...ne of the shipwreck or shortly thereafter, members of the crew are reported to
... a heavy chest, or box, high up the slope of Neahkahnie Mountain and buried it. The
...ations between the crew members and the Indians began to deteriorate and a battle occurred
with all the new settlers being killed.

Although the Indians knew of the treasure, it is said that after the battle they made no
attempt to unearth it, as they did not recognize gold or silver as being valuable, which is what
the cache is presumed to hold.

The buried treasure has been searched for by many people, but none have found the gold,
despite various interpretations of inscriptions contained on two rocks near the beach, which are
believed to relate to the hidden cache.

Q: Could you give me the general locations of five lost gold mines in Oregon?

A: There is supposed to be a lost gold mine, called the Tillamock, located in Washington
County.

In the area of Diamond Peak, the lost French Cabin Mine waits for rediscovery, in Lane
County.

There is a story that tells of the Four Dutchmen Lost Gold Mine near Prineville.

Along the east side of the Wallowa Mountains near Mount Joseph, the Nez Perce gold mine
and the John Cash gold mine are said to be lost. It is believed by many, that these two mines are
one and the same.

Here are two in Josephine County: the Wolf Creek mine and a mine on Miller Creek.

Q: Do you have any information on sixteen mule-loads of gold hidden by Indians near Crater
Lake National Park?

A: In the 1850's, after they had been mistreated by a group of renegades, several Indians
robbed them and threw sixteen mule-loads of gold dust and nuggets into a ravine somewhere
between the Rogue and Illinois Rivers, in the Muckhorn Mountains. This has never been reported found.

Q: Do you have any information on a cache buried in back of the post office at Swan Lake,
Oregon?

A: The rich gold loot from several stagecoach holdups is said to be buried in what was once a
potato patch located back of the old post office in the village of Swan Lake, then a stage
station on the line from Klamath Falls to Lakeview. Many searches have been made for this
treasure, but as the site of the original post office cannot be determined, it has not been found.

PENNSYLVANIA

Q: Where is the "Coalbeds" and did a gang of outlaws operate there?

A: In 1788, a gang of outlaws operated near Wilkes Barre at a place called the Coalbeds.
They raided farms and robbed travelers in the area. They were finally driven away by the Pennsylvania militia. Their hideout was four log cabins near the Susquehanna River. Legends of
buried gold at their hideout hidden by this gang, still circulate in the area.

Q: Has silver ever been found in Pennsylvania? If so, where is the general location?

A: There is a long-standing legend of an Indian silver mine and cache of silver ingots being
hidden in the area of Deep Run, Pennsylvania. This location is almost exactly on the state line
of Pennsylvania and Maryland. However, most people believe the mine and cache to be within
Adams County, Pennsylvania. The location and events covering this site were described in
papers over 100 years ago:

The story goes that a German silversmith named Ahrwud was allowed to work a mine owned by local Indians. When Ahrwud's daughter betrayed the Indians' trust by stealing silver items from the mine, father, daughter and mine vanished.

The papers mention a stream and a large flat rock. Steps underground are mentioned, with the cryptic notation that they "should not be mistaken for nature's opening."

The location is approximately one-and-one-half miles out of Union Mills, at the base of a hill. There could be some truth to this story as the mineral conditions are right for silver in this area.

Q: I have heard of a place called Spanish Hill in Pennsylvania. Were the Spanish that far north?

A: Spanish Hill or Carantouan is first mentioned in writing in 1614, on a Dutch map. In 1795, a Frenchman, Don de Rochefoucould-Lian-Court, on a visit to the junction of the Chemung and Susquehanna Rivers wrote, "Four or five miles to the north, I saw a mountain in the shape of a sugar loaf, upon which are to be found the remains of some entrenchments. The local inhabitants call them the Spanish Ramparts." In the 1840's, a medal was found that was proved to have been made in 1550. Later, a Spanish sword, crucifix and a black, waterlogged boat were found.

Local tradition says the hill was used by Mound Builders, early French, Iroquois Indians, and by three soldiers from a Swedish boat that was blown off course. All of this is theory. The evidence and most oft repeated stories, say the ramparts were built by the Spanish about 1550. The early Indians told that men in iron hats came to the mountain to escape other men that were after them. The Indians called the mountain "Espana" or "Hispan" and said that none of their ancestors would visit the place. The men were supposed to have carried large chests full of round discs (coins) with them to the mountain and buried the chests in a cave. Both parties of Spanish were attacked by Indians and all were killed.

In 1810, Alpheus Harris, a surveyor with a party of men sent to define the New York-Pennsylvania boundary line, told of talking to the few Indians still living in the area. They would not approach Carantouan and said the spirits of the dead men guarded the money chests.

In the 1820's, Joseph Smith (founder of the Mormon Church) is known to have searched Carantouan for the money chests with a divining rod, without success. Others have searched unsuccessfully. As far as can be learned, the chests of coins are still there.

Q: Did a doctor that had been a pirate with Captain Kidd bury treasure in Pennsylvania?

A: A persistent legend in the county of Bucks, involves the mysterious Dr. John Bowman, who built a log cabin, sometime around 1700, in what is now Washington's Crossing State Park, on the Delaware River. Washington used Bowman's Hill as a lookout point prior to the battle of Trenton.

Dr. Bowman, some said, had been a member of Captain Kidd's crew, and had received a share of the pirates' booty. According to history, a Dr. John Bowman was captured and forced to sail with Captain William Kidd, as a ship's surgeon. About 1696, Bowman came up the Delaware River seeking refuge. He made one more trip with Kidd, then returned to the cabin he had built on a hill overlooking the Delaware River. Kidd was caught and hanged in London, and Dr. Bowman never went to sea again. He died in the cabin he built and it is believed that his share of the booty during Kidd's pirate raids is buried near there.

Q: Do you have the story of a document, similar to the Declaration of Independence, that was drawn up then hidden in Clinton County?

A: Somewhere on the grounds where Fort Horn stood, is a document of priceless value. This was put into an iron box by the citizens of Pine Creek in July 1776. This document was a Declaration of Independence from the Crown of England, stating that the citizens of the settlement were free and independent. It was probably written within hours of the Declaration accepted by the Continental Congress in Philadelphia.

In 1778, the Six Nations, with the help of the British, all but wiped out the white settlement of Pine Creek. After 1779, when General Sullivan broke the power of the Six Nations, the settlers that remained returned to Pine Creek. Fort Horn had been burned and no trace of the town could be found.

Strange, that two documents of almost the same words could be written, although neither party knew that the other had been written. One is lost to history while the other became the greatest document in history. Our Declaration of Independence is secure, while the lucky person, if anyone ever does, that finds the Pine Creek document, will have something priceless. This is an unusual treasure, but one worth the effort of checking out.

Q: Is there a lost treasure from an airplane crash near Mt. Carmel?

A: In June, 1948, an airliner crashed into Mount Carmel. The story is that there was $250,000 aboard the plane. This money was in packets that were jettisoned just prior to the crash. None of the packets of money have been reported found. Wreckage of the plane was found over a wide area. Several reports put this crash in Northumberland County. But the County Clerk, at Bloomsburg, tells me that the incident happened in Columnia Conty.

I quote this from the New York Times, June 1948: "Authorities were searching today for an air express package containing $250,000 in small bills believed jettisoned before the crash of a United Airlines DC-6 near here (Mt. Carmel), June 17th. A postal authority said the parcel of money weighted 240 pounds and contains bills in $1.00, $5.00 and $10.00 denominations."

Q: I am sure you have been asked this question before, but what is the Dent's Run Treasure?

A: The Dent's Run treasure is said to be lost somewhere in the rugged, sparsely populated area where Elk and Cameron Counties meet. According to legend, a young Union Army lieutenant was commissioned in 1863 to transport a false-bottomed wagon containing 26 gold bars, weighing 50 pounds each from Wheeling, West Virginia, to Washington, D.C.

Hoping to avoid Confederate troops, the lieutenant took a northern route. His plan was to bear northeast to the village of Driftwood on the Sinnemonhoning River in Cameron County, then build a raft and float down to the Susquehanna, on to Harrisburg, and eventually by land to Washington.

His party travelled through Pittsburgh, Clarion and Ridgeway, eventually arriving at Saint Marys in Elk County. They left St. Mary's for Driftwood one Saturday night in June, and were never seen again.

In August, the expedition's civilian guide wandered alone and hysterical into Lock Haven, about 40 miles southeast of Driftwood. He claimed all the other members of the expedition died in the snake-infested wilderness and the cargo was lost. Some believed him, but the army was suspicious. The guide was questioned and kept under surveillance for years, and Pinkerton agents were called into the area. But the gold was never found.

Q: Where did the Kirk gang operate and did they hide any money?

A: One of the long held legends around Uniontown, concerns that of the Kirk Gang. The exploits of this band of outlaws are said to have ranged from Morgantown, West Virginia, to the National Pike in Pennsylvania, during the 1800's. A book called "The Rover's Den" was written about this gang in 1865. The story goes that in 1804, the band set up a hideout in Dulaney's Cave (now Laurel Caverns) and buried a large amount of stolen money inside the cave. The outlaws were finally all killed but their reputed cache was never reported found.

Q: What is the story of a train robbery where the robbers blew themselves up and the money was lost?

A: In 1927, a pay car for the coal mines was blown up by two men. A large charge was used and the car and occupants were blown apart. More than $27,000 was spread over an area of 700 feet. Almost all of the greenbacks were recovered, however, $6,000 in coin still lies scattered in that particular section of woods located near Wilkes Barre, in the vicinity of Espe Gap.

Q: Do you have any information on a copper strong box full of money near the Delaware Water Gap?

A: Hidden somewhere within the Delaware Water Gap, lies a copper strong box filled with payroll for a railroad construction gang; buried there by the paymaster when he became ill and died soon after from a heart attack. The key to this chest was recovered near the site where he beached his canoe, but the chest has never been found.

Q: Was there ever a woman counterfeiter in Pennsylvania?

A: One of the few women counterfeiters to ever operate in Pennsylvania was Ann Carson. She and two companions also robbed cattle drovers. At one time she had an elaborate scheme to kidnap the governor's son and exchange him for her lover, Lieutenant Richard Smith. However, the scheme failed and Smith was hanged. The money she obtained in her outlaw career, is believed hidden somewhere near her home.

Ann often masqueraded as a Quaker Lady and passed a considerable amount of imitation money. She was finally caught and sent to prison, where she died in April 1824.

RHODE ISLAND

Q: Did counterfeiters ever operate in Rhode Island, if so, where?

A: At Old Potters Pond, located about three miles from Wakefield, there is a legend of a counterfeit press being lost. In the early 1700's, a gentleman by the name of Potter was making a pretty good copy of the King's money and spending it as well. Things were going along just fine, until one day, the King's soldiers made a raid. However, Mr. Potter threw his press into the pond and made good his escape. No report was ever made of the counterfeit money or press being found.

Q: Do you have anything on Robbers Corner?

A: This site was located near Wickford Junction. It was named Robbers Corner because of the large number of stagecoach robberies that took place there. Several local stories tell of bandit caches in the area.

Q: Would you give an opinion as to whether or not there is treasure buried on Block Island off the coast of Rhode Island?

A: Block Island is popularly believed to be one of the hiding places of Captain Kidd's treasure as well as other pirates' treasure. The island has been gone over many times by enterprising treasure seekers, and it is told that some booty has been found. In 1689, French privateers captured Block Island and made it a base for their operations on the Atlantic Coast. Some of the many treasure tales which still keep searchers busy along the island's coast are connected with these privateers.

Q: Is there a treasure location on Conanicut Island?

A: Captain Kidd is believed to have buried loot on this island. Also, Thomas Paine, one of Kidd's crew, is supposed to have buried his share of a pirate raid at a place called Cajacet, on Conanicut Island. It is thought that other pirate caches are also on this island.

Q: Was there a pirate named Charles Harris and did he bury money in Rhode Island?

A: A treasure chest belonging to the pirate Charles Harris, who was hanged at Newport in 1723, is at the base of Newport Cliffs. The chest is 20" x 12" x 12" with the contents unknown. It was found in 1949 and was covered by the sands and lost again before it could be taken up.

Q: Could you give me a list of ships that sank off the coast of Rhode Island?

A: The Vineyard Sound Lightship sank in 1944, with some artifacts being recovered in 1965. The Atlantic sank off Point Judith in 1846.

The Adventure was sunk by the pirate, Bradish, in 1699, and an estimated $2,000,000 was on board when she went down.

The steamer, Fairfax sank in 1898, just off Sow and Pigs Reef, and the SS Silvia sank in 1908, just a short distance away.

A German U-boat, loaded with $1,000,000 in jewels hidden in ammuniton shell cases, sank in 1945, just off Point Judith.

The Princess Augusta, a British frigate, sank on December 27, 1738 on "Hummock" on the north tip of Sandy Point, Block Island, with $100,000 in gold and silver bullion. The craft carried the personal possessions and antiques of the Protestant Palantines, persecuted for their religious beliefs.

.e pirate Blackbeard ever bury any money at Providence?
:beard landed at Providence in 1716 and is believed to have buried a treasure there at

: there buried treasures that the pirate Joseph Bradish buried near Rhode Island?
:s, evidence points to the fact that Bradish did bury two caches, one on Long Island of
)0 and the other on Block Island of $200,000.
Bradish turned to piracy when he was a young man and died on the gallows in London in
1700, carrying to his grave the secret of these two pirate treasures he had buried in America
during the previous year. The exact amounts are not known, but historians say they are valued
at approximately $500,000. To the best of anyone's knowledge, neither treasure has been found.

The first trove was buried at Montauk Point, Lond Island, about March 19, 1699. The second
was buried on Block Island, off Newport County, Rhode Island, the following month.

Q: What is the story of a lost bell in Rhode Island, and why would it be so valuable today?

A: The bell you mention has quite a history. The reason the bell would be so valuable is, it is
supposed to have been made of almost pure silver which gave it a tone impossible to duplicate
today.

Another reason for its value, is the history connected with the bell: The bell was made by
Peter Seest, in Amsterdam in 1263. It was brought to this country in 1664, where it hung in a
church near Providence. The bell was later taken down and was to be hung in an English
convent but was lost. It turned up again aboard a British ship, during the War of 1812, when the
ship was captured by Americans. Taken back to Providence, the bell resumed its place in the
church tower. In 1891, it disappeared and has never been recovered. Needless to say, the historical value of the bell would be priceless today, also the two to five hundred pounds of almost
pure silver would be worth a small fortune.

Q: Can you supply me with information on the pirate, Thomas Tew, and did he bury any
booty in Rhode Island?

A: Nearly three hundred years ago, Captain Thomas Tew, a noted privateer, turned pirate,
retired to a life of ease at Newport, Rhode Island. He had accumulated a considerable fortune
which was well hidden from prying eyes.

In his "Directory of Buried or Sunken Treasures and Lost Mines of the United States", Thomas Penfield stated that Tew's booty was worth in the neighborhood of $100,000. Today, its
increased value can only be guessed at.

Old shipmates lured Tew out of retirement for just one more voyage from which he never
returned to enjoy his fortune, secreted somewhere in or near Newport. To this day, the old
pirate's loot has never been recovered.

Information on the pirate, Joe Thomas Tew can be found in these books: "Calendar of State
Papers, America and the West Indies, 1702-1703", "Pirates of the New England Coast," and
"History of the Pirates".

Tew never left any indication of where his Newport treasure was hidden. Neither, has anyone
ever reported finding it.

Q: Have you heard of a lost gold mine is Moosup Valley?

A: It seems unusual that there could be a lost gold mine in Rhode Island, but such happens
to be the case. It was worked in Moosup Valley near Foster Center in the late 1700's. Forgotten,
it was rediscovered and mined from 1812 to 1825, but was then lost again. Gold was also found
near Johnston, but the deposits were too small to mine.

Q: What is the treasure of John Kafke?

A: I have very little on this location, just that Kafke buried a cache of gold coins near Liberty, Rhode Island. The local library can probably help you.

SOUTH CAROLINA

Q: Where was the Confederate Treasury captured when the Civil War ended? How much was missing?

A: Union army records show the Confederate Treasury was headed south, and when the boxes and kegs were captured and opened by Union troops, somewhere south of Sandersville, Georgia, only $25,000 in gold sovereigns were found. Records show that several stops were made in South Carolina, at both Chester and Newberry, but what happened to the three hundred thousand dollars that was missing is not known.

Q: What is the story of the cutter Beaufort and her immense cargo of pieces of art that sank off the coast of South Carolina?

A: For over one hundred and eighty years, a valuable cargo of art treasures has lain undisturbed on the bottom of the sea, just ten miles off the entrance to Bull Bay, South Carolina. The treasure went down with the ex-U.S. Navy gunboat Beaufort, built in 1799 for river patrol and coastal defense. The small sailing 'galley'—Beaufort was only 50 feet long—proved impractical for the latter use, and was soon sold to private ownership.

Now skippered by long-time mercenary-privateer Allen Winslow, the Beaufort fit nicely into the smuggling trade between America and the West Indies. The trail of this illicit trafficking began in Europe. Rare antiques, porcelains, statuary, heirloom jewelry and other valuables were stolen from various private collections or museums in England, France and Italy. These treasures were then shipped to various British-held islands in the West Indies. From there, men like Winslow ferried them to the United States and arranged for their sale on the cultural black market in New York City.

It was on such a voyage that Winslow and his ship met with disaster. On a bright August afternoon, Beaufort left Grand Bahama Island sailing for New York. In her open hold lay crate after crate, packed with all manner of small antiques and objects d'art—alabaster eggs from France, numerous sets of ornate silverware, silver candelabra, jewelry boxes, mirrors of silvered Venetian glass, and other such delicate artworks of great value.

Winslow intended to head straight for Cape Hatteras in North Carolina and then swing west to a direct heading for New York. Instead, at sea, he chose to follow the southern coastline to avoid the beginnings of a storm gathering along his former course.

Winslow made good time, sailing without incident past Florida, Georgia and well along the coast of South Carolina. Just off Charleston harbor, Beaufort was confronted by a Federal revenue cutter. A mate immediately summoned the skipper from his cubbyhole. The captain of the Federal ship shouted a challenge, but not the one Winslow expected. The carefree but bored government crew wanted to stage an impromptu race!

A confused, still nervous but greatly relieved Winslow readily agreed. Separated by only a few yards, both ships headed north under full sail for some twenty-five miles, neither one gaining advantage over the other.

The wind gusted crazily and the cutter abruptly veered hard to the right, shearing off the entire bow section of the Beaufort. The ocean surged into the open galley, swamping her instantly. Within seconds, the splintered ex-gunboat settled from view in the dark waters, the crates of art treasure vanishing with her.

The cutter was brought under control and hove to, managing to rescue Winslow and his entire crew. The Federal captain remained unaware of Winslow's occupation or Beaufort's illegal cargo. Winslow and his crew were deposited at Charleston along with profuse government apologies.

Winslow is believed to have returned to his questionable career, while the Beaufort and its incredible fortune in art was left submerged some ten miles off the South Carolina coast.

Q: Has gold ever been found in South Carolina?

A: Yes, gold has been found. The Haile Mine in Lancaster County was still producing gold in 1942. Begun in 1828, the Haile Mine was soon followed by mines in McCormick, Chesterfield and York Counties. A 27-pound nugget, called "Sheephead" was found near Smyrna. Gold bearing gravels occur along Saltlick Branch and Goldmine Branch near Hickory Grove, and along

Wolf Creek. A letter to the State Department of Minerals and Resources at Columbia, South Carolina 29221, will give you more information on where gold can be found.

Q: What is the story of Manchester, South Carolina? Is it a ghost town and was a large amount of Confederate supplies lost near there?

A: This information is on a historical marker at the former site of Manchester: "A flourishing town once stood here; settled before 1799; Stagecoach on Wilmington and Manchester R.R., 1852-1872. (Station was 1 mile S.E.); Noted for its taverns, horse racing, games of ball-alley, and other contests; Raided by Union troops, 1865; Abandoned by railroad, 1872, in favor of Wedgefield."

A large amount of Confederate equipment was thrown into Wateree Swamp after it had been amassed between Manchester and Sumterville, about 11 miles away.

Q: What was aboard the Confederate vessel the York Castle when the Union Navy sank her?

A: The York Castle was carrying over 1,000 rare English Enfield rifles and $300,000 in gold planks. These now lie on the seabed in the depths of Long Bay, off South Carolina.

Q: Have diamonds ever been found in South Carolina?

A: Yes, in Spartanburg County.

Q: What is the story on the Six Mile Tavern treasure, near Charleston?

A: About five miles from Charleston, on U.S. 52, near the Navy Yard, was the site of the Six Mile House, a tavern and stagecoach stop that was operated in the early 1800's by John and Lavinia Fisher. This couple had a murder and robbery surprise ready for their guests, especially if they were wealthy.

Due to the fact that a couple of skeletons turned up in the tavern cellar, an irate mob had a necktie party for them in 1820. Soon after, people began searching for their ill-gotten gains and the search has continued up until the present time.

Q: Do you have any information on a South Carolina Tory bandit named Bloody Bill Bates?

A: A Tory bandit named Bloody Bill Bates used the mountain area near Travelers Rest and Greenville to hide caches of stolen goods, horses, loot, etc. He was captured one day and shot, at the Greenville jail, without telling where he had stashed his loot.

Q: Could you tell me of the location where Confederate weapons were dumped into a river?

A: There were an estimated 100,000 different weapons dumped into the Congaree River near Columbia. This armament was put there when it was captured by Union General Wm. Sherman, when he passed through Columbia in 1865 on his "march to the sea". The purpose was to keep Confederate guerrillas from using it.

Q: Can you tell me what the Melvin Purvis treasure is all about and where it is supposed to be buried?

A: Agent Melvin Purvis retired from the FBI in 1936. He had been involved in some sensational gang arrests and in the killing of John Dillinger in Chicago. After retirement, Purvis became a newspaper publisher in Florence, South Carolina, and earned a reputation as a money-making big spender. Early in 1960, Purvis died of an accidental or self-inflicted gunshot wound.

Rumors said that he left a fortune buried on a farm he owned in Darlington, South Carolina. Treasure hunters worked over the area, but nothing is known to have been found.

Q: Are there any hidden treasures in South Carolina?

A: There are many treasure sites in and around Charleston—in fact, throughout the entire state, and there are also some underwater sites in the coastal waters. There was heavy concentrations of military activity during the Civil War, so if you like hunting for Civil War relics, you could find them almost anywhere in the state. Here are some specific leads to help you get started. You can probably find additional information by doing further research.

It has long been believed that a treasure was buried near the place known as the Church Street Pirate House in Charleston.

Treasure of the pirate, Murrell, is believed buried in the marshes at Murrells Inlet, located on the coast not far from the North Carolina border.

It is believed that Blackbeard buried a huge fortune in the great swamp, west of Charleston. The South Carolina Historical Society, 100 Meeting Street, Charleston, SC 29401, can probably help on this one.

Many treasure hunters believe treasure is buried along Little River, in Horry County, since it was known as a pirate hangout dating back to colonial times. Also, along Little River, at Tilgmans Point, more pirate treasure is believed to be hidden.

Finally, near old Fort Randall in Horry County, treasure hunters have looked for buried gold.

Q: Is there any buried treasure near Jamestown?

A: There are two different treasures believed to be buried near Jamestown:

In the vicinity of the Santee River near Jamestown, a story has been prevalent for years that a cache of Confederate gold, worth over $200,000 is buried. This gold was supposedly captured from a Union paymaster.

Berkley County legend tells that $63,000 in gold and silver coins are buried on the grounds of the Old Hampton House. This site is on the Santee River north of Jamestown.

Q: What is the story of Rufe Lakers' cache?

A: Rufe Laker is believed to have cached a hoard of gold and silver coins in the vicinity of Cross Hill in Laurens County, that has never been reported found.

SOUTH DAKOTA

Q: I need the location of bandit loot in Custer County, South Dakota.

A: The sum of $140,000 in gold nuggets, dust and coin being sent by stagecoach from a mining camp in the Black Hills to a bank in Sidney, South Dakota, was taken by three bandits who held up the stagecoach in 1877 (in what is Custer County today) and temporarily escaped.

A sheriff's posse pursued them up several unidentified creeks, north of Fairburn, and killed or captured gang members, but the gold was not in their possession. One of the bandits, before being hung, stated they had hidden it along a creek in their flight, but he could not identify the particular creek. This money is still in the strongbox that was taken from the stagecoach. The bandits did not know how much loot they had acquired; the record of it was kept by the mining company, now nonexistent.

Another story is that one of the bandits escaped. Years after, he confessed that he had returned to recover the treasure, but was never able to find it.

Q: Is there a lost silver mine in South Dakota?

A: By the time Jerry Hardy drifted into the town of Pactola, situated on Rapid Creek, in the Black Hills of South Dakota, it had long been known as a gold camp. Placer gold was first washed from the stream bed in July, 1875, even before it was legal for white prospectors to be in the region.

Hardy, a prospector from Wyoming, was lured into the Black Hills by the fresh placer finds. He was a loner, so rather than live in town, he built a small stone cabin in Rainbow Canyon.

One day in May, 1877, Hardy rode excitedly into town clutching a leather bag full of rich ore. However, it wasn't gold but high grade silver.

A silver rush quickly gripped Pactola, with nearly every miner taking off into the hills searching for the fabulous silver mine.

Through it all, Hardy kept the secret of his mine. For three months, he showed up in town every Wednesday with freshly dug ore, buying provisions and tools. Then two weeks passed without a single sign of the lucky prospector. A group of concerned miners rode to his cabin to see if anything was wrong. They found Hardy inside, shot three times in the head. The killer or killers were never found and no more silver was ever brought into Pactola.

Somewhere within Rainbow Canyon, there is a rich lost lode of Black Hills silver.

Q: What is the story on Squeeky McDermitt's lost gold?

A: Squeeky McDermitt is believed to have cached $35,000 in gold bars, stolen from a Homestake Mine shipment, in the vicinity of his cabin. This cabin was located north of the junction of Prairie and Rapid Creeks, between Mystic and Rapid City.

Q: What is the story of the Thoen Stone?

A: In 1883, Louis Thoen, building a house at the foot of Lookout Mountain near Spearfish, South Dakota, found a flat piece of sandstone on which has been scratched this message.

"Came to these hills in 1833, seven of us, DeLacompt Ezra Kind G.W. Wood T. Brown R. Kent Indian Crow all dead but me Ezra Kind Killed by Indians beyond the high hill got our gold June 1834."

On the reverse side of the stone was carved:

"Got all gold we could carry out Ponys all got by Indians I have lost my gun and nothing to eat and Indians hunting me."

This historic stone is preserved today in the Adams Memorial Museum in Deadwood, South Dakota. Since Thoen found the stone, considerable other evidence has been discovered. The gun lost by Ezra Kind, the only survivor, was found near the stone and the skeleton of a man believed to have been Ezra Kind was found later, dead from an Indian attack, or of starvation. Also, prospectors have found gold dust in a stream not far from the stone, and because placer gold is not found in this stream, the particles are believed to have been a part of Ezra Kind's hoard.

In 1876, hunters found two skeletons in the hills to the northwest of Spearfish. They were lying beside a crude breastworks of stone. They are believed to have been with the mining party. There have been many searches for the gold indicated by the Thoen Stone, and many have searched for the gold believed to have been buried by Ezra Kind, but all without success.

Q: Was the Metz family really massacred by Indians and how much gold did they hide?

A: In 1876, at the head of Red Canyon, about 12 miles south of Custer, the Metz family buried or hid $5,000 in gold dust while camped for the night. The following morning, the entire family was massacred by Indians. The slaying of the Metz family is recorded history and there seems little doubt but that this treasure is still where Joseph Metz placed it.

Q: Can you tell me anything about a sunken ship treasure in Pierre, South Dakota?

A: In the 1860's, an unidentified vessel carrying gold bullion was wrecked in the Missouri River, off Pierre, before a permanent settlement was located there. The cargo of gold from the mines of Montana was valued at $500,000. Reports at the time said the site of the sinking was near three towering cottonwood trees growing close together. In Riverside Park in Pierre, at Missouri Avenue and Crow Street, there once stood three trees answering this description. They were known as The Three Sisters.

In 1922, a company was organized and sank a shaft in the solid ground near the three trees, where the river had flowed before changing its course. Neither the gold nor the ship was found.

Q: Is there treasure on Bogus Jim Creek and what does it consist of?

A: According to the stories, General George A. Custer camped with his command on Bogus Jim Creek. It is near the town of Nemo, northwest of Rapid City. General Custer, finding himself overloaded with arms, ammunition, whiskey and a chest of money to pay the soldiers, is said to have cached it on Bogus Jim Creek.

He intended to go back along Bogus Jim Creek in three or four days and pick up the cache. However, pursuing hostile Indians, his command left the region and never returned to recover the cache. Army records show that no officer was charged with the loss.

Q: Is there a miners cache on Lookout Mountain in South Dakota?

A: Indians killed a group of gold miners in 1865, but two managed to escape up Blacktail Gulch taking with them $25,000 in raw gold. This was cached on Lookout Mountain near Spearfish. Indians related that "much gold" is hidden on this mountain.

Q: Do you have any information on a gold treasure buried in Gordon Stockade in South Dakota?

A: The treasure was buried on French Creek. In the spring of 1875, John Gordon, the expedition leader who built the stockade, and Eaf Wither went out to bring back supplies. They were arrested by troopers fro trespassing on Indian land.

When the news reached Gordon Stockade, several men departed, taking their gold with them. One was Henry Thomas, who packed his placer gold in saddlebags. He was headed southeast along French Creek, four to six miles from the stockade, when he spotted Second Cavalry troops camped for the night. They were headed for Gordon Stockade to arrest those who had remained behind.

Withdrawing from sight, Thomas buried the saddlebags containing the gold. Thus, if the troopers caught him, they could not confiscate his gold. He then crossed French Creek and headed south for his home in Sioux City, Iowa. While en route, he took sick and died suddenly.

Gordon Stockade is six miles east of the present town of Custer, near Stockade Lake on U.S. Highway 16. The stockade has been reconstructed alongside a monument commemorating Mrs. Annie Tallent, a member of the party. No record can be found of this gold ever being recovered.

Q: It is said that a stagecoach treasure is buried on Hat Creek in South Dakota. Can you give me some details?

A: In 1887, the Sidney-Deadwood stage was held up about four miles south of Battle Creek in what is now Custer County, and a few miles south of the present town of Hermosa. The strong box was taken, as well as money and jewels, from the passengers. It is said, the bandits fled to their headquarters along Hat Creek, where the treasure was concealed until all the gang was present and it could be divided. Shortly after the holdup, a number of the bandits were killed, including the one entrusted to hide the treasure. The exact site of the gang's old hideout along Hat Creek in Custer County is no longer known.

Q: What is the story on the Indian, Gray Foot's, treasure?

A: South Dakota Indian legends and other sources tell of a Santee Indian named Gray Foot, who told his sons, in a deathbed confession, that he had buried a flour sack partially filled with gold coins near Long Lake in what is now Marshall County.

He said he was a member of a band of Santees, who attacked an agency—possibly the one called the Lower Sioux or Redwood Agency, near the present site of Morton, Minnesota, during the Minnesota Massacre of 1862. During the raid, most of the soliders stationed at the agency were killed.

After the massacre, the Santees discovered that a payroll had arrived just prior to the attack and that a table in one of the agency buildings was heaped with gold coins. Each Indian took a portion of the payroll, with Gray Foot recalling that he stuffed a flour sack nearly full, tied it to his horse, and escaped westward.

Following the raid, the War Department issued a warning that any Santee with gold in his possession would thereby be considered guilty of murder. This, said Gray Foot, caused him to bury his share of the stolen gold between two straight willows at the east end of Long Lake in August of 1862. The treasure has never been reported found.

Q: What do you have on the story of a washtub of gold?

A: An old prospector, by the name of Shafer, is reported to have buried his half of a washtub full of placer gold near his old cabin, two miles out of Hill City, in what is now the Black Hills National Forest. The gold was buried in 1882 and has never been reported found.

TENNESSEE

Q: What do you have on the Brixie Gang?

A: In 1864, the Brixie Gang was operating around Hillsboro. They heard of a farmer named Cefe Wenten that did not trust banks and had buried his money on his farm. The gang hanged Wenton in an attempt to make him tell where the money was. They then tortured and shot his wife and children, but no money was found. Many people have searched for what is believed to be a $40,000 hoard, but no report of it having been found has been made public.

Q: Did Jesse James bury money in Tennessee?

A: Jesse James and his gang are supposed to have buried $80,000 near Nashville. The money was from a bank robbery in Missouri. It is known that Frank James did hide out three miles from Nashville, where he owned a farm, in 1881, after robbing the Chicago, Alton Express train. This cache has never been reported found. The local library may have newspaper clippings telling of the story.

Q: Is there hidden treasure in or around the old John Brown Tavern?

A: Near Chattanooga is the old John Brown Tavern, built in 1803. Brown, an Indian half-breed, would check each traveler passing through the tavern. If their property seemed valuable, he would rob and murder them. To cover his crimes, he would break up the wagons and throw them into the river. He also owned a ferry at the site. Recent dredging operations have proven part of this legend to be fact as numerous parts of wagons have been found. The stories of buried money around this old tavern and ferry could be true.

Q: Can you tell me anything about the W.G. Seal treasure?

A: East of Sneedville, on the Clinch River, in Hancock County, is where W.G. Seal owned and operated a legal distillery in the 1800's. He was also a prosperous farmer and cattle trader. It is known that he accumulated a half bushel of gold and silver coins. A large part of this money he buried near the distillery. When his second wife died, Seal seemed to lose all desire to live and a short time later, joined his two wives in death. The buried coins have been searched for but have never been found.

Q: Has the Owl Creek Treasure been found?

A: I cannot say if any treasure has been found unless I find it. Here is what I have, briefly, on the Owl Creek Treasure:

An estimated $1,000,000 worth of silver coins, gold jewelry and flatware is buried somewhere near Owl Creek, one and one-half miles northeast of Lexington in Henderson County. This treasure was buried by soldiers during the Civil War. Twenty-three acres of ground in the area are pitted with holes dug by treasure hunters, who have searched in vain. According to local historians, the treasure has never been found.

Q: I have heard of two brothers named Farrington, that were outlaws in Tennessee. What do you have on them?

A: Two brothers that rode with Quantrill's guerrillas during the Civil War, were named Farrington. After the war, they organized an outlaw gang of five members, all from western Tennessee. During 1871, they robbed two different trains near Union City, of $51,000. They also robbed a train near Moscow, Kentucky, of $16,000 in 1870. (It is believed the Jesse James gang was falsely accused of some of the Farrington gang's robberies.)

The gang had a hideout on the west side of Reelfoot Lake, in a swamp, called Lesters Landing. They would escape by flatboats down the Mississippi River, while posses searched for them on land by horseback. The gang was finally broken up when one of the brothers drowned while trying to escape a posse, and the other was hanged at Union City. There are persistent rumors that the gang buried several caches of money at their hideout in the swamp.

Q: Do you have any information on a group of French army deserters that buried money on the Elk River?

A: In the 1690's, a small band of French deserters from the army in Canada, came to the Elk River section in Lincoln County, and lived for several years near where Coldwater is today. Their leader was named Jean Couture. They could be called the first outlaw gang of south-central Tennessee.

The gang traded with the Indians and local stories tell that after taking their furs to New Orleans, they always returned to this area. Several people believe caches of gold were buried where they had their camp. Could be some truth to this. The Indians had no use for gold coins and the Frenchmen could not spend them in Tennessee. Eventually, all the Frenchmen died and very few people know of this possible location today.

Q: Has silver ever been found in Tennessee?

A: I quote from a history of Tennessee written by James Adair: "Within twenty miles of Fort Loudon (built by the British in 1756-57 on the Little Tennessee River)... there exist silver mines so rich that by digging about ten yards deep, some desperate vagrants found at sundry times, so much ore, as to enable them to counterfeit dollars to a great demand, a horse-load of which was detected, in passing for the purchase of Negroes in Augusta."

According to Ramsey, a Tennessee historian of the early 1800's, "A tradition still continues of the existence of the silver mines mentioned thus by Adair. It is derived from hunters and traders who have seen the locality, and assisted in smelting the metal. The late Mr. Delozier, of Sevier County, testified to the existence and richness of mines of silver, one of which he had worked at, in the very section of the Cherokee country described by Adair."

In 1762, Henry Timberlake explored and mapped the Cherokee country along the Little Tennessee River. He heard continuous stories of rich silver mines in the area being worked by the Indians, but he never learned of their locations and most of his maps, charts and notes were lost in an accident.

Q: Are there buried treasure sites in Macon County?

A: Here is one you might check on: Around 1910, two brothers named Jones, lived in a cabin at Russell Hill. They never married and both were known as misers in the community. They raised corn, tobacco and hogs, which they always sold, keeping just enough money to live on. The rest was converted into gold and silver coins. They did not trust banks and kept all their money hidden on the farm. When they died, within a few months of each other, they had to be buried at the county's expense and their farm was sold at auction. Several searches of the farm were made but no money was reported found.

Q: Did the Cherokee Indians bury treasure near Flat Creek?

A: During the Cherokee Indian removal in 1838, some of the Indians were brought through Maury County, where they camped for several days. The story persists that a large treasure was buried near Flat Creek. There could be some truth to the legend, since in the 1920's, several Indians came from Oklahoma and camped in the area for several days. They searched the woods and creek for signs, left by their ancestors, that would show where the treasure was located. They were never able to find the symbols and none of the treasure was found, because the Indians were watched day and night.

Q: What is the story of the Jacob Roaks' treasure?

A: Jacob Roaks died about 1874. He was a well-to-do farmer of Maury County. The Roaks' farm was located near the Sowell Ford on Duck River. Jacob is said to have buried money in several different places on his farm. He always said, "I have money buried somewhere in the cedars." This was a large cedar tree grove that was near the river.

About 1900, two boys named Gilliam, were plowing where a corn crib had stood on the Roaks' farm. They found a skillet full of gold coins, believed to be one of Roaks' caches, a small one. There are still several that have never been reported found.

Q: Could you give me several treasure locations in Maury County?

A: During the battles around Columbia during the Civil War, a Confederate payroll was supposed to be hidden in a cave on Duck River, at Buzzard Roost. The soldiers that hid it were killed and it has never been reported found.

Symbols are carved on the bluffs overlooking Duck River that are believed to be Spanish. The inscriptions are thought to tell of treasure hidden in the area by a group of Spanish soldiers in the 1500's. It is known that DeSoto came through the area in 1541.

Legend has it, that Frank and Jesse James hid stolen money in the Duck River Bluffs. Frank was asked about this in 1915, by a newspaper reporter. He admitted spending the night at the Nelson House in Columbia, after the gang had robbed a Muscle Shoals payroll near Florence, Alabama, in 1881. Frank said he didn't know what the other members of the gang did with their share, but that he was never in Maury County again.

An old lady in downtown Columbia, hid some gold coins on the McGraw stable lot and died soon after. Newspapers of the 1870's, report people searching for this cache but no report was made of it being found.

During the Civil War, an ammunition wagon overturned on Rutherford Creek. The cannon balls went into a deep crevice where they could still be seen, but no one could figure a way to retrieve them. A smart treasure hunter might be able to figure out how to get them out.

A two gallon bucket full of coins and currency is supposed to be buried on the bank of a small stream near Spring Hill. This was hidden by a hermit in a brushy thicket, a few hundred yards from the shack the old man lived in. He later went insane and was never able to recover the money.

During the Civil War, William Younger buried $300.00 in gold along a fence row on his farm near Sante Fe. The fence was destroyed during the war and the money was never recovered.

TEXAS

Q: Do you have any information on a lost cache of gold that was buried by the Spanish in Aransas County?

A: There is an old story, that a mule train loaded with pay for Spanish soldiers, left its planned route to escape pursuing Indians. When overtaken near Falso Live Oak Point, at the southern tip of St. Joseph Island, the money was hurriedly buried before the party of Spaniards was wiped out. It has been pointed out that the pay trains carried more specie than commonly thought, because the risk of getting safely through the wild and inhospitable country was so great, that enough money was carried to pay the troops for an extended period of time. St. Joseph Island is across Aransas Pass from Mustang Island.

Q: Has platinum been found in Texas?

A: A lost platinum mine is located on the East Fork of the Brazos River. Two prospectors who originally worked the mine were suddenly killed by Indians and the site was never relocated.

Q: I have heard of a buried treasure south of Beeville, Texas. Do you have anything on this?

A: A Brownsville man started out for San Antonio with $40,000 in gold. He was camped just south of Beeville when he noticed a group of riders approaching in the distance, and suspected they were bandits. Removing the coals from his campfire, he dug a small hole beneath the bed of ashes, placed his gold in it and rebuilt the fire over the spot. Leaving the fire burning, he mounted his horse and galloped off, but the riders soon overtook him. Stubbornly refusing to tell where his gold was hidden, he was forced into Mexico with his captives, placed under guard and repeatedly tortured.

Escaping eventually, he returned to Texas and made a frantic search for the gold under the old campfire bed, but was unable to find it. He secured the aid of others and revealed that the campfire had been built between two oak trees on the west side of the old Brownsville Road, just south of Beeville. So far as is known, the gold has never been recovered.

Q: What is the story on the robbery of a passenger train in Terrell County and the loot being buried in Brewster County, sometime during 1891?

A: In 1891, a passenger train was held up and robbed near Sanderson, in Terrell County. The six masked men made off with $50,000 in silver dollars. Texas Rangers under a Captain Jones, picked up the trail of the bandits and followed it southwest towards the Rio Grande. When it became evident the robbers had split up, the chase was dropped. Later, another detachment of Rangers came upon the robbers' camp on a canebrake along the Rio Grande north of Bowuillas. Seeing the Rangers approaching, the outlaws rode off with the lawmen in hot pursuit. The bandits were finally traced to a camp near Ozona, in Crockett County. When overtaken there, the leader was killed and his three companions were captured. They were carrying their provisions in Wells Fargo money sacks, but they had little money on them.

One of the captured bandits revealed that the money was buried near Sue Peak, north of the Rio Grande and near their canebrake campsite in Brewster County. A search of this site turned up nothing more than some more empty money sacks. Supposedly, this treasure has never been found.

Q: What is the Mose Jackson Treasure and where is it generally thought to be?

A: Mose Jackson, an early settler in the southeast section of Mills County, is said to have once sold his cattle for gold. Placing the coins in a fruit jar, Jackson and his wife left their house to bury it, watched from the window by their two small children until they disappeared from view. A few days later, Mose and his wife were killed by Indians as they gathered pecans on Pecan Bayou. The children were taken captive by the Indians, but were rescued shortly by Rangers. They could give only vague directions as to where the treasure was buried and it is said never to have been found.

Q: Could you give me some information on one of the caches made by the famous bandit, Pancho Villa?

A: Pancho Villa's fabulous loot is reportedly hidden or buried in several locations in Mexico. Less familiar, is the story of his treasure hidden or buried on Franklin Mountain—the large mountain that towers over El Paso from the north. There are no estimates of the wealth the bandit is said to have left on Franklin Mountain.

Villa is known to have taken a large sum out of Mexico prior to taking up residency in El Paso. What he did with his money is a mystery that has never been solved. Most likely he did not place any of it in American banks, because he did not trust them, and it is believed that he did not take any of the wealth with him when he returned to Mexico. What, then, did he do with it?

One explanation is that he packed his Dodge touring car with trunks filled with valuables and hid that loot in a well protected cave which he had found on Franklin Mountain. Another version of this story is that the wealth was buried, not by Villa, but by a trusted lieutenant. When this man died suddenly shortly afterwards, the only clue to the spot where he had deposited the treasure, was a rock carved with the word—"ORO."

Q: I have heard of a lost ledge of gold bearing ore west of Alpine. What information do you have on this?

A: West of Alpine, U.S. 67-97 and the Southern Pacific Railroad tracks, both wind their way through Paisano Pass. When the railroad was being built through this area, an engineer named Hughes was assigned to a worktrain. He spent his leisure time collecting rock samples along the right-of-way. After the tracks were laid, Hughes took some of the specimens with him to Denver to have them tested. One sample proved to be rich in gold. Certain that he knew exactly where it had come from, Hughes quit his job and went in search of a black ledge in Paisano Pass. The gold ore was not there. Over the years, Hughes patiently searched a large area along the railroad tracks but failed to find the lost ledge.

Q: Is there a wrecked pirate ship at the mouth of the St. Bernard River? What is the story of buried coins connected with this ship?

A: Rumors of a pirate ship wrecked at the mouth of the St. Bernard River, in Brazoria County, have persisted for more than a century. It is said that the ship put into the river about 1816, to escape a hurricane. Before the vessel was destroyed by the storm, the crew took ashore and buried, a treasure estimated at $10,000,000. When the storm was over, only one of the pirates remained alive. He is said to have settled down as a fisherman on Matagorda Island, and frequently displayed gold coins. He admitted to having been a member of the ill-fated ship, but insisted he had not participated in the burial of the treasure, and therefore knew only generally where it was hidden. In support of this story, it is said that Indians living in the area told early settlers of seeing the wreckage of a great ship after a storm had passed.

Q: Is there a buried Mexican payroll near San Jacinto?

A: On April 21, 1836, just a few miles north of the Brinso home, west of La Porte, General Sam Houston surprised Santa Anna's Mexican army which was camped on the plains of St. Huacinth (San Jacinto). The Mexican army funds, amounting to over $12,000, is reportedly buried in the general vicinity.

Q: If true, what is the largest treasure in Texas that you have information on?

A: As you said, if true, this is probably the largest. Coronado's fantastic $60 million treasure is said to be buried somewhere on an 80-acre pasture on what was known as the Sems Ranch in 1809, near Clyde, midway between Abilene and Cisco.

Q: Could you tell me the different treasure stories connected with Espantosa (ghostly) Lake in Texas?

A: There are several stories told of hidden treasure concerning Espantosa Lake. Here are three of them:

One—This story tells of a wagon train loaded with silver, gold and other valuables, that camped one night beside the lake. Suddenly, while all were asleep, the ground on which they were camped, sank and every member of the party was drowned. None of the treasure was ever recovered.

Two—Another, is that a Mexican pack train loaded with gold and silver bullion camped here. They expected to be attacked by Indians, so they buried the bullion. The attack came the next day and all the men were killed. The only survivors were two women who were taken captive by the Indians and kept as slaves for several years. When they were released, one of them tried to lead a party to the location of the fight, but she could never find it.

Three—It is believed that beside this lake, the so-called lost colonists of Dolores met their fate. They were the survivors of 59 immigrants, mostly English, who came with Dr. John Charles Beales to found a colony between the Nueces and the Rio Grande. In March 1834, they reached their destination, which they named Dolores, about 25 miles above the present city of Eagle Pass. The colonists suffered from the beginning. Their crops failed, they became desperate. Many finally sought homes in other places. In March, 1836, a few days after the fall of the Alamo, the last of the colony—eleven men, two women and three children—set out for San Patricio or some other coast point in the hope of returning to England.

There was no road to the coast and their wagons made slow progress. Late in March, they remained in concealment for several days to avoid Santa Anna's invading army, whose supply trains they heard and whose soldiers they dreaded no less than the Indians. On April 2nd, they resumed their march and about midday camped at a large lake, which is believed to have been Espantosa. What money the party had remaining was buried for safekeeping. A few hours later, they were attacked by Comanches, all of the men killed and the women and children captured. This lost cache was never reported found.

Q: Was silver ever found in Texas?

A: Yes, according to legend (and in some instances, recorded facts) silver has been found in several places in Texas. You might want to search for this silver outcropping:

Shortly after the close of the Civil War, pioneer settler L.J. Dailey and a few of his friends took their hunting hounds out for a walk, in the area southwest of the town of Simberly. In climbing a bluff, Daily grabbed a protruding rock and it broke off in his hand. Noting that it was unusually heavy, he placed it in his pocket and continued the chase. It was several days later that Dailey examined the piece of rock and made the discovery that it was high-grade silver ore. He thought he had picked up the sample in Shelton Holler or nearby. He retraced his steps as nearly as possible, but was unable to identify the bluff. Working with others at a later date produced no better results, and the search was abandoned.

UTAH

Q: I need a location of bandit loot in eastern Utah, can you help me?

A: Hope you can find this one: It is believed that somewhere near Skull Valley, a cache of $10,000 worth of gold bullion lies buried at the edge of the Sevier Desert in western Utah.

The loss of this $10,000 worth of gold ore was one of the very few times Orrin Porter Rockwell, Utah Territorial Marshal, ever failed to recover robbery loot, or get his man.

A stage robbery took place near Simpson Springs in the 1860's, and the lone bandit had picked the most unlikely spot and method to use. Pretending to be hurt, he caused the stagecoach to stop. After taking the bags of gold bullion and loading it onto a packhorse, the bandit headed south. The stage continued on to Simpson Springs, where Marshal Rockwell happened to be. When he heard the story, Rockwell started after the bandit. After several days of trailing, he located the outlaw's camp at the mouth of Cherry Creek, in what is now Tooele County.

Taking the bandit prisoner plus two bags of bullion to Lookout Pass, the bone-tired marshal went to bed. Sometime during the night, the outlaw escaped. When Rockwell delivered the two bags to Wells Fargo, he was shocked to learn there had been three bags of bullion and that $10,000 was still missing.

Although a search of the outlaw's campsite at Cherry Creek was made, the bullion was never reported found.

Q: Did Brigham Young have a secret cache of coins?

A: Because of the Mormon War in 1857, Brigham Young buried a vast hoard of gold and U.S. money in and around St. George and continued to add to it until his death. Three different caches were found in 1963 and 1964, and it is believed that much more remains buried in the area.

Q: Do you have the story on a lost flask of gold (weight about 100 lbs.) in Tooele County, Utah?

A: This little known cache of gold in the town of Gold Hill (a near ghost town), in Tooele County, is almost certainly still there. Back during the Second World War, an old prospector known only as John lived on the north side of town. As his age advanced, John began losing his mind. After a while his actions became so violent the sheriff was called. John was taken to Tooele for psychiatric treatment.

When he again became rational, he told the sheriff he had $200.00 in a bank in Ely, Nevada, and asked the sheriff to get it and give it to a friend for safekeeping. When the transfer of the $200.00 was finished, John insisted on returning to his shack to get what he called a "flask of gold." He claimed he had found it in the desert and that it had been stolen from a smelter.

The sheriff and hospital officials assumed the flask was just a figment of John's imagination, so he was left in the institution for treatment. A short time later, the sheriff met an employee of the Utah Highway Department, who told him of a visit he had made to John's shack some time before the old man went crazy. John was trying to open a large flask and told the highway employee he had to leave.

The employee noticed wheelbarrow tracks coming from the old man's pickup truck parked near the shack. The sheriff and highway employee made several searches around the shack, but could not locate the gold filled flask.

About two years later, John was released from the mental institution. He got his $200.00 and left town. The shack was watched but the old man never returned. It is believed that in his disturbed mental condition, John probably forgot about the flask.

Several searches have been made for this flask, but no report is known of it being found. Since it weighed about 100 pounds, the old man didn't transport it too far, since he had to use a wheelbarrow to carry it.

Q: Have you ever heard that the treasure of Montezuma is in Utah? If so, where is the supposed location?

A: The $10 million treasure hoard of Montezuma, supposedly consisting of gold, silver, and precious gemstones, is reported to be somewhere in the maze of passages that honeycomb White Mountain near Kanab.

Q: What is the story on the robbery of approximately $105,000 in cash and $40,000 worth of jewelry that is supposed to be in Box Elder County, Utah?

A: On the night of October 11, 1881, three masked men held up a Colorado and Southern Railroad train just north of Colorado Springs, Colorado. How the larger part of the loot ended up in Box Elder County, Utah, takes some explaining:

A few days after the robbery, the express company announced the loss of $105,000 in cash and $40,000 worth of jewelry, mostly watches and diamond rings. A sheriff's posse followed the outlaws northwestward, but lost their trail near the Continental Divide. Eventually, the bandits were identified as E.E. "Jack" Wright, George H. Witherell and George Tipton, all well known, wanted outlaws.

Later, it was learned the three robbers had worked their way across Colorado and Wyoming, into Idaho. From there, they followed the Bear River southward into Utah. They made camp about four miles north of Corinne. Most of the Colorado loot was buried here, but each man kept a few hundred dollars, along with one ring and one watch. The few pieces of jewelry the men kept, led to their downfall.

One robber lost his watch in a Corinne monte game. The winner showed the watch to a jeweler friend, who identified the stolen timepiece by the manufacturer's serial number in the case. Eventually Wright and Witherell were arrested, tried in Colorado and sentenced to long prison terms.

Tipton, though badly wounded, managed to escape and fled the area. He was taken in by Laf Roberts, a rancher who took pity on him. Before Tipton finally died of his wounds, he told Roberts a disjointed story of the robbery and gave him a rough map of the treasure's burial place along the Bear River. Roberts searched for the buried loot, using the map Tipton had given him, along the Bear River, and located some of the markers indicated. During his search,

Wells Fargo agents notified him that anything found would be seized, and that he would probably be sent to prison. After locating a few scattered watches and rings, Roberts abandoned the search as not being worth the time and danger of being locked up.

Although the story of the Bear River treasure is well known and is authentic, no record can be learned of it being found.

Q: What is the Mine of Lost Souls?

A: The Mine of Lost Souls, a fantastically rich Spanish gold deposit, lies at a point where two streams come together in a remote canyon in the Unitah Mountains. A natural stone bridge is located in a side canyon, not far from a cave containing skeletons and a store of silver bars hidden nearby.

Q: Do you have a story of a lost army payroll on the San Rafael River?

A: Sometime in the late 1870's, two army officers enroute to deliver a payroll of $60,000 in gold coins, made camp at a spring near the headwaters of the San Rafael River. Aware they had been trailed by Indians that entire day, they anticipated an attack at dawn on the following day. Deciding to make a run for their lives, they buried the heavy bags of money near the spring, mounted their horses and rode out. They were immediately attacked by the waiting Indians, but the soldiers managed to fight them off and made their escape.

Deciding to have the money for himself, one of the officers killed the other and rode back to his headquarters where he reported that his companion had been killed by Indians and that they had stolen the payroll. The story was not believed and the officer was court martialed and sentenced to 20 years in prison.

After serving his term, the ex-soldier returned to the area of the spring and made a long, but fruitless search for the buried gold. The spring had dried up over the years and other landmarks had changed or disappeared. The treasure is supposedly still there.

Q: I have heard of a crucifix of gold buried in Utah. Do you have any information on it?

A: The Treasure of the Golden Jesus, a huge crucifix of gold and 40 burrro loads of other treasure, secreted in 1810, is believed buried in a cave somewhere between Boulder and Escalante.

Q: Has lead ever been found in Utah?

A: The Sevier Desert stretches from the northern tip of Sevier Dry Lake across Juab County to the Tooele County line. It is a barren area of shifting sand dunes, sandhills and hummocks. About 1900, a miner from Mammoth, exploring these shifting sands, found a low ledge of mineral bearing rock. His samples assayed high grade lead ore, but he was employed in the Mammoth mines and did not return to the area for several weeks to place his location notices. He could find no trace of the ledge and concluded that moving sands had hidden it. As far as is known, the outcropping has never been found.

Q: Please give me a treasure location in Morgan County.

A: A location worth researching, that is almost certainly overlooked by treasure hunters, is the area between Farmington and Centerville in Morgan County. In 1923 and 1930, floods from several canyons took seven lives and caused over a million dollars in damage.

Spewing mud, debris and rocks weighing up to 30 tons each, the outpour blocked the highways and a railroad, smashed homes, wreacked havoc on farmlands and destroyed irrigation sources.

Several stores were destroyed, so this is a good place to check with a metal detector for the thousands of items (in the form of coins, jewelry, tools, et cetera) that were lost by the residents.

Q: Did the Donner Party bury treasure in Utah?

A: At a little spring north of Pilot Peak, the Donner Party buried a large store of gold and silver coins as they labóriously moved their group along the trail, only to later experience the ill-fated trek at Donners Pass. This is why so little was found at the site of the tragedy. Old family records verify that a large amount of treasure was being transported, the capital for the starting of a new way of life for the entire wagon train.

Treasure found in one afternoon.

Author in workshop.

Found in old house.

Old Missouri house where Jesse James stayed.

Pot of coins found by treasure hunter.

Hunters at Ohio River.

VERMONT

Q: Is there a cache of gold coins on Stannard Mountain?

A: Yes, there is supposed to be a melted cache of coins that were in a house which burned in 1916, on Stannard Mountain, out from the small town of Stannard, in northeastern Vermont.

The location of where the house stood can be reached by going through Walden, past the old Fairbank's Mills and up the Stream Mill road. Take a left at the fork and go about three-fourths of a mile. No report of this being found can be learned.

Q: Can gold be found in Vermont?

A: Yes, gold in small quantities can be panned in the streams of the Berkshire and Green Mountains regions.

Q: What are the Bristol Money Diggings in Vermont?

A: In 1800, an old man named De Grau appeared in Bristol (then called Popock) in Addison County, and spent several months digging in a nearby rocky area, known locally as "Hell's Half Acre." He finally revealed that he had many years before, been a member of a party of Spaniards who had found and mined a rich vein of silver which they smelted into bars. Then, forced to leave the area for some unknown reason and unable to transport all the silver bars, they concealed the ones left behind in a cave.

Of the party, only De Grau lived to return, but his search for the silver bars proved fruitless and he finally concluded that the cave had been covered by a rockslide. Many years later a crude crucible, evidently of Spanish origin, gave added credence to the story.

Q: Is there any pirate treasure in Vermont?

A: Two Spanish silver dollars were found in 1839, by workmen building a canal near Bellows Falls. It is believed that this was only a sample of a vast pirate hoard that Captain Kidd supposedly buried near Bellows Falls.

Q: What is the story of a Confederate raid into Vermont in 1864?

A: At four P.M., on October 19, 1864, a band of 25 men swooped down from Canada and caught St. Albans—15 miles south of the border—by surprise. They robbed the city's three banks of approximately $200,000, stole 25 horses and set fire to the hotel. Five citizens were shot, one fatally. In less than a half-hour they were gone.

A group of irate citizens formed a posse to trail the raiders, and the Rebels were followed across the border into Canada. Eleven were captured and $75,000 was recovered. As they were captured in Canada, they were turned over to Canadian authorities. On December 14, the Secretary of War in Washington was informed that the court in Montreal had released the St. Albans raiders on a technicality.

On this note the incident drops out of the war's official records—except for one item, still to be found in some Confederate records. It says that somewhere in the Canadian wilderness, or perhaps between St. Albans and the U.S.-Canadian border, seven canvas sacks are hidden in a pine grove among some rocks. These sacks contain $120,000 in gold.

All this was brought to light by the death of an ex-Confederate soldier from Mississippi, who had taken part in the raid and escaped capture. According to his diary, the weight of the gold slowed their escape and so he and two other men hid the money in a pine grove beside the trail, among some rocks. No record can be found of its recovery.

Q: I thought Gardiner's Island, where Captain Kidd is supposed to have buried one of his treasures, was in New York. But I heard of another Gardiner's Island in Vermont, where treasure is supposed to be buried. Is this correct?

A: Yes, there is a Gardiner's Island in Lake Champlain. It is off Long Point, Addison County, Vermont, is privately owned and has its own buried treasure story.

After Ethan Allen's capture of Fort Ticonderoga during the Revolutionary War, several British soldiers who had escaped, were seen carrying a heavy box onto Gardiner's Island. They left without it and naturally it has always been presumed that it contained treasure. A great deal of digging has been done for the chest, but so far as is known, it was never located.

Q: Where is Smugglers Notch and what is the treasure story connected with it?

A: Smugglers Notch is a pass in the Sterling Mountains near Stowe. The area was used in the War of 1812, to smuggle contraband into and out of the United States, with the caves in the area sometimes being used to store or hide the goods. During World War I, Prohibition and World War II, other illegal operations were carried on in the area, making it a good location to check with a metal detector.

Q: I am told there is a buried treasure on Ludlow Mountain in Vermont, can you verfiy this?

A: I can't say whether or not it is true, but there is a tale of buried treasure on Ludlow Mountain. About 200 years ago, a party of ten Spaniards, carrying a large amount of gold, passed through this part of Vermont on their way to trade with the Indians. Eight of the travelers were taken ill and died. The other two, unable to carry the gold, buried it on Ludlow Mountain not far from the Camel's Hump, a well-known landmark. One of the two is said to have returned years later, but was unable to locate the cache.

Q: What is the story of treasure on Stave Island off the Vermont shore in Lake Champlain?

A: A strange tale of treasure is told about Stave Island, north of Mallett's Bay and just off the Vermont shore in Lake Champlain. One day a laborer was eating his lunch alone in the island's pine woods. Glancing idly up toward the sky, his eye was suddenly attracted to a human hand, with pointing finger, carved on a tree trunk. At first he did not think it odd, but then it dawned on him, the finger might be pointing at something interesting.

Climbing the tree, he sighted along the pointing finger. Strangely enough, it directed the man's line of vision toward a large flat rock in a small clearing. Once again on the ground, the man struggled to lift the rock, but it would not budge.

At home that night, the laborer kept thinking of the finger and rock and the possibility of buried treasure occurred to him. Could this rock conceal one of the troves he had heard of years ago?

It was certain that the rock in the forest could not be moved without help, so with the assistance of an elderly boathouse keeper, he returned to the island a few days later. A caretaker spotted the two men equipped with pick, crowbar and shovels landing on the beach. Surmising that the two interlopers were seeking buried treasure, the caretaker roughly informed them that any treasure dug up, would have to be turned over to the island's owner.

A couple weeks later, the caretaker changed his mind. He called upon the laborer and offered to permit him to dig, providing they shared anything found equally. For some reason, there was a delay in the digging, and suddenly a forest fire swept Stave Island. Every tree became a charred ghost. The pointing finger vanished, but the buried treasure still haunts the island.

Q: Can you give me any information on the General Gates, a ship that sank near the Vermont coastline?

A: A treasure is lost near Colchester Point, on Lake Champlain. Nearby is Colchester Reef, on which is located a steel tower with its light constantly winking at night. It was here, the schooner General Gates sank, depositing a fortune of $45,000 in silver coins on the reef. This money is believed to still be there, but very few details are known.

Q: Do you have any information on the Birch Hill Silver Mine in Vermont and was gold and silver ever mined in Vermont?

A: It is hard to believe, but for several years Vermont ranked only behind California and North Carolina in the mining of gold and silver in the United States. There are several unconfirmed stories that Spaniards mined precious ores in Vermont as well as in other New England states.

The legendary Birch Hill Mine is so named because of its supposed location on Birch Hill near Pittsford. It is said to have been worked by a Spaniard, who melted its ore into bars and, fearing the Indians, buried the bars at his mine and fled to Spain. A company was formed in Spain and some years later its members returned to Vermont and made a fruitless search for the silver mine and hidden bars.

A lost Spanish gold mine and a cache of gold bars nearby, is also located in the vicinity of Otter Creek, in Addison County.

Q: Do you have any information on Vermont's Gold Brook?

A: Prior to the Civil War, an old Vermont trapper used to trade his marten, mink, fisher and otter pelts at a general store in Burlington. After he had filled several boxes with groceries, new traps, a new axe, a shovel and other necessities, he would return to the counter for a talk with the proprietor. When he was certain no one was watching, he would plunk down a small handful of gold nuggets, which he exchanged for cash. He would never reveal the source of the yellow metal, although everyone knew that his trapline was at the foot of Mount Mansfield.

For years the old man continued this practice, but one spring he failed to show up as usual. He had died during the winter—without telling anyone where he had found his gold. Within a few years, the story of the gold was all but forgotten by the citizens of Burlington.

In the spring of 1859, a man named Slayton, was fishing in a stream (later named Gold Brook) at the foot of Mount Mansfield, when he noticed some bright flecks in the water. Gathering a few, he went to Burlington, where he was told that the flecks were gold. No one has ever known how much gold Slayton found, but it had to be considerable as he showed considerable signs of prosperity after this. Before he died, Slayton was interviewed by a curious reporter. He swore that the gold discovery was genuine and that Gold Brook was the source. While some small nuggets can be found in Gold Brook and other streams in Mount Mansfield, the mother lode has never been found.

VIRGINIA

Q: Has gold ever been found in Virgina?

A: Near Dillwyn, in Buckingham County, was the most notable gold mining regions in the country, before the California gold rush in 1849. The Morrow Mine, opened before 1835, was one of the earliest gold mines in which underground mining was used. It was worked at a profit for a number of years, then finally closed. There are many other now unworked mines nearby.

During the early part of this century gold was discovered near a site called Great Falls, in Fairfax County, on the Potomac. Located in a corner of boundaries that include the states of Maryland, Virginia and Washington, D.C., this site yielded $10,000 in gold nuggets to one man alone who picked them from a small stream.

This small stream empties into the Potomac River, just downstream from Great Falls and along the old C & O Canal that was built to carry boats plying the Potomac around the impassable area of the falls. A great flurry of excitement was short-lived though, because the free gold that lay in the bed, soon played out, and when working the rose quartz in the area proved more costly than the worth of the gold extracted, mining soon slowed to a halt. As far as is known, it was never reworked, other than for a number of "weekend" miners in the area recently. With the price of gold what it is today, this would be well worth looking into.

Q: Could you give me two locations of possible Civil War treasure in Virginia?

A: It has been estimated by historians that over $2,000,000 was buried by different southern families around Lynchburg, in Bedford County, during the Civil War. This consisted of coins, jewelry and other valuables. In numerous cases, the people never retrieved their caches. The Historical Society of Lynchburg, might be able to help on this one.

It is believed that considerable treasure in the form of coins and jewelry is buried in different places along the south banks of the Appomattox River west of Petersburg, in Chesterfield County. This was hidden during the seige of Petersburg by the southern families to keep Union soldiers from getting it.

Q: What is the story of the Jim Surry treasure?

A: Looting and caching of treasure was widely indulged in by both factors during the Civil War. It was practiced by some of the regular army units and by freewheeling guerrillas. As a precaution against just such looting by invading troops, many plantation owners in Virginia, Louisiana, Mississippi, Alabama, Georgia and the Carolinas, buried millions of dollars worth of family jewelry and heirlooms.

One such hoard awaiting discovery, consists of approximately three million dollars worth of gold and silver plate and jewelry contributed by patriotic Southerners to the Confederate Treasury in Richmond. It was meant to purchase arms and ammunition from England.

118

All of this treasure was safely transported to Richmond, during February and March, 1865. But the night of April 1, 1865, two days before the fall of the city, a band of guerrillas led by a former Confederate sergeant, Jim Surry, murdered the four-man Treasury guard and fled with the entire amount.

They got as far as the James River, where they found themselves trapped between pursuing troops from Richmond and reinforcements marching northward from Petersburg. There they buried the treasure, just before Surry and his eleven followers were killed to the last man.

Q: Did some slaves murder their owner and hide his money in Virginia?

A: In 1818, three slaves murdered their owner, a Doctor Berkely, on his estate near Winchester, in Frederick County. After the murder, the Negroes took a medical bag containing an undetermined amount of money, which they in turn, were afraid to keep. The bag and money were buried near the slave quarters. Three days later, the Negroes were caught and hanged without telling where they had buried the money. The cache was searched for by the doctor's family but was never reported found.

Q: Do you have any information on the Widlerness Road treasure?

A: On the old Indian Trail, that later became part of the Wilderness Road, cut by Daniel Boone in the 1770's, was a tavern and stockade built about 1770. This later became a favorite stopping place for pioneers heading west. The owner is supposed to have worked a gold mine in the vicinity and became quite wealthy but was later killed by Indians. The story goes, that he buried a sizeable amount of gold near the tavern. There could be some truth to this since it was a long, dangerous trip across the mountains to any kind of bank, the nearest located at Alexandria and Richmond. This tavern stood about two and one-half miles east of Cumberland Gap, near Ewing in Lee County, on the north side of route 58.

Q: Was silver ever found in Virginia?

A: In 1802 a Frenchman, Louis Michelle, with several men, came through a gap at Harpers Ferry, and traveled south along the Shenandoah River to Powell's Fort near Bluemont in Loudoun County, where they found evidence of Spanish silver mining. Because of English jealousy, the Frenchmen concealed the mines and returned to Canada.

Q: Where is "Haunted Woods" and is there a treasure story connected with this place?

A: "Haunted Woods" is in Matthews County, and there are two very good treasure locations there:

About five miles from the town of Matthews Court House is a wooded area locally called "Haunted Woods" or "Old House Woods." A large treasure consisting of coins and jewelry is supposed to be hidden in this area. The treasure of coins and jewelry is supposed to be hidden in this area. The treasure was collected by English Major General Charles Cornwallis during his southern advance and before his surrender to the American Colonials at Yorktown. According to legend, Cornwallis (before becoming surrounded at Yorktown and Glouchester Point) sent six soldiers with a wagon to bury this treasure. The men buried the wagon load of contraband (estimated at over $1,000,000) in the area of "Haunted Woods." On their way back to Yorktown, they were ambushed and killed by members of the French Navy who were fighting with the Colonials. With them died the location of Cornwallis' treasure.

Another treasure believed to be buried in the "Haunted Woods," is that of England's King Charles II, during the late 1600's. Charles anticipated an attempt to take his throne, so he sent several trusted men to Virginia to bury a large hoard, so that if necessary, he could flee to the colonies and have money to live on. It is known that among King Charles' treasure was a collection of ancient Roman coins that would be priceless today.

King Charles' men were supposed to go to Jamestown, find a likely spot, bury the treasure and return. Instead, they made a mistake in navigation, sailed up Chesapeake Bay and supposedly buried the treasure near the mouth of White Creek in the area of "Haunted Woods." King Charles had them executed for their mistake when they returned to England. The secret of the treasure location was lost.

Q: Is treasure buried in Prince George County?

A: It is an historical fact that England helped the Confederates during the Civil War. She sold guns, ammunition and other supplies to the South. It is also known that several large loans were made to the Confederate Cabinet in Richmond that was never paid back.

A local legend in Prince George County tells that $10,000,000 in gold on loan to the South, from the British Government, is buried somewhere near Hopewell. This happened during the last months of the war, when so many defeats and confusion existed for the rebels. Jefferson Davis is supposed to have had this buried, in the hope that the South could retrieve it later and continue the war after the Confederate capital was moved from Richmond. The loan was in gold and silver bars that the South intended to mint into coins.

Q: What do you have on the Cousins' treasure?

A: A man named Cousins, lived on a farm south of Hopewell during the 1920's. He was a well-to-do farmer, and had saved a sizeable fortune in gold and silver coins through the sale of tobacco, hogs and cattle. Immediately following the economic crisis of 1929, Cousins buried three half-gallon fruit jars full of coins near his home. He was accidently killed and never told his family the hiding place of the money.

Q: Could you help me with information on Captain John Mosby?

A: In March of 1863, General Edwin H. Stoughton of the Union Army was captured by the Confederate guerrilla leader, John S. Mosby, along with several other prisoners. The General had in his possession over $350,000 worth of gold plate, jewelry, silver tableware and gold coins that his men had looted from southern homes. Captain Mosby marched the General and his men to Culpeper, where they were turned over to Rebel General, J.E.B. Stuart.

About midway between Haymarket and New Baltimore, Mosby, accompanied by only one sergeant, James F. Ames (Ames was captured and hanged at Front Royal by Union General George Custer, a short time later), buried the sack containing the $350,000 between two pine trees, marking the trees with knives. Mosby expected to return in a few days and retrieve this loot. The fortunes of war and the fact that Mosby and his men moved about so much, made it impossible for him to return. When the war ended, Mosby disbanded his men and went to Bristol where he practiced law.

Shortly before his death in 1916, at the age of 83, he told some of his close friends. "I've always meant to look for that cache we buried after capturing Stoughton. Some of the most precious heirlooms of old Virginia were in that sack. I guess that one of these days someone else will find it."

No report has been made of this cache ever being found.

Q: Can you help me on a cache made by a newspaper reporter in 1932?

A: A newspaper reporter covering the presidential campaign in 1932, is supposed to have accumulated $250,000 through "gifts" given to him not to expose several unpolitical deals that he had learned about. The reporter is supposed to have buried about $245,000 of this on his farm seventy-five miles southwest of Arlington, in Fairfax County.

WASHINGTON

Q: What can you tell me about the treasure associated with St. Mary's Mission in Washington?

A: St. Mary's Mission was founded in 1889 by Father Etienne de Rouge, who devoted his personal fortune to bringing Christianity to the Indians in the nearby area. The treasure supposedly buried on or near the grounds of the mission, is that of old Chief Smitkin, who as a successful cattleman, always demanded payment in gold when he sold his herds. Hoarding his gold, Smitkin is said to have accumulated a fortune of well over $20,000. When the old Indian died in 1918, his money could not be found, nor had he ever told anyone where it was hidden or buried. His son made repeated searches for it and came to the conclusion that the money was buried on the grounds of St. Mary's Mission, or close by.

Q: Is there a gem location in Washington called Happy Hills?

A: Yes, Happy Hills is in Okanogan County, Washington, and a drive to its aventurine deposits from the city of Okanogan (anyone there can tell you how to get to Happy Hill) will add about 16 miles to your car's speedometer. Aventurine is a sparkling green gemstone of the quartz family and can be used in jewelry, paperweights and bookends.

Q: Will you please give me some information on the Victor Smith treasure?

A: Victor Smith was a debt-ridden newspaperman from Cincinnati, Ohio, who came to Port Angeles, Washington, in 1860. He moved there in order to work as a Special Agent for the Treasury Department, an appointment given him by the Secretary of the Treasury, Salmon P. Chase, in payment for a political debt. In time he became Customs Collector for the Puget Sound District, and built a home in Port Angeles and a building which he rented to the government, to house the customs activities.

After a fairly severe flood in Port Angeles, not long after Smith had settled here, a strongbox from Smith's home was reported missing. It contained, among other things, $1,500 in legal tender notes and $7,500 in $20 gold pieces.

In February, 1861, Smith's brother Henry, who had been appointed a lighthouse keeper nearby, appeared in justice court in Port Angeles and testified that his brother's strongbox was concealed in a nearby Indian village. Shortly after, eight Indians were arrested and one was convicted, but no trace of the strongbox or its contents was discovered. It has long been believed that the Indians who stole the strongbox, buried its contents very close to Port Angeles.

Q: Is gold still being produced in Washington?

A: Washington is one of the few states in which gold production has increased in recent years, mainly because of the output of the Knob Hill Mine in the Republic district, and the Gold King Mine in the Wenatchee district. The state's total output from 1860 to 1965 was about 3,671,000 ounces. Gold was first discovered in Washington, in 1853, in the Yakima River Valley. Placers were worked along most of the major streams of the state through the 1880's, but most of them were depleted by the early 1900's. Lode deposits were found in the 1870's and eventually supplanted placers as the chief source of gold.

Q: What is the story on the Scarborough treasure?

A: $50,000 to $60,000 worth of gold ingots, in a small barrel was buried in or near the Fort Columbia Military Reservation in Pacific County, by Captain James Scarborough, a Scottish sea captain and trader.

In the 1830's, Captain Scarborough sailed his ship into the Columbia River and decided to return and settle permanently. In 1840, he took out a donation land claim of approximately 640 acres, which included the family home of the ancient Chinook Indian Chief, Comcomally, who had died in 1831, during an influenza epidemic. The site of the home is near Battery Two of the present Fort Columbia Military Reservation.

Shortly after settling, Captain Scarborough established a lucrative fishing trade, purchasing salted salmon from the Indians and shipping it to the eastern United States and Europe. Most of the money which he received for the fish, was in the form of gold ingots, and these, according to legend, the captain buried near his home.

Scarborough died in 1853, and although his Indian wife supposedly knew the location of his buried wealth, she never revealed it to Scarborough's son, Ned who conducted several hunts for the cache before dying at the age of eighty, at his home in Cathlamet.

Q: Do you have any information on the Lost Logger Cache?

A: There is a well-documented and still undiscovered cache of gold coins on Vashon Island in Puget Sound, between Seattle and Tacoma, Washington. The treasure is thought to be buried on the banks of Judd Creek near the community of Barton.

This lost treasure centers around Lars Hanson, a lumberman, who worked in this region in the 1870's. Settling in the community, he married a young Indian girl, who was soon assisting him in his business. The girl, suspicious of thieves, buried a number of gold coins from the sale of lumber in a hiding place known only to her. She was killed shortly afterward in an accident and Lars Hanson was unable to recover his money.

Q: What are the facts behind a mining boom that once took place near Rogersburg, Wash., as the result of a lost mine and treasure story?

A: The town of Rogersburg, at the junction of the Snake and Grande Ronde River, was born as the result of frequent mining booms, and experienced regular stampedes through its existence.

One gold rush occurred in 1865 as the result of a lost mine story that originated in 1860. According to the unconfirmed story, three men had beached their canoes on a sandbar where the Shovel River joins the Snake River. They spent the night there, and in the morning found a placer so rich that they quickly picked up a pail full of nuggets.

Since they were short of supplies, the men headed for Walla Walla to outfit themselves—but first they buried the pail of gold. While in town, one man was killed and another died of natural causes. The third man mysteriously disappeared.

Prospectors made trips into the area from time to time, but in 1865, when the story became more widely known, a stampede resulted. Nothing was found but searches are still being made for the lost pail of gold and rich placer deposit on Shovel Creek.

Q: I can't find Spring Valley, Washington, on any map. Can you tell me where it is, and if it is true that an outlaw treasure is buried there?

A: The district around Fruitland in the southwestern corner of Stevens County was once called Spring Valley. It was also called Robber's Roost, and is said to have been one of the toughest hellholes in the early days of the state—a rendezvous for outlaws and cattle thieves.

An outlaw named Slim Watson is said to have buried a considerable fortune at Robber's Roost, before making a trip back east. He told some pals the approximate location of his cache, and when he failed to return, they searched for it but did not find it.

Q: What is the lost mine of the Klickitat Indians?

A: The lost mine of the Klickitat tribe, on the Little Klickitat River in southern Washington, was reported to be the richest gold mine on the Pacific coast. Lewis and Clark saw the gold from the mine being prepared for shipment to England, by a Hudson's Bay factor in 1806. Traders working for the Northwest Fur Company were next to buy gold from the Klickitat Indians.

The gold found, was in the form of wire stringers, nuggets and uneven slugs. By 1875, only one aged Klickitat Indian knew of the mine's secret location. Trying to trail him to the mine and failing, disgruntled white renegades killed him in a fit of anger.

Q: Where is the graveyard of ships in Washington and was any treasure lost in these wrecks?

A: Within an area of 20 miles off Sand Island, between the years 1600 and 1870, more than 600 ships were lost at the mouth of the Columbia River, among which were some 80 treasure laden vessels whose gold and silver cargos are estimated to exceed $100 million.

Q: Who was Harry L. Sutton and did he bury any treasure in Port Townsend?

A: Harry L. Sutton was the son of a wealthy Boston owner of a fleet of clipper ships. Involved in a fight in which two men were killed, Sutton fled Boston aboard one of his father's ships and arrived in Port Townsend, Washington in 1862. He opened the Blue Light Saloon on Union Dock and immediately attracted a following of thugs and toughs.

One of the many enemies made by Sutton, was one Charles W. Howard. When Howard ignored the warnings of friends and went to the Blue Light to settle a matter with its owner, Sutton met him at the door with a gun and killed him.

Sutton immediately fled, but was later arrested in Port Angeles. Tried for the murder of Howard, he was sentenced to five years in prison, but with the aid of outside friends, he soon escaped and was never known to be seen in Washington again. He is believed to have been killed in a shooting scrape later in California.

It was common knowledge in Port Townsend, that Harry Sutton had profited handsomely in the saloon business. It was known also that, there being no banks, he took long weekly walks into a forest back of Ben Pettyrove's orchard to bury his money. As far as is known, none of Sutton's money has ever been recovered.

Q: Do you have any information on a lost safe in Commencement Bay that contained $3,600 in currency and gold coins?

A: In November of 1894, a hard rain had fallen for several days and had weakened the earth on the hillsides overlooking Commencement Bay. Suddenly, the whole mass gave way. Two million cubic yards of dirt and mud crashed into the bay, carrying all before it, including 1200 feet of dock.

When stock was taken by the townspeople, it was found that an area 250 to 300 yards long had dropped into the bay, causing a small steamer, the Orion, to sink.

A 7,000-pound safe owned by the Northern Pacific Railway was also lost in the debris. It contained $2,400 in cash and $1,200 in gold coins. Experts say the treasure would be worth over $24,000 today.

The safe should lie somewhere southeast of the present stevedoring docks at the mouth of the City Waterway.

WEST VIRGINIA

Q: Do you have any information on a cave filed with old guns near White Pine?

A: About fifty years ago, a young man named Wease was picking berries when a rain storm caused him to seek shelter in a cave near White Pine in Calhoun County. He later told that the floor was covered with old rifles and boxes. Because of his excitement and after being told by his father never to go back, Wease forgot the cave's location. It is believed the cave holds a cache of guns that date to the Indian Wars of the 1780's.

Q: What is the story of a lost gold or silver mine being found during the 1950's but which was lost again?

A: Sometime during the 1950's, two deer hunters discovered an old mine shaft in Clay County. The mine, which they explored, proved to have a very rich vein of gold. There were also relics of mining nearby to indicate that at one time, it had been worked, but not recently. The shaft was in a heavily wooded area and was well concealed. It had been pure luck that they found it.

They were naturally excited about the find and completely forgot about hunting deer. When they left the area, they vowed they would return and reopen the mine, but they failed to take into account the terrain and the identifying markers to lead them back. The two men returned to their jobs and waited until they again had the time to return, but when they finally did return to the area, they could no longer find the mine shaft. This mine is still waiting to be found. The Starcher family of Clay County, has all of the story on this, all but the exact location of the mine.

Q: Did counterfeiters operate in West Virginia and where did they obtain their silver ore?

A: Before the Civil War, a silver craze struck the area of Doddridge, Lewis and Harrison Counties. Small amounts of silver were found by different people. A hole in the side of a mountain on Dry Fork, near Big Issac in Doddridge County, is the entrance to what was once a cave with a smelter for melting ore and counterfeiting silver dollars.

In 1929, Solomon Day, aged 86, gave this account of the story to a newspaper: "The silver was pure, there was no doubt of that, and was gotten from several different places. The crime was in using a Government stamp on the coins. A prominent farmer, named Abraham Collindaffer, told me of seeing as much as a half-bushel of silver dollars and there was every reason to believe that plenty of silver existed in the region. A man named Childers, made the money molds in his blacksmith shop. When officers went to arrest him, he escaped by swimming a large creek. He was never seen again. A gang passed the counterfeit coins up and down the West Fork River."

"What finally broke up the gang, was the arrest of Issac Perine, the gang leader. He was put in prison for a term. When he was released, he assaulted a young girl, a mob took him to Tom's Fork and he was never seen again. So he didn't get any of the silver he knew about. Some people still look for these mines and buried silver, but so far as I know they have never been found."

Q: Is there a treasure near Gauley Bridge?

A: Where the Gauley and New Rivers unite to form the Great Kanawha River in Fayette County, is an old bridge built in 1822. It was erected and burned three times, the last time by the Confederates in 1861. Stories have persisted for years of money being buried near this old bridge on at least two occasions, during the Civil War. A check of county records in Fayetteville could reveal more information on this.

Q: Can you tell me anything about the treasure at St. George Chapel?

A: At the site of the St. George Chapel, near Charles Town in Jefferson County, is supposed to be the location of at least one buried treasure. During the Indian Wars, 1774 to 1790, landowners of the area would hide or bury their valuables near this chapel, because for some reason the Indians would not molest it. Several of the landowners were killed and never retrieved these caches.

Q: Has the treasure of Moishe Edelman been found?

A: I cannot say if the Edelman treasure has been found but here is the story on it:

When the old peddler, Moishe Edelman was gasping his last breath in the 1930's, he told the doctor these directions to the four chests of money he had saved and hidden: "Go along the hard road until you come to Fry (a small community about halfway between Huntington and Logan in Lincoln County). Go toward the little town of Leet, across the mountain. At Leet, the Laurel Fork empties into the Big Ugle River. Go up the fork for a mile or two until you reach a large rock. Directly across the road from the rock, in a small bend in the creek, are the chests of coins. Dig along the banks." As of the last report I had, these chests have not been found.

Q: I know several different treasures were hidden during the Civil War in West Virginia. Do you have one in Logan County?

A: According to an old story in Logan County, told to me by a 94 year old man in 1958 (his father had been in the Union army and had told his son the story many times), a Union payroll of $6,000 in gold is buried on the west side of the Guyandotte River, near what is now the little town of Chapmansville, in 1864. A Yankee patrol was carrying the money to troops on the Tug Fork of the Sandy River. After crossing the Guyandotte River, they ran into a group of Confederates and guerrillas.

During the fight all but two of the Federals were killed, and the survivors taken to the Rebel camp. One of the Yankees told the Rebel officer they had been transporting a payroll that they buried during the fight. (The Rebel officer did not believe their story.) The prisoners were then shipped further south to a Confederate prison. There could be something to this legend, since a lot of fighting did take place along the Guyandotte and Sandy Rivers and near Chapmansville. A check of Union army records during the Sandy Valley Campaigns might pay off.

Q: Is there an Indian treasure somewhere near where old Fort Seybert stood?

A: Here is the story briefly of Fort Seybert. In 1758, a band of Shawnee Indians attacked Fort Seybert, located in what is now Pendleton County. Those settlers who escaped the massacre gave the following account of their captivity:

After leaving the site of the fort, the Indians led the settlers along a pathway still known as the Indian Trail, which crosses South Fork Mountain, on to their destination in the Ohio River Valley.

The valued possessions and treasures belonging to the settlers were collected in an iron kettle, a pole was inserted through the handle, and two braves carried the treasures. As trudging up the east slope of South Fork Mountain became more burdensome and the fear of pursuit made faster travel advisable, the two Indians fell behind the traveling group.

When they joined the captives and the other Indians, they were empty-handed; apparently, they had hidden the treasure in the mountain. It is doubtful that the Indians later returned to claim the valuables as this was their last known raid in the area.

Somewhere along this old Indian Trail is a cache of priceless valuables that as far as records show, has never been recovered.

Q: What do you have on three Italians that killed several men then buried the money taken from the bodies?

A: About 1900, three Italian railroad construction workers killed fifteen of their fellow workers in camp to get the money they were saving to send back to the old country. The money was divided with each share equaling about $5,000 in coin. The men split up and one of them went through Marlington on the railroad tracks. Since the money was heavy, he thought he would hide it and go back for it later. On a moonlit night, about two miles below Marlington (in Pocahontas County), he spotted a V-shaped field which came down to the Greenbriar River, on the west side. At the river's edge, there was a rock cliff, with a large number of flat rocks at the base. He supposedly buried the money under one of these rocks.

The man was caught shortly thereafter and died in the electric chair. He told the story to a fellow prisoner, who later looked for the treasure but could never locate it.

Q: Did Ike and Ed Colter bury any treasure in Pocahontas County?

A: Ike Colter lived with his uncle, Ed Colter on a small farm near the head of Laurel Run in Pocahontas County. The mouth of Laurel Run is nearly opposite the small town of Denmar. One day, Ed Colter came in from plowing and was shot in the back just as he was hanging up a bridle on the barn door. Ike was accused of the murder, but it could not be proved. Both Ike and Ed did not believe in banks and were known to have money stashed away. As a small boy, Dewey Purr (now deceased) went to the Colter house and Ike asked him to bring a digging tool, called a mattock. When Dewey brought it to him, Ike said, "Your eyes would pop out if you knew how much gold this mattock has buried."

Today the house is gone, but the bricks from the chimney can still be found in the corner of an open field, used as a "primitive camping ground" for the Watoga State Park.

Q: Do you have any information on the Spanish mining any gold or silver in West Virginia?

A: This is a condensed version of the story of a lost silver mine in West Virginia, giving the essential facts and directions:

"About Indian Camp on Indian Camp Run (in Upshur County), there is an interesting tradition of a lost silver mine and a fabulous buried treasure of silver bullion. The mine's origin antedates the Revolution, with some apparent foundation of truth. The mine was worked by a party of Spanish and English adventurers, who were nearly exterminated by their Indian allies. At the Indian Camp, in 1883, I was shown the ruins of the 'silver mine,' but I was never able to locate the vein of ore. I was also shown a small polished stone disc, pieces of basketry and a piece of drossy metal that had been taken from the waste of this mine, which upon examination, proved to be silver."

"I also examined a figure, or symbol carved on a large sandstone boulder, in a nearby rock shelter, known as the 'Chimney Rocks,' it crudely represented the compass with four points of directions shown. On July 15, 1867, Dr. L.S. Farnsworth found some legendary rock inscriptions on the head of Stone Coal Creek. In company with Valentine Lorentz, Farnsworth visited the area, and on an immense flat rock was found the inscription."

"About three-quarters of a mile northwest of this carving was found an upright stone bearing this inscription 'S,' the 'S' is thought to mean silver. Three-fourths of a mile further northwest, a small rock shelter was found. Back from the entrance, was a large stone slab several feet across that had fallen from overhead. Carved in the roof of the shelter was a circle with the four points of a compass. Across the surface of this circle was a well defined 'pointer' like the needle of a compass. In 1883, several ancient tools were found in a cave on Grass Run Creek, close to Indian Camp. They were described as 'strange looking.' It is believed by several historians and researchers, that straggling bands of early Spanish explorers from the Southern Tide Water penetrated the Virginia and Kentucky wilderness, where they found gold and silver. They were either killed or absorbed into the Indian tribes through marriage."

The story of the lost mine was first written by Lucullus V. McWhorter of Buckhannon, West Virginia, in 1915. Indian Camp is located on Indian Camp Run Creek, about fifteen miles south of Buckhannon, on Route Four.

WISCONSIN

Q: A few years ago there was a lot of excitement about a treasure found near Eagle River. It was believed that not all of it was found. Can you give me some details?

A: Until he died in May, 1950, no one knew that R.C. Bennett had been putting part of his large fortune into the ground because he distrusted banks and paper money. Following directions left in a note, his wife went to the fruit closet, in the basement of their farm home and dug up 60 tin boxes buried in the floor. They contained $40,000 in nickels, dimes and quarters, all neatly wrapped in paper. Bennett had been a shrewd businessman, and friends estimated his wealth to be in the millions. It is suspected that his main hoard was never recovered.

Q: Can you inform me if all the Thomas Burke treasure in West Allis, Wisconsin, has been found?

A: When an expressway was being built through West Allis in 1962, workers dug up $7,700 in cash. It was claimed by Mrs. Thomas Burke, whose house, from which she had been evicted, once stood on the site. Mrs. Burke said another $8,000 or $9,000 was still in the ground, presumably under the expressway or near it. The money had been buried in glass jars over the 34-year period the Burkes occupied the site.

Q: Do you have the story of an Indian cache of gold in Wisconsin?

A: A story passed down through several generations of residents of Arena, Iowa County, Wisconsin, tells of the robbery of a Mississippi River boat which was transporting gold to St. Paul in the early 1880's.

The two outlaws who committed the crime were Indians, who fled eastward to a cave location high up in Coon Rock Bluff, where they supposedly hid the gold. The amount that was taken in the robbery has never been determined.

Later, the Indians were killed during an attempt to capture them, but no trace of their stolen gold was ever found.

Q: Do you have any information on the buried treasure of Bogus Bluff, in Richland County, Wisconsin? What is its value and where is Bogus Bluff?

A: A treasure of unknown value was supposedly robbed from a boat carrying pay for the soldiers stationed at Fort Winnebago. It is said the outlaws cached the loot somewhere on Bogus Bluff in order to make their escape, but that none of the bandits recovered any of it. Bogus Bluff is on the Wisconsin River between the towns of Gotham and Port Andrews.

During the Civil War, Bogus Bluff was the headquarters of a band of counterfeiters. The cave they operated from is still known as Counterfeiters Cave. Led by a man named Ellis, the gang was finally rounded up at Boscobel and put out of business. There is a story that they left treasure buried in or near the cave, but whether this was genuine or counterfeit money is unknown.

Q: What is the William Snow treasure in Wisconsin?

A: Back in the 18th century, William Snow was one of a small band of pioneers responsible for opening up the Northwest. Near the present-day village of Osceola, on the St. Croix River of western Wisconsin, Snow and his party were attacked by a contingent of Indians and French soldiers. Snow was carrying a large quantity of English coins and other valuables, but he succeeded in burying his treasure just before the enemy struck.

Interested parties should probably concentrate on the wooded bluffs and river banks west of Osceola, for rivers were the traditional highways for movement of men and supplies in the 18th century and shorelines were favorite depositories for treasures buried "on the run."

Q: Was a cache of coins made during the Indian uprising in Wisconsin during the 1860's and was it ever found?

A: Back in the nineteenth century when the Minnesota Sioux were on the warpath, white settlers living as far away as eastern Wisconsin grew fearful. They knew that treaties previously ratified, were unsatisfactory to both whites and redskins, that the restive Indians had little understanding of private ownership of land or the papers they'd signed with the federal government, and wanted only to continue in their former life style.

So it was that the residents of Hartland, Wisconsin, 15 miles west of Milwaukee, were terrified by the news of this latest insurrection. A fleeing refugee had evidently spread the alarm of imminent attack and the townpeople fled in panic. However, one wealthy woman took time to snatch up all her silver and family treasures and bury them.

The Indian attack never came and the villagers soon returned to their homes. The woman, unfortunately, was unable to recall where she'd hidden her worldly wealth. Somewhere in the area east of Hartland lies the wealth of a pioneer settler, a treasure which has never been found.

Q: What is the story, briefly, of a French soldier cache in northwestern Wisconsin?

A: In south-central Dunn County, in northwestern Wisconsin, a company of French soldiers were moving northward along the Red Cedar River in the early 1700's. Suddenly, a band of Indians was sighted and the troops hastily retreated.

Weighted down by an assortment of cumbersome weapons and supplies, the French troops stopped just long enough to bury some of their equipment—and a sizeable amount of gold—on the west bank of the river before fleeing for their lives.

Some local residents claim the treasure is concealed in a cave near Pinnacle, a landmark near the village of Irvington.

Q: Do you have anything on an army courier hiding gold in Pepin County?

A: In the middle of the nineteenth century, a courier on horseback was transporting government gold. Just east of the city of Durand, he was spotted by Indians who gave chase. Some say the Indians were after the horse and not the gold. But the rider, entrusted with federal money, was taking no chances of being ambushed and robbed. He stashed the gold and fled at a gallop. The gold has never been recovered.

Q: I have heard of Paul Seifert's cave, what is it?

A: When Paul A. Seifert emigrated from his native Austria to the United States, he brought with him a love of adventure and exploration. Settling on the banks of the Wisconsin River in Gotham, Wisconsin, he became immediately enchanted with the picturesque river bluffs.

One day, while exploring these bluffs near the "lost" village of Richland City at the mouth of the Pine River, Seifert located the opening of a cave. With difficulty, he worked his way through the narrow passageway and found himself in a chamber filled with jewelry, ancient pottery vessels, stone and copper implements, bones of extinct animals, and Indian skeletons.

Seifert sealed the cave by blasting rock over the entrance. Insofar as is known, all attempts have been unsuccessful at locating the cave, and the contents of Seifert's treasure cave still await some lucky treasure hunter.

Q: Is there a cache of buried money on the Mattrick farm near Beaver?

A: In April of 1925, county authorities were summoned to the Bottlieb Mattrick farm near Beaver, Wisconsin. They found 22 men digging, guarded by a group of excited farmers who were armed with shotguns to protect the diggers.

Investigation revealed they were searching for part of a little-known treasure. It was part of $11,200 stolen the previous year, by Martha Battaglan, daughter of the farm's owner. She was believed to have buried a big share of the loot on the farm, only a part of which had been recovered.

Martha was arrested for the theft in October of 1924, in St. Paul, Minnesota. She was brought to trial in Marinette and pleaded guilty to larceny. She was sentenced to five years in prison.

During her trial, Martha confessed to having stolen the money and said she had buried part of it on her father's farm. The rest she hid at her home in St. Paul.

About $3,000 of the money was recovered from the farm and several thousand more was found at her St. Paul home. Still missing were several thousand dollars and Martha would give no inkling as to where it was. Many believe it was buried on the farm but never recovered.

Q: Did you ever hear of the $50,000 hidden by William Tompkins, four miles south of Madison?

A: For many years, treasure hunters have searched for a large cache of $50,000 on a farm bordering Highway 51, four miles south of Madison. This money was buried by an early settler, William (Bill) Tompkins, who brought the sizeable nest egg with him from the east. Tompkins made a comfortable living, farming and fishing in the neighborhood of Portage. When he died, his family made a futile search for the hidden money, but after a while gave up in disgust, and sold the farm.

Several years later, Tompkins' daughter found a crudely drawn map among the old man's belongings. Was this a key to his buried wealth? Perhaps, but when the daughter asked the new farm-owner's permission to make a search, she was rudely refused. Even when she offered to share the wealth, the answer was still no. Instead, the farmer figured he could find the secret cache and keep it himself.

The man searched everywhere with poor luck. All he ever found was some coins in tin cans while digging post holes. The remainder of Tompkins' trove is still safely hidden.

Q: Have you ever heard of a paymaster's chest of gold being in Lake Mandota?

A: Oldtimers tell of an incident that happened in 1828, when a detail of soldiers was carrying a chest of coins from Fort Dearborn in Chicago, to Fort Crawford at Prairie du Chien. The troops were being followed by a strong Indian war party. It was winter, and the soldiers decided to escape by crossing the ice on Lake Mandota, the present site of Madison. Halfway across, the war cries of the Indians in close pursuit became louder. To lighten their load and speed up their escape, the soldiers dropped the paymaster's chest through a hole in the ice. Relieved of their burden, the troops managed to save their scalps and reach the safety of Fort Crawford. To this day, the chest of coins is still mired in the bottom of Lake Mandota.

Q: What is the story of a cache of government bonds worth $50,000 in 1883, being hidden near Glidden?

A: In the latter part of the nineteenth century, James Beckey and his wife lived near Eau Claire, Wisconsin. In 1883, Beckey's wife suddenly left him. He became morose and despondent and finally moved to the north woods. There, about 25 miles from Glidden, in Ashland County, Beckey built a hut and lived the solitary life of a hermit. He was a very wealthy man and had taken with him about $50,000 in government bonds that he proceeded to hide either in his hut or somewhere in the woods on his property.

In 1893, Beckey was found dead in his hut. Searchers from Glidden combed the premises but found only 15 cents. The cache of government bonds still has not been located.

WYOMING

Q: Do you have the location of a bandit cache in Albany County?

A: Sometime in the 1800's, a lone bandit used a clever ruse to rob a stagecoach near old Fort Laramie, about three miles south of the present town of Laramie, in Albany County. The stage carried guards because it was transporting a chest containing $40,000 to meet the payroll at Fort Laramie. The bandit, however, managed to get the chest and waved the stage on. Fearing pursuit by the soldiers, he hurriedly buried the chest near the scene of the robbery and marked the spot by driving a kingbolt, from a broken-down wagon, into the ground. The outlaw was captured a few days later and confessed the crime. Hoping to gain last minute clemency, he told of burying the chest. He was then given western justice and promptly shot.

An immediate search was made for the chest. When it was not found, the searchers concluded that the bandit had given them false directions. In 1928, a farmer plowing along the old stagecoach road found a kingbolt driven into the ground. He knew of the buried treasure chest and is presumed to have searched for it. He was apparently unsuccessful. A few years later he died, without any evidence of sudden wealth.

Q: What is the story of the lost Jim Shaw Gold Ledge?

A: In the late 1890's, Jim Shaw was with a hunting party near Mountain Home in the Medicine Bow Range, in the southwestern corner of Albany County. It was early fall and a light snow was on the ground. When an elk crossed the meadow ahead of the hunters and headed into the timber, Shaw told his companions to go on ahead with the wagon and make camp on the Laramie River while he stalked the elk.

Shaw soon lost the trail of his quarry. When it started snowing again, he turned back to rejoin the party. He was picking his way down a steep hill when he slipped into a hole. In working his way out, Shaw seized a ledge and a piece of rock broke off in his hand. He noticed at once that it was laced with wire gold. Examining the ledge further, Shaw found it to be rich in gold. He gathered all the ore he could carry and went on to the camp.

No one slept much that night. It was agreed that the entire party would follow Shaw to the site of his find the following morning. But by morning, there was a foot of snow on the ground, and the snow was falling harder. The trip had to be postponed for several days. As soon as the weather cleared, the party started on their quest up the mountain. They spent ten days scouting the country for the ledge of quartz but failed to find it.

The next year, Shaw and a companion spent a month fruitlessly searching for the lost ledge. The following two years, Shaw made frequent and prolonged searches alone. On his last trip into the region, he had an encounter with a bear and was badly mauled. He gave up the search and so far as is known, Shaw's ledge of gold is still lost.

Q: Has the Big Baldy Lost Gold Mine been found and what is the story on this mine?

A: Bald Mountain, or Big Baldy as it is known locally, is a barren, dome-like highland that rises above the black-timbered slopes of the Big Horn Mountains. Big Baldy stands south of where Alternate U.S. Highway 14 crosses Sheridan County into Big Horn County.

Q: Can you give me any information on the Lost Stranger Gold Mine?

A: The Sierra Madre Mountains are a short range along the eastern slope of the Continental Divide, southwest of the town of Saratoga, in the south-central section of Carbon County. Indian legends have long told of rich veins of gold in this region, and rims of placer shafts and tunnels of an unknown age and origin have been found. But little gold has appeared. It is an area marked by many ghost towns, and some prospecting still goes on.

In the early days, Ed Bennett operated a ferry across Encampment Creek about 12 miles below Saratoga. One evening, a bearded stranger rapped on Bennett's cabin door, then collapsed at his feet. Taking the heavy pack from the man's back, Bennett helped him to a bunk. The stranger was desperately ill with fever. After several days, his condition improved and he accepted Bennett's invitation to stay at the cabin until he was completely well. He and Bennett became quite friendly. When he was ready to leave, the man insisted upon paying his benefactor for his kindness. Bennett declined to accept anything. Still insistent, the guest went to his pack and pulled out a sample bag filled with gold dust and nuggets.

Bennett acquired from him the information that he had found the gold in the Sierre Madre Mountains which he had left before being snowed in for the winter. The man announced that he was going east. He said he would return in the spring and take Bennett to the mine. The stranger never returned. Bennett spent the rest of his active life searching for the Lost Stranger Gold Mine in the Sierra Madres, but he never found it.

Q: Do you have the story of a buried army payroll in Converse County?

A: Soon after the close of the Civil War, a band of outlaws held up an army paymaster on his way to Fort Fetterman, then fled into the mountains south of Glenrock. The paymaster's chest contained $40,000. The robbers were tracked down by a cavalry detachment. In the ensuing fight, all the robbers were killed. Before his death, one of the outlaws declared that the gang had ridden far up Deer Creek and made camp near a cave where they cached the $40,000. This has never been reported found.

Q: How much money did Butch Cassidy bury near Crowheart?

A: Somewhere in the Wind River Mountains, near the town of Crowheart, George Leroy Parker, better known as Butch Cassidy, is said to have cached $70,000. Cassidy was known to have visited the vicinity frequently. At one time, he "horse ranched" near Crowheart. Discreet neighbors appeared not to notice that, somehow, he always sold more horses than he raised. Older residents of Crowheart say that Cassidy returned to the Wind River region to look for the buried loot in 1936, some 27 years after his reported death in South America. There was, and still is, much controversy over Cassidy's alleged death in South America. Many people who knew the genial outlaw, support the belief that he did return to the United States and made a search for the loot in the Wind River region, without success. The treasure is believed to be on the Wind River Indian Reservation.

Q: What are "pothole" gold deposits and have any ever been found in Wyoming?

A: Here is the best location I have on "pothole" gold:

Brown's Hole is a valley crossed by the T-shaped junction of the state lines of Colorado, Utah, and Wyoming. In the nineteenth century, mountain men held an annual rendezvous at Brown's Hole. Sometime in the late 1830's, three trappers, after attending the meeting, started north to trap beaver. They headed into what is now called the Grand Canyon of the Snake River. Finding the water at low season, they climbed up the high-walled canyon. Somewhere in this canyon the trappers found a large number of potholes along the river's edge. In the gravel at the bottom of these potholes they picked up nuggets of gold. Each of the trappers took as much as he could carry.

John Schuman, one of the trappers, sent some of the nuggets to his sister, a Mrs. Tyrell, in Ilinois, describing the place where they had been found and declaring that there were quantities of the gold nuggets.

About 40 years later, in 1870, Mrs. Tyrell told her son Robert and his friend Normal Ezell of the potholes and showed the nuggets her brother had sent her. In the summer of 1871, the two young men went to the Grand Canyon of the Snake, found the potholes without any trouble, and took out about forty pounds of gold merely by selecting the largest nuggets. Eventually, they had to flee because of hostile Indians. Taking the gold they had gathered, they returned to Illinois. Seven or eight years later, young Tyrell returned to the Snake River, but this time he failed to find the potholes of gold.

In 1887, Elmer Nastron, a relative of the Tyrells, went to the Snake River Canyon. After much searching, he discovered that the potholes had been covered by an enormous rock slide. By moving great piles of rock and earth, and almost losing his life in the attempt, Nastron took out almost $50,000 worth of nuggets. It is believed that the potholes are now covered by new rock slides.

Q: Did Joseph (Jack) Slade bury any money in Slade Canyon?

A: Slade Canyon, also known as Sawmill Canyon, is a few miles northeast of Guernsey. The canyon is named for Joseph A. (Jack) Slade, who for a time was superintendent of the Overland Stage Line between Julesbury, Colorado, and Salt Lake City, Utah. There is a persistent story that Slade, while with the stage line, headed a gang of outlaws who made their headquarters at Slade Canyon. The specialty of the gang was robbing emigrant trains of their stock and valuables. The stock was often sold back to the persons it was stolen from. Many searches have been made for caches of gold, jewelry and other valuables the outlaws are said to have buried in Slade Canyon. Slade was later hanged by vigilantes in Virginia City, Montana, for riding a horse into a general store and shooting the canned goods from the shelves.

Q: Can you help me with a treasure near Fort Fetterman called the Hog Ranch Treasure?

A: The site of Fort Fetterman is on the south bank of the North Platte River, a few miles north of Douglas. Across the river and seven miles to the north of the fort was the inevitable Hog Ranch. Hog Ranch, was the local name for the saloons, brothels, dance halls and gambling houses, which were the natural addition to military posts on the Plains. To these places came soldiers, cowhands, trailhands and others to spend their pay. A small cemetery ususally held the bones of the slow and the careless.

When Fort Fetterman was abandoned in 1882, the Hog Ranch was acquired by Jack Saunders and Jim Lawrence. They operated it until 1886, when Saunders was killed in a fight with Billy Bacon. It is said that Saunders regularly buried his share of the income from the Hog Ranch, but it has never been found.

Q: Do you have anything on the Walker Mine?

A: In the Big Horn Mountains, west of Sheridan, it is said, are the remains of an old cabin that marks the site of a gold mine once worked secretly by a man named Walker. The location of the cabin was well known at one time, but it was not associated with Walker's mine. Since then, all searches for the ruined cabin have failed.

CHAPTER TWO

MISCELLANEOUS QUESTIONS AND ANSWERS

The following questions and answers, while they do not give treasure sites, will be of general interest to all treasure hunters on a variety of subjects.

Q: What interest does the United States Government have in buried treasure when it is found?

A: This question was put to the Treasury Department and here is the reply received from the acting director of the Mint:

"In the absence of complete facts, it is not possible to determine the interest of the United States Government in buried treasure. However, in the absence of some claim of title to the treasure, any amount which might be payable to the Government, would probably be determined by the applicable Internal Revenue laws. The Bureau of Internal Revenue has indicated that in general, the value of buried treasure discovered by an individual, the owner being unknown, will constitute taxable income to the person who discovers it for the taxable year in which he reduces it to his undisputed possession."

Q: Why are so many treasure stories labeled "Legendary", when treasure hunters are only interested in the real thing?

A: Only a small percentage of treasure stories can be completely verified and documented, but the treasure hunter should bear in mind that a very thin line often separates fact from legend. In fact, many legendary treasures have turned out to be the real thing. The serious treasure hunter, while aware that fact is to be desired, does not turn his back on the so-called legendary treasures. There are on record, many instances of a legendary treasure being considered with tongue in cheek, only to turn out to be the real thing.

Q: You've said there is money hidden in every county in the United States. I am unable to see how this could be true.

A: The answer is simple and logical. For instance, during the four year period from 1960 to 1964, more than 600 million half-dollars were minted. Where are they? These coins are not in the banks, and are for the most part, hidden in homes or squirreled away in private caches. To go a little further, there were millions of mercury dimes minted, but where are they today? The same goes for Lincoln-head pennies minted prior to 1959 and quarters before 1964. Silver dollars have also disappeared. Most of these coins have been hidden or lost and will eventually become treasure.

Q: Have you ever heard of money lights and what are they?

A: Mysterious lights are sometimes associated with buried treasure, supposedly hovering over the treasure site. They invariably occur in swampy areas. The Latin name of this phenomenon is "ignis fatuus", which translates into something like "fools' light", from a supposed tendency to mislead travelers. This eerie phosphorescent light which hovers or drifts along a few feet above the ground on dark, moist nights has never been satisfactorily explained, although it is generally thought to be generated by marsh gases, from decaying animal matter or vegetation. The lights have been called "will-o'-the'wisp," "ghost lantern," "jack-o'-lantern," "marsh fire" and other more or less fitting names and many superstitions have surrounded them. Their ability or reliability in indicating treasure in any form, is still an unanswered scientific question.

Q: Where can I get detailed information dealing with army and land office activities prior to 1900?

A: Contact the National Archives and Records Service, General Services Administration, Washington, D.C. 20408. You can write to them but it may take months to get an answer. It might take two or three trips to Washington, to actually see the records you want to inspect.

Q: What is gold and where is it found?

A: Gold is a soft, yellow, corrosion-resistant, highly malleable and ductile metallic element, that is used as an international monetary standard; in jewelry, for decoration, and as a plated coating on a wide variety of electrical and mechanical components.

Scientists believe that the precious metal originated from a combination of gases and liquids rising from deep within the earth's core and moving to the surface through cracks, or faults, in the crust. By unique processes, the gold was combined with silver in a natural alloy called an electrum, as it was also combined with quartz, calcite, lead, tellurium, zinc and copper.

Gold is found in lode deposits, in placer deposits and as a minor element in sea water. Lode deposits are "veins" in the earth's "skin". Placer deposits are found in the beds of streams and rivers, and consist of grains of gold or large particles, called nuggets. These grains and particles have been washed out of and carried away from upstream lodes by surface water—usually flood water.

There are two types of placer deposits: "Eluvial" deposits, found close to the originating lode, and "Alluvial" deposits, found at considerable distances from the original lode.

Gold is seldom found in an unalloyed, or pure state. A varying proportion of other minerals are usually present. Of the total gold contained in the earth's crust, man has secured only .0000186 of one percent of it! The main deterrents in obtaining more gold at the present time are, the high cost of searching for its exact location, mining, and processing it. Identification: Gold has a metallic luster, such as copper. It cannot mark paper but can be scratched with a knife or sharp instrument. Specific gravity is 15.6 to 19.3 (very heavy).

Q: I found a lucky penny from the 1933-34 World's Fair. Could you tell me where I can have it and other coins appraised?

A: Usually the best place to get a true evaluation of coins is from your local coin dealer. Most of the time he will buy your coins at a fair price.

Q: What treasure in the United States—buried, lost or sunken—has the greatest value?

A: A treasure of $20,000,000 in gold bars was smuggled into this country from Mexico, some time before the Gold Confiscation Act of 1934. This tops them all, and there is no less an authority for its existence than the United States government. This treasure became the official business of a federal grand jury investigation in Los Angeles in 1952, when a group of prominent Los Angeles citizens, acting for unknown parties in Mexico, attempted to arrange a sale of the gold to the U.S. Mint, in San Francisco. The court action received wide publicity—and was then suddenly hushed up.

Eventually the case was closed and none of the findings of the grand jury have ever been made public. The assistant U.S. district attorney who brought the case before the grand jury, later resigned to accept another federal post. Shortly afterward, he said there was no question about the existence of the gold and that it was buried "somewhere in northwestern New Mexico". He also pointed out that the finder of this gold is in for a lot of trouble unless it is turned over to the federal government. It is in this country illegally—and Uncle Sam wants it.

Q: Where can I get detailed maps of different states or areas of those states?

A: Contact the United States Geological Survey, G.S.A. Building, Washington, D.C. 20242, and ask for a topographical map price list of each of the states you want. The price lists are actually maps in themselves and are free. Then select maps for the area you want and order from the forms you receive. Maps cost in the neighborhood of $1.00 to $2.00 each. They are worth every cent of it.

Q: What is silver and where is it found?

A: Silver is a lustrous white, malleable metallic element used in : jewelry, tableware, coinage, photography, soldering alloys and electrical contacts. It occurs as native silver in large twisting, branching masses. Silver has been found and mined as an element alone, however the predominate source is not silver mines as such, but other metals' mines, especially copper, lead, gold and zinc, which produce silver as a secondary value or by-product.

Identification: Metallic luster, cannot mark paper, can be scratched by a sharp instrument, gray to black in color. Silver melts (or can be smelted from ore) at 1761° Fahrenheit. Specific gravity 10.5 to 14.6 (heavy).

Silver is found in several different countries: Canada, Germany, Norway, United States and Russia. Mexico is the world's leading producer of silver.

Q: If one finds an old mission treasure, can the Catholic Church claim it?

A: Certainly the church could claim it, but could the church make its claim stick? Generally, recovered treasure belongs to the original owner, or heirs thereof, but there are many other factors involved. This is a question for an attorney.

Q: During my research, I find it hard to locate any hard historical facts to substantiate the tales of lost treasure. Could you give me any advice on how to authenticate a treasure location?

A: 95% of the time the facts are there concerning a treasure location, but sometimes they are hard to find. The people that hid or buried their valuables most certainly meant to return and retrieve them at a more appropriate time. A time that, in numerous instances, never came. A friend, members of the person's family, sometimes even a stranger, was given directions to a location, often by a dying or incoherent person. Due to the amount of time, distance and effort involved, the person with the directions was unable to find the hidden valuables. These people told someone else or wrote the information down and it was passed on to others. Thus a treasure story or legend was born, and like all stories, some were exaggerated.

An occasional mention is made in history books of a ship's sinking with a valuable cargo, or of a train or bank robbery, thus research into written history is the major key in obtaining hard historical facts. County and state records, old newspapers, historical societies, government census, senior citizens, surveyor's and geologist's reports are all invaluable aids in authenticating a treasure site. But regardless as to what extent your efforts may be in research, there will always be a doubt until the treasure is actually found.

Q: Does the government of the United States have researchers employed to look for Confederate and Union gold lost during the Civil War?

A: Not to my knowledge. I posed this question to the Treasury Department, in Washington, and they said "No".

Q: Would you give me a brief history of the Natchez Trace and would it be worthwhile to investigate for buried treasure?

A: No equivalent length of road in America is richer in treasure lore than the historic Natchez Trace. The sites of all but a few of its inns are completely lost today. If found, each could produce a storehouse of relics.

The Trace was a wagon road following old Indian trails. It started at Nashville, ran through what are now Davidson, Williamson, Lewis, Wayne, Maury, Lawrence and Hickman Counties, Tennessee, then entered the northeastern corner of Mississippi, passing through the present counties of Jefferson, Clairborne, Hinds, Madison, Attala, Leake, Choctaw, Webster, Clay, Chickasaw, Pontonoc, Lee, Prentiss, Tishomingo, and ended in Adams County, at Natchez, Mississippi. The land over which the trace extended was owned by the Choctaw and Chickasaw Indians. It was they who granted the United States the right to widen the trails into a wagon road. The Indians, however, reserved the right to maintain the necessary inns and ferries along the route. The inns were spaced about 20 miles apart.

The Trace was under the supervision of the Post Office Department as a post road. Mail carriers, traders and flatboat men followed it northeast. A stream of settlers afoot, on horseback and in wagons traveled southwest over it. All who traversed it, carried with them much or all of their fortune. Those going southwest, took all they had for a new start in the west. Those returning east, bore the proceeds of the merchandise they had flatboated to Natchez or New Orleans. To fasten on this stream of wealth came the known outlaws: Murrell, Mason, Hare and the Harpes. They branded the early 19th century as the "Outlaw Years," and until 1835 made the Natchez Trace a dark and bloody ground. It was popular belief that these outlaws buried treasure at convenient places along the Trace in order to recover it easily when it was needed. A few caches have been reported found, but the areas along both sides of this historic road are still a treasure hunter's paradise.

Q: I am an avid Civil War buff. Do you have an address where I can obtain maps of different battle fields, showing the disposition of troops, both North and South?

A: The best place I know to obtain the kind of maps you want is this address: Library of Congress, Geography and Map Division, Washington, D.C. 20540. Ask for their bibliography, Civil War maps and annotated list. This list will show most of the battle sites of the Civil War. They can photoduplicate any map for you.

Q: I have researched a large number of legends of lost gold and silver mines that the Indians supposedly worked in the eastern United States, before the white man came to America. I can't find any written record or authentic proof left by the Indians that these "lost" mines ever existed. Would you please explain to me how the Indians mined gold and silver with flint tools, where and how these legends started and why they have persisted until the present?

A: First, the eastern American Indians knew little, if any metallurgy before the white men came. The only tribe of Indians that did any mining of silver and gold were the Cherokee. This was in a crude manner, mainly to obtain metal for trinkets.

Occasionally, an Indian would find and keep as a curiosity, a pretty stone, nugget of gold, silver or copper that was worn smooth, usually by a stream. Native copper was beaten into crude forms of arrowheads, knives and trinkets by a few Indian tribes around the Great Lakes region, but the widespread use of gold, silver and precious stones was mainly in South and Central America. The eastern Indians had no written language, except a few symbols that they carved into trees or rocks. These usually indicated water, trail, a good camping spot, or danger from other Indian tribes.

As to how the legends started, the Indians quickly learned the white man's greed for riches, so in a large number of instances, the stories were simply made up by the Indians. If you will read almost any early history book, you will find that it wasn't until *after* the first white men came into the eastern United States, that gold, silver and other minerals were found, because they were looking for a quick way to get rich. The Indian had no use for gold or silver, except to trade for guns, tools and whiskey. Alcohol and white man's diseases did more to destroy the Indian's way of life than all the guns and bullets ever manufactured.

The reason these legends persist today is, people want to believe them (there is a little hope and greed in all of us). They make good stories to be told around a campfire or when a group of treasure hunters get together. Man has always had his myths, legends, folklore and dreams, so they are good because without a heritage and dreams, man cannot exist.

Q: What is emerald composed of and has any been found in the United States?

A: Emeralds come from beryl, which is a silicate of two light metals, beryllium and aluminum. Industrial beryl sometimes occurs in huge crystals and has been found in Colorado, California, New Hampshire and Maryland. When beryl is green, it is emerald; when blue or blush-green, it is aquamarine; when pink, it is morganite; all are beautiful gems. Quality emeralds have been found in North Carolina and California. The best ones have been found in Maine.

Q: Why is it that dowsing seems to be on the downgrade among treasure hunters? I have tried every known method, school, rods, forked sticks, et cetera, but cannot make any of them work. How were the early Spanish able to find so much gold and silver ore through dowsing?

A: You just answered the first part of your question yourself. Although I am sure there are persons that can dowse successfully, I have never seen one. I always ask a dowser one question, why aren't you rich? A dowser would not need an author, publisher or anyone if he could dowse successfully. The early Spanish did not, I repeat, did not depend on dowsing alone in their search for minerals, it was but one part of their methods. That is another misconception generated by treaure hunters and dowsers.

During all expeditions by the Spanish, when in search of minerals, or new lands, a priest was taken along. This man was trained to take ore samples, test them, and observe outcroppings and indications of ore bodies. He was also the cartographer. (The average Spanish soldier could not do this. He was there to protect the priest and expedition only.) That is why even Coronado and Cortez would ask their priest's opinion before making a decision.

A priest was the judge, father confessor, and sometimes leader of an expedition. The Spanish, like all men, suffered from the worst disease a human can have — greed.

Q: Could you tell me where to write for information on meteorites?

A: The people at this address can give almost any information that you want concerning meteorites: American Meteorite Laboratory, P.O. Box 2098, Denver, Colorado 80201.

Q: I keep reading of gold west of the Mississippi River. Has any ever been found in the eastern United States?

A: Gold has been found in small quantities in most of the eastern states. Panning is one method that is used in locating gold in the streams. Here are five states worth checking into: Michigan, Virginia, Indiana, North Carolina, Georgia and Alabama. Write the Geology Department (usually located in the state capitol) of each state you intend to visit. They will send you information on locations where gold has been found.

Q: Why is the hobby of treasure hunting the most popular, in numbers of people involved, than any other in the world?

A: I would say that there are three reasons for the popularity of the treasure hunting hobby. First, this is one of the few hobbies that will pay for itself if one keeps searching. With a little research and a metal detector, almost anyone can find something of value.

Second, we all hope or dream of finding a gold mine, oil well, or some type of riches. As we live out our daily lives, it is this dream that helps us over the rough spots that our way of living and society, seems to put in our paths.

The third reason is, I believe, psychological. I wrote the following some time ago. It just about sums it all up.

"To people interested in treasure hunting, no explanation of the desire to search is needed. To those not interested, no explanation will make them understand. There is something about this "thing" that gets into a person's blood. It is a condition known as treasure hunter's fever. Its boundaries are unknown and unlimited. It affects, in some manner, about one-fifth of the population of the world."

"The cure (not really searched for) is unfound. It has been known to cause the pulse to quicken in young and old, the eyes to glaze over, and has sometimes caused babbling and incoherent speech in individuals. It will make people get out of bed at 4:00 A.M., walk uncounted miles, fail to eat properly, search numerous places, spend thousands of hours in research and traveling and hundreds of dollars for equipment and expenses, freeze half to death in winter, and almost burn up in summer. But no true treasure hunter is concerned with any of these conditions. After finding one treasure, sometimes only a coin or an old bottle, the condition worsens. The only known permanent method of curing oneself of this malady is suicide."

Q: Why is it that the treasure magazines do not devote more space to small localized treasure stories that cover the whole country instead of large known buried treasures that the average treasure hunter can't afford to search for?

A: There are several reasons for this. Printing space is limited, the high cost of printing, payment of authors, postage and handling, et cetera. Most treasure magazines try to print a variety of stories, product reports, pen pal sections, letters to the editors, question and answer columns and advertising, so there is something that will appeal to all readers. When you consider that sometimes over 100,000 people will read a current issue of a treasure magazine, it is impossible to please everyone.

Q: I know most of your questions are about treasure locations but mine is about metal detectors. What is the best detector on the maket today for coin shooting?

A: It is impossible to say which manufacturer makes the best detector. There are several good ones on the market. I suggest you visit a dealer in your area and have him demonstrate different brands and models. Explain to him what you intend to do, and I am sure he will be able to advise you as to the detector that is best suited for your needs.

Q: Where can I obtain information on aerial infrared photography and radionic photography used in identification of minerals and does this method work in treasure hunting?

A: I recently began studying this method of treasure hunting myself. This is a theory concerning the location of minerals through Satellite Imagery. It is sometimes referred to as Geophotography.

135

In some cases this type of photography will actually show mineral outcroppings, sinks, underground streams, mine tailings, diamond "pipes" and faults in the earth's surface. The address to write for information is: National Cartographic Information Center, 507 National Center, Reston, Virginia 22092. Phone 703-860-6045. Enclose topographic maps of the area you are interested in. Also tell them which type of photos you want: color; infrared 1:24,000 scale, color photography 1:24,000 scale or black and white 1:20,000 scale. This is a very interesting theory concerning treasure hunting.

Q: Is lead associated with silver ore in its natural state? Also, what connection is there between lead and uranium?

A: Lead as well as other minerals are associated with both silver and uranium. In some instances, the radioactive decay of uranium will eventually result in the formation of lead. All lead deposits should be checked for the possibility of both silver and uranium.

Q: I have heard that ambergris is a very valuable substance used in the making of perfume. A friend of mine tells me that it can be found occasionally along the seashore and could be classed as a treasure found. How could this be so, when a metal detector is not used? Also, how much is the stuff worth and what does it look like?

A: We normally think of treasure as being in the form of gold, silver, artifacts, paintings, bullion or jewels. While these are sometimes priceless, there are many other forms of treasure worth just as much. Ambergris is one of them. It is used in making perfume after being dissolved in alcohol, as a stabilizer for the fragrances. The color is grayish or yellowish-green and feels spongy to the touch.

Sometimes it may be almost as hard as rosin because of exposure, or can resemble a piece of fat. Small smounts of ambergris can be found washed up on coastlines almost anywhere.

Ambergris is formed in the stomach of whales and is something the whale burps up. While this substance may look, or feel, unpleasant to some individuals, when you consider it is worth about $5,000 a pound, it could pay anyone to forget their feelings and search for it along a coastline.

Q: Could you tell me where to write for information concerning all types of mining?

A: This is the best place I know. Contact: Chief, Office of Mineral Information, Bureau of Mines, Room 1035, Columbia Plaza, Washington, D.C. 20241. They have booklets and technical literature on mineral production, consumption and research, and abatement of environmental pollution associated with minerals. Most of this literature is free.

Q: I have made several searches for treasure, but it seems that something always happens so that I cannot get to search the way I want. There have been too many changes in the land during the last few years. Do you have this problem?

A: Yes, I have had this problem in several places I wanted to search. I would research a site, then make a trip to the area, finding that in all too many instances, time and progress had caught up with the treasure hunter (me, in this case). In some areas complete towns have disappeared, others have grown, and streams and roads have changed their courses. Places that were farms a few years ago, are now shopping centers. Also, road and dam building, strip mining and housing projects have so changed different areas that sometimes it is impossible to locate a treasure that was hidden, even a short time ago. Usually the older the treasure site, the more changes there will be and the less chance there is in finding what was hidden.

Q: Could you give me an address where I can obtain a list of "gold hoarders" the Government is supposed to have? I read somewhere that a list was made by the Treasury Department in the 1930's of businessmen, bankers, et cetera, that the Government knows did not turn in all their gold.

A: You have quite a theory and it just might pay off. I assume you want to contact the Treasury Department at their address today. Here it is: United States Department of the Treasury, Washington, D.C. 20220.

Q: I know this is not a question on a treasure location, but I would like to know when coins were first minted and what was used for trade before coins?

A: What was called the barter system, was used thousands of years before coins were invented. This was a measured value of one product in exchange for another. There were many problems to this system, so finally, metal in coin and bar design came into use. These metal items could be made in different weights, were easier to transport and store.

The Chinese are believed to be the first people to use metal money. They made miniature spades, knives and other tools in bronze about 1100 B.C. The first actual coins were made in Lydia, now Turkey, about 600 B.C. The Romans made coins, called denarius, in the 300's B.C. Paper money developed from a custom in England, in the 1600's. People stored their gold and other valuables in a bank-like depository and were given receipts which were used for money. The first banks (as we know them) came into being shortly after 1650.

Q: Could you tell me where I can obtain the addresses of all the historical societies in the United States? Is this information in book form?

A: Yes, there is such a book. You can order it from American Association for State and Local History, 1400 Eighth Avenue South, Nashville, Tennessee 37203. The book costs $24.00 and they require a check or money order in advance.

Q: I have heard that diamonds have been found in other parts of the United States besides Arkansas. Is this true? And how would I recognize a diamond in its natural state? What are alluvial diamonds and how are they mined?

A: This is unusual, four questions in one, but here are the answers. Yes, diamonds have been found outside Arkansas. Kentucky, Indiana, West Virginia, North Carolina, Georgia, Alabama and California are a few of the states diamonds have been found in.

A diamond in its natural state usually feels greasy and rough. Alluvial diamonds are those that have been washed out by a stream or broken away from whatever formation they were originally in. These can be obtained by panning, sifting or a type of suction pump can be used on the bottom of streams to remove the silt down to bedrock. Thick oil is sometimes used, mixed with sand and gravel. The diamonds will stick to the oil when being washed out of a pan.

Q: Where can I obtain information on all ships that have been wrecked in the Mississippi River?

A: To my knowledge, no such list has ever been compiled. It would have to be obtained through several sources, such as reports in the Government Archives in Washington, D.C., old newspaper files in towns along the Mississippi and records of navigation companies engaged in Mississippi River commerce. One can only guess where these might be.

Q: Can you stake more than one claim, side-by-side? How big does the discovery hole have to be, and tell me a little about the $500 worth of work that must be done on each claim. Also how does a person obtain a lease to prospect and mine minerals on government lands.

A: You can stake a dozen claims to cover a desired area, if they are open to location. Depending on state laws, you do not have to have a "discovery hole." An outcropping can be considered a valid discovery.

The $500 worth of work you mention, is known as "annual expenditure or assessment work" and can be in the form of actual labor or in physical improvements on the claim. The building of a road, core-drilling or any other expenditure of money or labor will qualify as long as it definitely contributes to the development of the property.

I quote in part, a letter I received from the Department of the Interior, Bureau of Mines. "The Bureau of Land Management, U. S. Department of the Interior, Washington, D.C., negotiates leases on acquired federal lands. You should apply to the B.L.M. with a map of the area you want to lease. The map and application are then sent to the National Forest Service, which is part of the Department of Agriculture, for verification of the map and approval of the application."

"You can expedite matters by obtaining the cooperation of the local forest ranger. If he will look over the area and make the map or approve your map before you send the application to B.L.M., there should be no delay when B.L.M. sends the application and map to the Forest Service for verification and approval."

"You can get a prospecting permit from the local Forest Service office, if prospecting is necessary to determine the area you want to lease."

Q: Do you know who first started keeping records of hidden treasure in the United States?

A: The earliest record I can locate of anyone researching treasure sites was in 1770 (there could have been earlier ones), when Silas Hamilton, a leading citizen and large landowner of Whitingham, Vermont, started keeping an account on everything he could find about buried treasure. The present whereabouts of Hamilton's journals (which were extensive) are not known, but they would be invaluable if found.

Q: I am an avid treasure and coon hunter. I own several hounds and two metal detectors. I have heard that dogs have been trained and used by different police departments to locate marijuana. Could one be taught to smell out different metals? If so, how are they trained?

A: I have just recently obtained information on this relatively unknown method of prospecting. Dr. Harry Warren, a professor of Geological Science at the University of British Columbia, in Canada, states: "Specially trained dogs can find copper, lead, zinc, nickel, even gold and silver. They do a very good job and work faster and more economically than an ordinary prospector. The animals are conditioned to detect the smell of sulfides, metals mixed with sulphur. A conservative estimate is that a dog can find as much as 20% more than a man and can be trained to detect the smell of rocks the prospector can't even see, in extreme cases, as much as six feet deep. Prospecting dogs have been used widely in Scandinavia, but American miners have been slow to accept them."

"The idea sounds stupid to those people who don't know how simple it is. Because of ignorance they are turning down a technique that could save many hundreds of thousands of dollars. Dog owners can train their own pets to find precious metals. If you can teach a dog obedience, he can be trained to find gold."

John Brock, president of Welcome North Mines, in Vancouver, says: "There have been six instances where dogs trained by Dr. Warren have located ore-bearing boulders that have been mapped and traced back to their original source. In one case, a prospector working with a dog, located boulders which were traced back to a valuable deposit of uranium. The dogs are invaluable. They greatly speed up the process of finding mineral deposits."

James McDougal, manager for the Falconbridge Mines in Canada, agrees with Warren and Brock that using dogs is a bona fide technique. Their sense of smell is 100 times that of a human.

Q: I read somewhere that certain plants can detect atomic fallout or natural radiation. Is there any truth to this? The information might be helpful to treasure hunters in different areas.

A: Yes, with the large number of nuclear plants being built in the United States and the search for uranium, this information could be helpful. Garden Magazine recently reported that the Japanese are planting Spiderwort around nuclear plants as radiation detectors. The wild flower changes from blue to pink when exposed to atomic radiation, both natural and man-made.

Q: I have heard of an island in Lake Superior that is supposed to be all silver. How could this exist and why hasn't the ore been taken out?

A: The island is not all silver, although the mine is so rich it is sometimes called Silver Island. It is located about 75 miles north of Michigan's northern border, in some of the stormiest water in the world. During severe storms, waves almost completely cover the island.

Discovered in 1870, this fantastic lode has defied all attempts at mining since 1884. Between 1870 and 1884, a large flood wall made of rocks and logs, held back the waves. A shaft was sunk 1,000 feet deep and more than $4,000,000,000 worth of silver was removed. Coal to keep the pumps going, failed to arrive before the freeze of 1884. Without the pumps, water flooded the shaft and mining operations had to stop.

It has been estimated that the supporting pillars of the mine shaft alone, would yield a million dollars in silver. The vein runs in a line south across Lake Superior toward Michigan's Upper Peninsula, where silver, gold, copper and iron have been found. Some people believe the silver vein begins on the Upper Peninsula of Michigan and then goes north to Silver Island.

Q: This is an unusual question concerning treasure hunting. "Are there any plants, grasses or trees, that indicate mineral deposits or water and what are their names?"

A: I am sure the answer will come as a surprise to numerous treasure hunters. The poppy flower (in its wild state) almost always indicates a copper deposit. Peppergrass and milk vetch, could mean there is uranium below their roots. The common horsetail plant has the ability to extract gold from the ground if the mineral is present. The chief value of the plant, however, is as an indicator of gold in a given location.

Hemlock and the holly tree are sometimes indicators of lead. Firs, junipers and yellow pines show where to look for gold. The rhododendron bush has been known to indicate coal and oil by the color shades of its leaves. Regardless of where you find willow trees, the cattail plant or swamp grass; they indicate water. Different types of grasses and trees are used to control erosion.

Plants, trees and grasses (in their natural state) can be important clues to locating mineral deposits and water. Searching in this manner is referred to as geobotanical prospecting. This little known science has been used by a select few for hundreds of years. The ancient Egyptians used this method in conjunction with dowsing. It is believed that the early Spanish Jesuit priests also knew this art and used it in our southwest. That is one reason why they were so successful in locating gold and silver deposits. Very little has ever been written concerning this method of treasure hunting.

Q: Would you please give me the names of the best books on all types of treasure symbols?

A: Here, in my opinion, are the best: Arnold Kortejarvi's "Handbook of Treasure Symbols"; William Mahan's "Early Spanish Treasure Signs and Symbols"; Thomas Penfield's "Treasure Signs and Symbols"; Forest Wade's "Cry of the Eagle"; and Campbell Grant's "Rock Art of the American Indian".

Q: I am an all-around treasure hunter but I like rock hounding best. I was told by friends that they had heard of a place in Virginia where natural stone crosses can be found. We have been unable to locate this site. Could you please tell us if such a place exists and where it is?

A: Yes, there is such a place in Patrick County, Virginia, and it is amazing. It is called Fairy Stone State Park and is almost hidden in the foothills of the Blue Ridge Mountains, near the small town of Bassett. The park is named for the curious little stone crosses that are found all over this area.

The fairy stone, or staurolite, is one of the strangest crystals in the mineral world. This is a little curio stone which is known as a good luck charm; a crystal formed into a perfect cross. It carries with it, an age-old tradition of good fortune—a cross to hang your troubles on, the mountain people say.

The crosses are found in three shapes, namely: Roman, Maltese and St. Andrew. About 85% of the staurolites found here are of the St. Andrew's variety and shaped like the letter "X". About 5% are perfect right angled Roman or Maltese crosses. The other 10% are classed as "bow ties" or large crosses formed in single staurolite crystals.

A six pointed staurolite is sometimes found, but they are very rare.

Q: Could you give me the name of the best book (in your opinion) on the ship wrecks in Lake Superior?

A: "The Great Wrecks of the Great Lake," by Frederick Stonehouse, probably gives the most comprehensive list of any book that has been written on the Great Lakes. Mr. Stonehouse lists hundreds of wrecks in Lake Superior, giving dates of sinkings, cargoes, specie and loss of life.

Q: Did the Cherokee Indians have any certain way, such as with a primitive dowsing rod, or witchcraft, to locate gold and silver? Recorded history tells that before they were driven out of Georgia, they had accumulated millions in gold and silver that they had to hide (in some manner), because the U. S. Government did not let them take it with them to Oklahoma. How were these places concealed?

A: Beginning in the early 1700's (after they learned the value of gold and silver) and continuing until about 1830, the Cherokee used this method (there were others), in locating different minerals. An elder would fast for about a week, then he would walk along a stream bed or ridge in early morning, usually in late fall or early spring. When he saw a place where "smoke" (steam) came from the ground, metal was almost always found.

When the Cherokee realized that they could not win and would have to leave, they decided to conceal the mines and caches. An individual, a family, or a group of several families would use natural or man-made caves to conceal the gold, silver and jewelry they had accumulated. A waybill was made for each site, so that the cache could be found if they ever had a chance to return.

For use in concealment, clay was mixed with animal blood and water. When it dried, it bonded together like our concrete. This primitive but effective mortar was used to fill in cave and mine openings (it also prevented cave-ins). Grass, bushes or moss were then planted to cover the site. In a few weeks all signs of the entrances were gone. Most of these secret places had a death trap inside, such as a large rock that would fall on anyone that did not know the way to get in. These were called "dead-falls". Then each family, or individual would make markings nearby. This could be anything: carvings, certain rocks, trees, mountains or streams.

After extensive research in the Cherokee culture, I believe their earthworks to have been exceptional because very, very few of these locations have been found by white men, even with our modern metal detecting equipment. I believe the majority of these sites are lost forever, unless accidentally found. About six generations have passed, since the Cherokee were forced from their homeland, most of the original waybills have been lost, the stories are garbled and even their own heritage has become legendary to the Cherokee.

Q: Could you tell me where the Valley of Rubies is located?

A: The locality between Franklin and Bryson City, North Carolina on U. S. 28, is known as the Valley of Rubies because of the large number of gemstones that have been found there.

Q: Mr. Henson, I think you're the top writer in treasure hunting today. Would you tell me how you are able to write on so many different states and treasure locations? I am sure you have your own methods of researching, but I would like to have an idea of how you learn so much on different areas.

A: I have been asked this question several times. Here is my answer: I have over 25 years experience in collecting material on different treasure locations. My library looks like it belongs in some university. I have over 15,000 books, magazines, newspaper clippings, articles, out-of-print county, state and federal bulletins, and brochures, all covering the entire country. My map collection would stagger your imagination. I have been offered $30,000 for my research alone. I have written eight books and have two manuscripts waiting to be printed, plus about 1,000 articles on different subjects for newspapers and magazines.

I travel upwards of 50,000 miles and probably contact 500 people a year, in search of new information. My mail normally runs from 5 to 25 letters a day. A large number of readers send me local newspaper clippings, county histories, old letters and maps, all pertaining to treasure locations I could not otherwise obtain.

I have history books that date back to 1800. It's amazing the (now) unknown treasure stories and locations some of these books contain. I have dozens of locations that I have never written anything about. Also, I have been an avid student of history and geography all my life. By having all this material indexed and my continual research, I am able to answer 99% of the questions I receive and I can write (where research and history will allow) with authority on any state in this country. These are part of my methods, the rest will have to remain a "trade secret."

Q: Is there any way I can tell if a stone is garnet without taking it to a jeweler?

A: One way to identify garnet, is to scrape its surface with the edge of a piece of broken china dish, this will leave a streak if it is garnet. I always carry a piece of this china in my field pack.

Q: Did the Spanish gold and silver mines one reads about, really exist in the southwestern United States, during the 1600's, were the priests successful in obtaining large amounts of gold and silver and where would the headquarters of the church have been at that time?

A: Yes, a large percent of the old legends concerning Spanish mining are true. As far as can be learned through research of old Spanish church records, gold mining was done by different Indian tribes under the direction of Spanish priests from about 1550 until the 1780's. After the

Indian uprising of 1765-67, few concentrated efforts were made to mine gold and silver by the church.

The priests were as greedy for gold as the Conquistadors, but in a more subtle manner. Actually they were more successful in obtaining large quantities of gold and silver than the Conquistadors, because they used the Indian's superstitious nature to their advantage through fear and in some cases outright enslavement. There is little doubt but that vast amounts of gold and silver were mined and secreted by the priests at different times and in different places during this period. Due to Indians, weather conditions and death, a large part of this is still waiting to be found.

The headquarters of the church, if such it could be called, was probably located in what is now Mexico City. At that time the city would have been only a cluster of missions with quarters for the priests and soldiers.

Q: What is the best book I can get that will list different treasure sites, old forts, Indian villages, houses, trails, et cetera, in different states?

A: I sould say "The Federated Writers Guide" for each state (these can be found in most public libraries), are the best sources of general information outside the professionally written treasure books.

Q: I have read most of your material in different treasure magazines and enjoy it very much, but I heard somewhere that you write on subjects other than treasure hunting sites. Would you please tell me some of your thoughts and experiences and what different types of writing you do?

A: I have to admit this is an unusual request, but I have received several such as this. Yes, I have written quite a few science fiction articles, based on facts learned through treasure hunting experiences (I plan on doing a book on this someday), folklore, fishing stories, humor, and I once won first prize in a state sponsored contest on poetry in Kentucky. I also do a weekly newspaper column on different subjects. But my first love is treasure hunting research and history. I feel that my purpose as a writer on treasure hunting should be to instill in the hunter correct information (as far as history and research will allow), reflection, decision then action. My philosophy is based on the belief that only by sharing leads and exchanging information can the full stories be learned and recoveries made.

One of the things I have learned in my 20 odd years of treasure hunting and writing is that you can get used to anything, even to the fact that perfection is only temporary. There is always something else waiting somewhere; another river to cross, a mountain to climb, a person to see, a trip to make, a job to do, and during all of this, there is still a road, either north and south or east and west that one has to take. I have learned that you have to be honest with yourself and take your own road, because at the end of it—with luck—just might be the thing you have been searching for and really want.

Q: In summing up your many years in the treasure hunting hobby, what would you say has been your greatest find?

A: This will surprise you but the answer is the friendship and integrity of the hundreds of people I have met and learned to care for throughout the treasure hunting hobby. Treasure can be found in many forms but camaraderie is the greatest of them all. I would not trade my memories and experiences for all the gold in Coronado's fabled Seven Cities of Cibola.

Civil War fort site.

Author doing research.

Where railroad "tank towns" stood is likely.

Abandoned farmhouses may be searched.

Parks are always a possibility.

Old fashioned cemetery in eastern U.S.

142

CHAPTER THREE

HOW TO RESEARCH TREASURE SITES

"Research (in one form or another) is the major part of any successful venture."

This chapter is written for those that want to know how they can research and obtain information on treasure locations, before investing money or equipment, or doing any hunting. The methods listed herein have proven successful for me:

Libraries... When you visit a library obtain a library card, this will help to avoid confusion and delay on later visits, when checking out books and miscellaneous material. Get to know the librarian and clerks, explain what you are looking for. They will sometimes know of an old book, brochure, federal, state or county publication that is not listed in the regular files. These items are sometimes stored for months, until they can be filed in their proper place by the staff.

Look in the library catalog or index file for the type of material you want, this can be found by using the author's name or the book title, in an alphabetical order. Locate the different departments that specialize in such subjects as history, mining, minerals, geology, federal, state and county publications, local authors, newspaper files, documents, maps or any subject that you want to research.

When checking a book for information look in the index first to see if what you are looking for is listed by name (this can save a lot of time). Start with (for treasure hunters): battles, bandits, counterfeiters, canals, forts, ferries, gold, gems, lost mines, legends, mining, minerals, outlaws, priates, silver, treasure, taverns. Almost anything you want can be found faster in this manner.

Most libraries have a room devoted to local and state history. This is where most of the existing histories, state, county, topographical and geological maps, atlases, journals and census records are located. The list is almost endless. Information on nearly any subject concerning a particular state can be learned here.

Check with the librarian on letters they have received from people interested in differen subjects, sometimes it's just what you are looking for. When checking newspapers and periodicals look in the "Letters to the Editor," "Pen Pals," "Readers Views," and "Questions and Answers" columns for names and addresses of people seeking information on the subject you are interested in, then contact them. Always enclose a self addressed, stamped envelope.

If you want a particular book and your library does not have a copy, they can arrange an inter-library loan for you from another library. Almost all libraries, historical societies, county and state offices are understaffed, so it is best to develop your own system of research. Leads to treasure sites can come from almost any kind of publication.

Usually there is a Xerox machine where you can make copies of whatever you like, so that you can study it later, or keep it in your files. Make certain you have pens and notebooks (the libraries do not furnish these). Always get the title, author's name and date of publication on all information. This is very important for use in later references.

Museums... Your local museum will usually have exhibits that can furnish information on minerals, gems, rock formations, types of strata in a particular state, ore samples, Indian relics, fossils, and other information that can be of value. Study the exhibits that interest you, learn when they were found and where.

Get to know your museum curator, he can usually tell you of local locations, that cover a variety of subjects that have never been reported.

Historical Societies... Usually for a small fee, you can join your local or state Historical Society. Through their monthly or quarterly publications, you can learn local history that has been well researched by a member or qualified author. Your membership card can be very useful to you, as a treasure hunter, when visiting other historical societies throughout the country.

Other sources of information... Postmasters and county clerks can be helpful, especially in a small town, as they will know most of the population.

Senior citizens (people over 65) will remember events of 50 years ago that younger people never heard of and they will usually talk to you.

The bankers in small towns may know of withdrawals of money that someone later buried.

Newspaper morgues, where all back issues of the individual newspapers are kept, are good sources of information.

Talk to landowners, they may know of Indian pictographs or other symbols carved in rocks that could be signs to treasure.

Your local metal detector dealer will have heard numerous stories of different lost treasures in his area.

Write the Secretary of State (your state), to obtain the latest state maps and brochures that describe and locate the different points of interest. This provides lots of information and the information is usually free.

For information on Civil War, Indian and other battle sites for relic hunting, contact the Civil War Roundtable or State Historical Society. This office is usually located in the (your) state capital.

Subscribe to or trade for all of the treasure magazines on the market that you can afford, this is your best investment. The stories have usually been well researched, sometimes with maps and photographs. File them for reference.

Executors of estates are good people to talk to. Sometimes money or valuables were buried or hidden that they need to locate.

Join a treasure club, and attend all the meetings you can. Most of these clubs publish a newsletter giving leads, stories of treasure found and names of people throughout a particular state that are devoted to the hobby of treasure hunting.

Historical markers erected along highways are a good source of information on old forts, battlefields, trails, old homes, early trading posts, ferries, and other data. Most states publish a booklet that tells where the markers are located and what they say (sometimes with additional information). Write the Historical Society in your state capital on how to obtain this booklet.

Look through old court records, family histories, old letters, diaries, journals, county highway records (they will have old road maps and survey reports). Check any source of information that might be helpful.

Spend the winter months in research. Check the routes, locations, contact landowners, and get your maps together with all the available information. Make sure you have all of the equipment you need and that it is in good working order. Plan your trips carefully.

Although history does not always agree on the manner in which events occurred, almost all stories, legends and folklore have a basis in fact, no matter how exaggerated they may have become. One should always try to get all of the available information on a treasure site from as many different sources as possible, because as in everything that concerns human nature, there is room for error.

Nothing can stir the human heart and imagination so much as the lure and fascination of hidden riches. A lead to an exciting and often profitable site can be an old map, history book, newspaper clipping, a legend, a rumor, sometimes only a whisper.

CHAPTER FOUR

TIPS AND TECHNIQUES

Coin and Cache Hunting

I have devoted more space and information to "coin shooting," because this is the type of treasure hunting that is done by the largest number of people, especially on weekends and during vacations. Only a small percentage of treasure hunters have the time and money to spend in research and travel that is usually necessary in locating a large cache.

Coin shooting... Very little research needs to be done on this type of treasure hunting. It is largely a matter of observation and logical thinking.

The tools... Coin shooting is an activity that need not be expensive. A metal detector and a screwdriver, knife or other narrow, pointed instrument and small bag to carry your "finds" are all the tools that are needed.

When using a metal detector to search for coins, keep the coil one or two inches above the ground. Adjust the instrument in your hand where it is comfortable to carry, then use a swinging motion from side to side, approximately three feet wide. Let each swing slightly overlap the one before, so that you cover the entire area. Move slowly and you will recover more valuables.

Most coins are found within two to four inches under the surface of the ground, so the problem of "digging" coins up is simple. With a little experience, you will be able to determine exactly where a coin is located as you pass the search coil over it. Then plunge a screwdriver or similar tool into the ground beside the point, and pry the coin to the surface with one continuous movement.

Another very good method to retrieve coins, when searching well kept lawns, is to stick a knife (with a six-inch blade) into the ground, make a circle, then remove the section of dirt and check it with your detector. If the coin is not in it, check further down. When the coin is found, place the plug of dirt back into the ground and step on it, this will hide the hole you have made.

Tricks of the trade and places to search... Professional or full-time coin shooters and treasure hunters invariably follow similar or identical pocedures. Here are a few of their secrets to help you become more proficient.

Check around picnic tables and park benches for coins.

When searching playgrounds, check the grass areas around the worn and eroded spots under swings, teeter-totters and other recreational equipment.

At fairgrounds and rodeo grounds, search around the ticket booths and both under and around the bleachers and other seating areas. Be sure to check the midway and parking lots.

Unpaved parking lots are always good for a few coins, keys and jewelry.

Rest areas along modern interstate highways are good places to search, and so are the picnic sites along highways.

Church yards, especially between the front door and the street, are good coin areas.

Amusement parks, almost a thing of the past, are productive areas even though some of them have been closed for years.

Country school yards often are surprisingly lucrative coin shooting spots, though the schools may have been closed in recent years.

Cemeteries are often good coin areas, and the places to look are along the lanes and the driveways.

Lovers' lanes, both the old and new, have always been lucrative search areas.

Not many of these are left, but the lawns and lanes around and near railroad depots are good places to search.

Livestock sale barns and pavilions are good spots for the coin shooter. Search the parking lots, around the food stands, and if you can get inside, search under the seats.

Nightclub parking areas and around such buildings usually provide a few coins, if not many.

Old time picnic grounds, where annual holiday and harvest festivals were held, are always good.

Race tracks, if you can get into them, are usually very good. Some of the old horse tracks have been closed for years, but you can usually get onto the property. Look around the old grandstands and the barns.

Service stations, especially the old ones in small towns, have lots of coins around them. Sometimes dirt has been filled in around the stations and the coins are deep.

Campgrounds along the old wagon roads are often good. These are generally off the beaten path, but some of them have been used up to recent years.

Resort areas are always good. The older, abandoned ones produce fine old coins, while the present, popular resorts, provide good late dated coins—and more are being lost every season.

State line markers are good. People stop to get their picture taken by the signs or markers, and while fumbling for their car keys or cigarette lighters, often drop a coin or two. Jewelry is often lost in these locations, too.

The parking lots at small airports are usually good. Look in the areas where visiting planes are parked.

Trailer courts are very good and are rarely searched. Check where the cars are parked and along the concrete ramps for each trailer space. If overnight facilities are available for trailer travelers, check these spaces carefully, as these people usually pack and unpack in a hurry, and they lose things.

Last but not least, don't forget motels. Check the parking lot, the lawns and especially around the swimming pool.

Any type of digging, such as road building, excavating for basements, housing projects and streets, are good places to search. Check old stream beds where rivers or creeks have changed their course; along river banks where people spend a lot of time fishing; beaches around a lake.

You would be surprised at the amount of money that is found with metal detectors on paved parking lots. The secret is to check the areas where dirt or mud from automobiles accumulates. Lots of people, at first, think it is ridiculous to consider searching a paved parking lot—that is, until they are reminded that dirt accumulates in spots on these lots and that coins are often concealed in the dirt.

The older the site you are searching, the better your chances of finding something of value (before tin and aluminum cans, tinfoil and bottle caps were used). Almost anything found today over fifty years old, is regarded as an antique and can be sold.

This is by no means a complete resume of the procedures of coin shooting, but there is enough information and good, solid tips given so that nearly anybody can apply themselves in their local community, for their own pleasure and profit.

Cache hunting... Remember, this type of searching usually involves more time, money, research and traveling than does coin shooting. When searching a house, look around fireplaces, door and window casings, under stairways, rugs, closet floors and ceilings. Sometimes there were secret compartments built into closets. (I once found a valuable cache closed up behind a staircase.) Watch for lumped or sagging places under wallpaper, floors and ceilings. Check under front and back steps, porch floors (coins fall through cracks), basements, especially in the corners and between the foundation stones.

In older homes look in yards where people used to sit in swings and on benches under shade trees (before fans and air conditioning), rock walkways, back doors where wives used to throw dish water. Spoons, forks and rings can be found.

Try to find the trash dump. This is the place for an old lamp, dishes, bottles or silverware. Be sure and label any antique you find with the place and date it was found. This will aid an antique dealer in putting a value on the item.

Large boulders were sometimes used as markers. Check an area of 50 to 60 feet around boulders, old trees, or rotted stumps, anything you think someone might have used as a starting point, or marker, when they buried their valuables. Also, search around any prominent landmark you think might have been used.

On farm sites, 50 to 150 years old, search around the barn and outbuildings. Remember, in the days of horse and mule power, the farmer spent most of his time around the barn. Always check out any fence rows that surround a farm house or outbuilding. A large number of farmers used what was called "post-hole banks."

In later farm sites (this may sound foolish, but I know a treasure hunter that recently found several hundred dollars in the tubing of an old corn-planter) search the farm machinery. Remember, today's farmer spends a great deal of time with his machinery, just as his counterpart did with work animals, 50 to 100 years ago.

The wells were another favorite hiding place for valuables. In old log cabins (still found in ghost towns and other out-of-the-way places) always search the "chinking" (mud used for insulation) between the logs. This was a favorite place for pioneers to hide coins and jewelry.

Use your imagination and logic-thinking freely. Search anywhere you think someone might have hidden or lost something.

This is not a complete listing of all the methods involved in cache hunting, but the procedures given have proven successful and will work for almost anyone.

The tools needed for cache hunting are: Metal detector, shovel, a small crowbar, knife, ground probe, a rock pick and a pack to carry whatever is found.

......

I have given only the basics in the chapters on research and coin and cache hunting because there are already several well written books on the market that deal with these two subjects.

Finally, remember, always obtain permission from proper authorities or landowners to enter any area, fill all holes you dig, do any repairs necessary to leave or restore the property just as you found it, and thank the party that gave you permission to search. Follow these procedures, which are very important, on all treasure hunts, should you want to return to an area for another search. Always extend these courtesies regardless of what type of searching is involved.

CHAPTER FIVE

TREASURE SYMBOLS

Since the dawn of mankind, symbols have played an important part in the life of humans. Early cavemen painted pictures and symbols on cave walls with sticks of charcoal. Each ancient civilization created its unqiue symbolisms and today's religions of the world have survived with the assistance of symbols.

When you have digested the treasure symbols in this chapter, you will have a much better understanding of this unique field of treasure research. Remember, each individual concealing a treasure was concerned with a common thought—that of being able to find the trove in the future when the need arose.

After one symbol has been discovered, the best way to begin your research is to first identify the symbol with the help of the information in this chapter. With even one character, the story can most likely be put together. When you find any symbol, don't disregard it. Record or photograph the symbol and save it for the future.

This listing gives most of the known symbols likely to be found in treasure hunting:

BURIED TREASURE SIGNS

   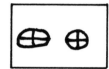

Any representation of the sun indicates mineral close by.	(Gold) Ore is short distance away.	Gold short distance away.	Variant signs of cross.

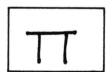  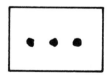 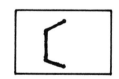

Treasure hidden in tunnel or mine shaft.	Treasure buried in mountains.	Treasure buried in cave or caves.	A tunnel.

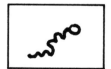  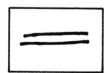 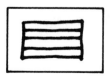

Snake in striking position. Pointing toward treasure.	Coiled snake. Treasure underneath.	Two straight lines. Double the distance of one.	Flight of steps. Treasure cave or shaft.

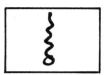

Snake going down tree. Treasure is on that side of it. Measure distance from tip to tail to ground. Step off ten times distance straight out. Should find either treasure or other sign.

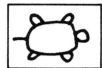

Turtle, or terrapin, head toward treasure, also means death, defeat, destruction, burial of possessions close by.

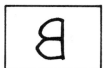

Means two deposits, mines, or caves, adjoining each other and the flat side of the sign could mean a mine shaft.

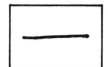

A straight line. A certain number of Veras to be measured off, the number usually being from 50-100 (A Vera is 33½ inches).

Animal tracks carved on something, points toward or back to treasure.

Sombreros indicate number of persons in party that buried treasure. May also indicate the number killed by enemy.

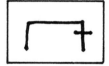

Cross inside could indicate church objects hidden in a cleft or niche, maybe a shallow cave.

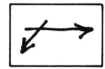

Two or more arrows connected. Treasure has been divided in as many parcels in direction indicated.

Moose, deer, or any animal carving, points to treasure.

Ore or treasure is in triangle of trees or rocks.

Rocks enclose treasure.

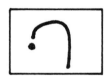

Treasure in middle of tree or rock triangle.

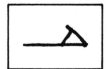

Treasure to one side of tree or rock triangle.

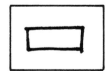

Treasure in box, cask or chest.

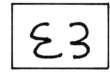

Change direction.

On line of treasure; also a landmark.

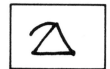 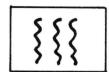 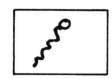 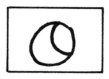

Deposit around bend, away from tree or rock triangle.	Treasure buried near a stream, or cross stream to get to it.	Snake going up tree. Treasure on opposite side. Go to next sign.	Go to right.

 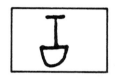 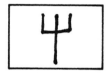 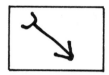

Mine, shaft or tunnel has been closed.	Spade, dig here.	Fork, handle points to treasure.	Pointing downward to treasure.

 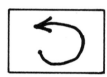 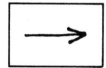 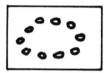

Arrow with heft inclined up. Sign further on.	Go around to left, follow bend in stream or trail.	Horizontal arrow without heft. Points to treasure or water.	Circle of rocks, treasure in circle.

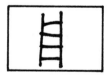 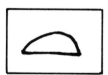  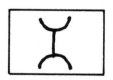

Ladder, climb up tree, cliff or hill to treasure.	Treasure buried in mound.	Under rock ledge or cliff.	Treasure in tunnel or cave, two entrances.

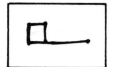

Pipe stem points to treasure, or go in opposite direction to another symbol.

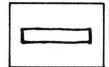

Flat stone, or stones, check bottom side for symbols.

Bell means mine or treasure is nearby, follow top point of bell.

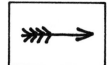

Arrow with feather heft. Flying away toward treasure.

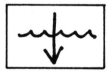

Large quantity of minerals or treasure nearby.

Treasure is below.

Treasure underneath this sign.

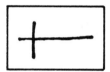

Treasure in opening close to mouth of cave or tunnel.

Treasure beneath water, stream, lake or river.

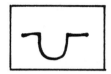

One day's journey to treasure.

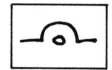

Look below for treasure or minerals.

The long part of the upright point to treasure.

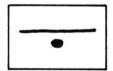

Treasure below.

Moon in clouds, look higher in mountain.

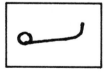

Follow curve in river or trail.

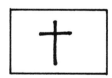

Rich objects of the church buried here.

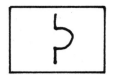

Mule shoe, lying horizontal to tree, but keep going.

Go to right.

Quarter moon—treasure below.

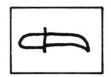

Bowie knife, pointing to treasure.

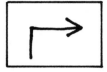

Proceed then turn right at another symbol or marker.

Spanish gourd. On way to spring water.

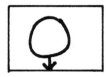

Mine or treasure below.

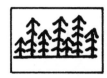

Treasure in woods or group of trees.

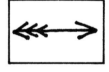

Wrong direction, go back.

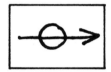

Points toward treasure.

Pointing to treasure.

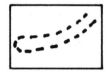

Trail or look for trail.

Treasure close by.

Two locations of treasure.

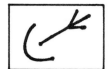  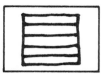 

Indicates mine shafts or tunnels.

 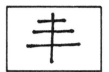  

Pertains, in some manner, to mining.

Chimney rock in N.Y. could be marker for nearby treasure.

Good place to search with metal detector.   Author detecting a park.

Old swimming hole with possibilities.   Deserted cabins may have treasures.

Around monuments are likely sites.   Author searches a playground.

CHAPTER SIX
HOW TO PAN FOR GOLD

With the high price of gold and since searching and panning for it has become such a large part of the treasure hunting hobby, this information can assist the novice in getting started and remind the professional of methods he may have forgotten.

The author makes no attempt to explain gold mining but deals with the techniques and tools of panning for gold that (with a little practice) can be used by everyone. Panning is a process of testing earth, sand and small gravel for gold content, not a method of obtaining gold on a large scale.

Since the primary purpose of this chapter is to help you find and pan free or placer gold, I will describe what you will see when you have gold in the bottom of your pan. From the smallest specks to the largest nuggets, the color will be yellow. Whether seen in sunlight or in the shade, there will be little sparkle to its color, nor will it glow, it is just a plain unchanging yellow. It will not flake apart when placed under pressure, such as you might apply with your teeth to a nugget. Hit it with a hammer, it will flatten out, but still remain in one piece. Slosh a little water around in the bottom of the pan and you will see sand, black sand, move rapidly under the action of the water, but the gold will move slowly as though it is anchored to its resting place. Gold is heavy, and with few exceptions, will be the heaviest mineral in your pan.

What tools are necessary for panning?... I would suggest the following items as a minimum start: A pair of tweezers; a first-aid kit (including a snake-bite kit); a small bottle or vial; two shovels, one large and one small; a pick; a garden trowel; a pair of waterproof boots (or a willingness to get your shoes and feet wet); a bucket (especially if you wish to save black sand); a small but stiff and heavy spoon for crevicing; and most important, a pan.

A gold pan is usually somewhere between 10 and 18 inches in diameter, with a depth of around two inches and sloping sides that angle at about 35 degrees. It is usually made of sheet metal, iron or steel; the more modern ones are made of plastic.

A 12 or 15-inch steel pan is hard to beat. It handles easily, doesn't hold too much gravel, and is easily blued. This process is quite simple to perform and is well worth the effort involved (it makes the gold particles easier to see in the bottom of your pan).In order to blue a pan, place it over the burner of a stove or in the ashes of a camp fire. Let it get good and hot, but not red, before removing it from the heat. Let the pan cool by allowing it to sit at room temperature (putting it into water while hot is likely to cause warping), and your're ready to try your hand at gold panning.

What areas to search?... The whole key to panning is to think of gold as a mineral with a higher specific gravity than anything else in the stream. Swift water will carry gold, slow flowing water will allow it to sink to the bottom. Investigate spots where the rate of flow decreases. This is where the gold is most likely to be.

Look in eddies, beneath waterfalls, wherever the water makes a pause or change of direction. Investigate the inside curve of sharp bends. Coarser and richer gold sinks first while the finer material is carried farther downstream. If your pan yields a showing of powdery or fine gold, try upstream for heavier pieces.

Once settled in a stream bed, gold will sift down through the sand and gravel. It will keep sifting down, because of its weight, until it eventually reaches bedrock. The values at bedrock are many times those on the surface and make it well worth the effort of shoveling away the overburden, if there are encouraging colors.

Pay particular attention to crevices and other irregularities in bedrock. These trap gold like the riffles of a sluice box and sometimes are incredibly rich.

Another way to find gold, is to pull up small clumps of grass or plants under the water or near the water's edge. Shake the roots and catch the sand in your gold pan for panning. Another excellent possibility is uprooted trees. Also, where a river or creek has changed its course, leaving the old stream bed dry. Culverts where streams wash gold down, are other good places to search.

Black magnetic sand is a good indication or gold. When it is seen, it's always a smart idea to check a few pans of material. The black sand is heavier than the surrounding sand and settles in about the same manner that gold does. If it is present, you can be assured that conditions are favorable for the deposition of gold.

Iron pyrite is "fool's gold." It is a mineral with a yellow color and glitters, but will break when struck with a hard object. Real gold will bend and can be flattened, but will not break apart.

Casual panning can be rewarding even in a heavily worked stream if you don't make the common mistake of thinking that the gold is distributed evenly over the stream bed. Concentrations of gold are located in spots. If you can find these spots, your take will be much greater than if you panned indiscriminately. (See illustration).

Wet panning... fill the pan nearly full of the material that you have selected for panning and place it in water deep enough to cover the pan and its contents. Work over the contents with both hands, breaking up the lumps and throwing out the stones. After the contents have been thoroughly disintegrated and the stones have been removed, grasp the pan with both hands, still under the water, at opposite sides of the top, for the panning operation. Holding the pan about level, give it a rotating motion, rapidly alternating the direction so as to agitate the contents and allow the heavy particles to settle to the bottom. Then move the hands until they are a little way back of the middle of the pan. This action tips the pan away from the panner.

With the pan in this inclined position, give it a circular, sidewise, shaking motion that washes the contents from side to side. This brings the lighter material to the surface and washes it toward the front or lip of the pan, while the heavy particles work their way toward, or remain, on the bottom. Some of the lighter material washes out of the pan. To remove more of the lighter material, cause water to flow over it by raising and lowering the lip of the pan through the surface of the water. An experienced panner usually scrapes off a considerable amount of this light material with his thumb. These operations are repeated until nothing but the concentrates (gold and the heavy minerals, called black sand) are left in the pan.

The concentrates are saved until a fair amount has been accumulated. Carefully panning the accumulation will considerably reduce the quantity. Removing the magnetic particles (chiefly magnetic iron) by the use of a magnet will reduce the bulk still more. This method works best when the concentrates are dry. Covering the ends of the magnet with paper or cellophane helps to keep it clean, since, on withdrawing the magnet from the covering, the particles drop. The larger gold colors can be picked out with a sharp-pointed pair of tweezers.

Dry panning... the dry, gold bearing gravel is dumped into a pan and shaken up, so as to bring the lumps and coarse stuff to the top. After they have been removed, the remainder is slowly poured, from about shoulder height, into a second pan which is placed on the ground. A strong wind blowing through the stream of materials winnows it and carries away the light fines. This operation is repeated several times until a concentration has taken place. The concentrates are then winnowed by tossing them up from the pan into the wind. Following this operation, the material remaining is panned just as in water. The concentrates from this panning are then cleaned further by blowing with the mouth.

Nothing more need be added to the above descriptions. It takes practice and experience to develop the technique that suits each individual. Whenever possible, the wet method should be used. It is much more efficient, and certainly a cleaner and more pleasant way of getting to the valuables.

Be sure to obtain all landowners' permission to search for gold (or any type of treasure) on their property.

Persons interested in panning for gold, can contact the Geology Department in their respective state capitals for information on where gold has been found and likely areas to search.

In addition to the twelve known gold producing districts, glacial gold has been found in small amounts in almost every state in the Union.

CHAPTER SEVEN

FIFTY PLUS TREASURE SITES

The following locations (one for each of the fifty states) are from the author's files. They have been thoroughly researched and as far as can be learned, the treasures have not been found. Several of these sites have been written about by other people, but no one has had access to the information this author has on file, which is printed here for the first time.

ALABAMA

A treasure site that is almost certainly overlooked in Alabama, is a small island (Dauphin Island) that was probably the first settled area of the state. Very few records exist that tell of the island's early history.

For the treasure hunter, one treasure story relates that a large, jeweled cross was hidden in a well. This valuable relic was stolen from a large church in Mexico, then smuggled into the United States. When the thieves could not dispose of it, the cross was put into a well in the hope they could return for it. The three thieves were later killed in Texas. Before dying, one of them told a Texas ranger about the hidden cross.

There are other stories of buried pirate loot, hidden jars filled with money and at least one location of a chest full of silverware that was buried during the Civil War.

For the person interested in metal detector sites, the island has been occupied by the Spanish, French and English. All of these armies had garrisons here at one time or another. Also, after the Civil War, the U.S. government had a camp of occupation there. For all treasure hunters, Dauphin Island is an interesting and possibly profitable site. The Mobile Historic Development Commission (the local historical society), S. Annex, City Hall, Mobile, Alabama 36601, can probably help with information concerning Dauphin Island.

ALASKA

These two locations, one of a lost outcropping of gold and another of a large amount of gold underwater have had very little, if any, searching done for them.

During the summer of 1881, two miners, named Bates and Harper, crossed the mountains from the Yukon River, to the Tanana River. While they were fording the north fork of Forty Mile River, Bates was swept off his feet by the fast moving current. After fighting the swift water for several yards, Bates was able to grab an overhanging tree limb and pull himself up on the river's bank. Here Harper joined him. They built a fire and decided to camp for the night. While gathering firewood, Harper noticed a ledge that had small gold nuggets in it. Taking several ore samples, the two men moved on the next day.

After several months of prospecting, the two returned to San Francisco, California. It was there they had all their ore samples assayed. Imagine their surprise when they learned the samples of ore they had picked up, when Bates fell into the river, assayed at $20,000 to the ton.

Harper returned to the area (Bates was unable to make the trip) the following year, but was never able to relocate the gold bearing ledge. The two men estimated the location to be twenty miles up from the mouth of Forty Mile River, on the right hand side. This is a good location for a modern day prospector with a metal detector to check into.

One of the best known and yet unsolved robberies in Alaska, took palce on the Yukon River. In early 1901, a steamer left Fort Yukon heading downstream with a large shipment of gold. A watchman had been hired to guard the shipment en route.

When the ship reached Victors Landing, on the Yukon, the watchman and gold were both gone. A search was made and the watchman was found hiding in a cabin behind the boat landing. Victor, the owner of the landing, was suspected of having planned the theft of the gold with the help of the watchman.

Victor had developed placer claims and it was believed by authorities that he intended to claim the gold came from his deposits. The watchman was taken to Fairbanks and tried for the theft. Although he claimed to be innocent, he was given a long jail term.

The jury agreed that Victor was innocent, that the watchman must have thrown the gold overboard with a buoy marker near Victor's Landing. He evidently planned to retrieve it later.

If the jury's conclusion is correct (and it seems to be the only answer) then somewhere near Victor's Landing, under a few feet of water, a fortune in gold waits for some lucky diver.

ARIZONA

This little known location of a large cache of gold in southern Pima County, Arizona, could very well be worth searching for.

In 1873, a Mexican prospector named Pedro Pedrillo, found a crude rock cross, bearing in Spanish, the instructions, "dig here." This was on the eastern slope of the Cocopah Mountain range. Pedro dug up a tin box which contained a scroll with this story: "On March 29, 1682, the Spanish ship, Isabella Catolica, wrecked off the coast of California. Captain Jesus Arroa and his crew of twentyfive men, with tools and weapons, started traveling east. They came to what is now the Cocopah Mountain range. Here they found placer gold and spent eight months collecting it. They planned to try and get to Mexico City with what gold they could carry but, unfortunately, Indians attacked the party while they were still mining."

A battle of two days, convinced Captain Arroa that they would all be killed. He thereupon wrote directions to where the mined gold could be found, then made a cross and buried the instructions beneath it. None of the ship's crew is known to have escaped the Indians."

In 1874, Pedro Pedrillo organized a search party to go to the Cocopah Mountain range. After several weeks of unsuccessful searching, the group gave up. To the best of known records, the gold has not been found. With modern equipment, a good prospector has a chance of finding this cache.

The location is in the Papago Indian Reservation. Permission to search will have to be obtained from the tribal council.

ARKANSAS

This lost silver mine in Arkansas has not been found. It is a recorded fact that the Spanish had several silver mines during the early 1700's, in what is now the state of Arkansas. One such mine was near the present community of Batavia, in Boone County.

The Spanish worked the mine for several years but due to Indian trouble, decided to conceal and abandon it. They planned to return when the area was more settled. Due to wars and the Louisiana Purchase of 1803, none of the descendents of the original Spanish miners ever attempted to relocate the silver mine.

In 1880, an old man that appeared to be Indian and Spanish, stopped at the general store near Batavia. Showing John Rea, the store's owner, an old weathered map, the man described the local terrain and told Rea that he believed the old Spanish silver mine was located on Pilot Knob, a local landmark. If this was the location, there should be a stream one hundred yards southwest of the large rock on top of the mountain. Rea assured the old man that his description was correct.

The next day, Rea, his sons and the old man went to Pilot Knob. After pacing off 200 yards north of the spring that formed the stream, the old man told Rea and his sons to dig. About six feet down the diggers came upon a cavity with a skeleton that had apparently been walled up in the cave.

Rea and his sons staked mining claims on all of Pilot Knob. When, after several weeks of mining and tunneling was done and no silver had been found, Rea and his sons gave up the search and went back to their store. The aged Indian left, still convinced that Pilot Knob was the right area.

Today, very few people know of this location. But with the current price of silver, it could be worthwhile for someone to try and locate this lost silver mine.

CALIFORNIA

This little known location of a half-gallon fruit jar full of gold coins would be well worth investigating. In 1910, Tad Tippet, an ex-slave, was a hired hand on the Harne Pruitt ranch near Placerville, California. While digging a posthole, he turned over a flat rock under which was a half-gallon jar of coins. Tippet took the gold to the owner of the ranch.

Pruitt was a greedy man. He told Tippet that since he worked for him, the gold belonged to Pruitt. The old Negro knew it was useless to argue, but he decided to watch Pruitt constantly.

After several weeks Tippet told a cowboy on a nearby ranch about what he had found. Soon it was common knowledge that Pruitt had the gold. Shortly after Tippet told the cowboy about it, Pruitt decided to rebury the coins which he had been keeping in his house, and started carrying a gun. Unknown to Pruitt, Tippet was watching him constantly.

Pruitt waited until after dark, then taking the gold and a shovel, he paced off twentyfive steps (Tippet, who was hiding in the barn, heard him counting the number of steps but could not see Pruitt because of the darkness.) and buried the jar full of coins.

As fate would have it, the next night two strangers that had heard about the gold came to the Pruitt ranch after dark. Getting the drop on Pruitt, they took turns torturing him, but Pruitt stubbornly refused to talk. The two men forced Tippet to watch.

They then turned their attention to Tippet. After stabbing Tippet several times, he told them he could not tell where the gold was because it had been too dark when Pruitt buried it. All he knew was, it was in the barn lot, twentyfive steps from the barn, but he did not know in what direction. The men then probed the ground around the barn but never found the money.

Stabbing the old Negro again, the two men left him for dead. After they had gone, Tippet managed to mount a horse and ride to town where he told the story of the attempted robbery and the torture of Pruitt before he died from his wounds.

Somewhere within twentyfive steps of the old barn site is buried a small (at today's prices) fortune in gold coins. The office of the land records could tell an interested treasure hunter where the Harne Pruitt ranch stood in 1910.

COLORADO

These three different locations of an estimated $1,500,000 each, in mined gold that were buried by a French expedition, in what is now the southeastern section of Mineral County, Colorado, could be well worth searching for, even if only one of the three caches were found.

The story is, that an expedition of 300 men were sent by the French government to explore the mineral content of the Louisiana Territory in 1790. The Frenchmen made their permanent camp near what is now Wolf Creek Pass. They found gold in large quantities and proceeded to mine it extensively. The gold was melted into bars and buried in three separate caches, all but several pounds they plannd to take with them back to New Orleans.

But misfortune struck the Frenchmen. They stayed longer than they had planned and their supplies ran out. At this time the Indians of the area began to make repeated attacks on the camp. After a few days of fighting, the Indians, and being near starvation, the French group was reduced to only seventeen men. The three remaining officers drew a map showing the gold's location. Further starvation and Indian attacks reduced the French force to two men.

These two managed to get away from the doomed camp and after an ordeal of several weeks, reached a French settlement at what is now Leavensworth, Kansas. They were in such a weakened condition they died, but not before giving to the fort's commander, the map showing the location of the three gold caches.

The French government sent parties in search of the gold but it was never found. For anyone interested in searching for this immense fortune, a starting point would be near old Summittville, because remains of the French mining activities can still be seen there. The three caches have to be in the immediate vicinity.

CONNECTICUT

Here is a location that is almost unknown. I obtained the details from an old newspaper clipping for October 19, 1901, in Bridgeport, Connecticut. "$101,000 was taken from the Adams Express Company at Pittsburgh, Pennsylvania, on October 9, 1901, by Edward George, an employee of the company."

"George was arrested at a hotel in Bridgeport, Connecticut, where he had been staying since October 12. He admits to having taken the money but refuses to tell where it is hidden. George had only $400.00 on him when he was arrested."

This would be a very good lead for an interested person to follow up through newspapers of the period.

DELAWARE

This treasure site in Delaware is almost certainly unknown. It comes from an old, undated newspaper clipping. In 1842 a man came to Newark and rented a farmhouse about five miles south of town. He never worked and spent all his time in searching for a symbol or carving supposedly cut into a large rock somewhere in the area. After several months of unsuccessful searching, the man who gave his name only as Thomas, confided to a nearby farmer what he was trying to find.

According to an old parchment map with directions that Thomas had somehow obtained (he never explained how), a pirate treasure was supposed to be in the area. The directions called for a large rock with an anchor and cable carved into it. The cable pointed toward the treasure site.

This cache had been made in 1728 by a pirate named William Neub, after a pirate foray in which considerable loot had been acquired, the money and jewels divided by the ship's crew. Neub realized that sooner or later the pirates would be caught and hanged, or killed in a robbery attempt.

Thinking he would be safe and maybe enjoy a full life, Neub left his pirate friends and traveled inland. Since he wasn't known and people in the lesser settled farm country did not ask questions, Neub thought he would be safe. All went well until farmers began to notice that Neub could not ride a horse and did not seem interested in farming although he always had plenty of money.

Finally a suspicious farmer, while on a visit to New Castle, told the authorities about the stranger. At this time, anyone suspected of being or having been a pirate, was given a quick trial and hanged.

One of the few friends he had made, tipped Neub off to what the farmer had done. Knowing he would be hanged if caught, Neub prepared to leave the country. Realizing he could take but very little of his pirate gains with him, because if he was stopped with a large amount of money he would be hanged for sure, Neub buried several thousand dollars on the farm. Since he had been a sailor, he used an anchor and cable carving as a marker, cut into a large rock. Neub got away safely but was never able to return.

Thomas left after failing to find the symbols. There could be some truth to this old story. I quote this from a letter written to the Board of Trade in London, by Nicholas Webb of New Castle, Delaware in 1699: "Many pirates have recently arrived in New Castle with riches from Madagascar and their booty is astonishing." It is also a recorded fact that Captain Kidd, Blackbeard and other pirates were familiar with Delaware waters. Coins of the period have been found along the beaches lending further credence to the story of William Neub.

FLORIDA

This approximately $2,000,000 in pirate treasure is recorded in the British Admiralty records. One of the most bloodthirsty pirates ever to sail was London born, John Rackman, known as "Calico Jack". For some reason, unknown to this author, historians have written very little about this free-booter.

Jack went to sea as a boy and rose to the rank of mate on a slave ship. He was so cruel and dangerous that even the slaver's crew (not exactly a group of choir boys themselves) put him ashore in Haiti.

In Haiti, Jack organized a crew that captured the brigantine, Fancey near Port au Prince. Making the entire crew of the Fancey walk the plank, Jack and his men hoisted the Jolly Roger, the symbol of a pirate Chip. Jack made his headquarters at first in Cuba, until he became so notorious that the Spanish sent warships in a special effort to catch him. Realizing that he could not fight the Spanish Navy, Jack moved to Oyster Bay, on the west coast of Florida and set up his headquarters ten miles up the Shark, or Lostman's River (historians generally agree that it was the Shark River). He continued raiding all shipping that he could take in the Caribbean and stored the booty at his new hideout.

In 1720 the Governor of Jamaica sent a warship with express orders to capture Jack and his crew. In November of that year the warship chased Jack's ship ashore, a short distance up Shark River, and captured the pirates that were not killed, in a pitched battle.

Taken in chains to Port Royal, Jamaica, the pirates were given a chance to tell where the estimated $2,000,000 in loot was hidden or else be hung. The pirates all chose to die. As far as can be learned, the authorities found nothing, which means that somewhere in the area, ten-miles up Shark River, an immense fortune waits for some lucky treasure hunter.

GEORGIA

If French records are correct, and there is no reason to doubt them, a good sized fortune is still buried near the forks of Okapilco and Mule Creeks in Brooks County, Georgia.

During the 1760's, when the Spanish began to blockade the port of New Orleans in a controversy over the Louisiana Territory, the French decided to send the major portion of their state treasury overland to a port in Florida, and there ship it to France. Since they had to travel through the Creek, Choctaw and Seminole Indian country, the French buried the treasury each night so that if they were attacked, the Indians would not get the money, which was mostly in gold coins.

After several weeks of slow travel through Indian country (at that time almost uncharted wilderness) the French reached what is now Brooks County, Georgia. It was here that such a concentrated attack was launched by the Indians, who had been following them, that all the French were killed except one, who managed to hide until the attack was over, then made his way back to New Orleans with a rough map of how far the party had traveled before the Indian attack occurred that killed all his comrades.

A party was sent by the French government to search for the dead men and the gold. The bodies of the Frenchmen were found but the treasure was never located. This would be a good place to search. Any artifact such as bullets, knives, et cetera, found, would pinpoint the battle site and the gold coins have to be nearby.

HAWAII

Since Hawaii is a fairly recent admission to the United States, it has not had the amount of research done into treasure locations that other states have, but there are several sites that would be of interest to treasure hunters.

One of the oldest stories in modern history concerns Captain Cook, the first man to circumnavigate the world. When he was killed by natives, in the Hawaiian Islands (historians and researchers differ as to what island Cook was anchored near at the time of his death) they had never seen any white men.

There is an old story that when the guns, lead, powder, the ship's treasury and other items were seized by the natives, they were taken to their king. Thinking the articles (since they did not know what they were, or their use) were magical instruments, the king ordered them buried.

It has been suggested by several knowledgeable people that this cache could be on the island of Kanai, because it is known that several treasures were hidden on this island by the natives in later years, especially that of King Kamehameha in 1810. This island could have been used as a depository by this line of kings for hundreds of years. There is a legend that an extinct tribe of small people lived here after their original home sank into the sea. These people were the guardians of all treasure that had been buried on the island for many years.

This island is a rugged, high-cliffed area with deep ravines. It is hard to reach, even by boat. Whether or not Cook's treasure (worth a fortune today) is on this island or not, will never be known unless it is found. But the island of Kanai seems to be the most likely area to search.

IDAHO

A few miles from three Creeks in Owyhee County, is an area that used to be known as Rye Flats. A historian that researched and believed the following story, gave me a few details on this treasure location several years ago.

A rancher named Hance, lived in Rye Flats, and supplemented his ranch earnings by allowing two outlaws to use his home as a hideout. He also participated in several robberies with them.

Hance's wife left him and the only other person on the ranch was an orphan boy that helped with the chores. The two outlaws heard of a shipment of gold that was being sent from Twin Falls to Boise. Leaving the ranch, the three men (the boy stayed at home) robbed the stage and obtained $40,000 in gold coins.

Returning to the ranch, the three hid the money in a small cave behind the ranch house. Sometime later, the rancher and one of the outlaws had a fight in which the outlaw was killed. His body was placed in the cave with the money. The other outlaw left the country.

Hance and the boy continued to live quietly until the rancher became ill. Realizing that he was dying, the rancher told the boy the location of the cave and the gold. The key to the gold box was in the pocket of the dead bandit.

After the rancher died, the boy finally found the cave, but because he was afraid of a dead man and also, that he might get into trouble over the gold, he left the cave alone and moved away. Several years later he told the story.

My historian friend checked this information. He found there had been a stage robbery and the boy's story and dates agreed. Also, a rancher named Hance had lived in the area. The cave is believed to be located a short distance behind where the ranch house stood, near the edge of the hills. For the interested treasure hunter, experienced in locating caves, there is an almost certain cache of gold coins waiting in the area of Three Creeks.

ILLINOIS

The supposed site of this treasure is known, but what is not generally known is that searchers have been looking in the wrong place. Most authors that have written about the 1,200 pounds sterling in English coins, which Colonel George Rogers Clark buried just prior to his successful attack on the British garrison at Kaskaskia, in what is now the state of Illinois, say the money was buried just before the attack. It was not — the cache was made over one day's march east of Fort Kaskaskia.

The reason for burying the coins was twofold. The pioneer soldiers under Clark were to be paid on the return trip after the fort was taken and if the Americans lost, the money would not fall into British hands.

As it turned out, Clark won, but on the return trip he learned that a flash flood had washed away the markers pinpointing the money's location. So, somewhere east of present day, Steelville, Illinois, a small fortune in English coins awaits some lucky treasure hunter.

INDIANA

An overlooked, or possibly little known treasure site, is that of an Indian treasure in Clark County, Indiana. The man that remembers the following story is still living at the age of 83.

Albert Schuller was twenty years old when a middleaged Indian came to his father's farm near Greenville, Indiana, and asked permission to search for a cave full of silver bars that had been left by his ancestors somewhere in the area, in 1820.

Given permission to search, the Indian spent several days on the farm, always looking for a large oak tree, which was a starting point. About ready to stop searching, the Indian finally asked Schuller's father if he could remember such a tree with a deer's head carved into it.

The elder Schuller remembered hearing his father tell of such a tree and markings. The tree had been cut down years before, but Schuller recalled where he had been told it stood. The Indian began searching again and a few days later told the elder Schuller that he had found what he was looking for. On leaving, the Indian said he would return in a few days.

About a week later he returned with twenty or thirty other Indians. They asked the elder Schuller if they could have a barbecue and explore the cave. The Schuller family watched the Indians butcher a beef and build fires, around which they danced for hours.

Two days later the Indian who had first visited Schuller, stopped by the farmhouse (the other Indians had disappeared, the Schullers never knew when they left or what they took with them) and told the family that he was leaving, but that if they could find it, there was enough silver left to shoe every horse in Indiana.

Schuller and his family searched for the next several days. All they found was a large empty hole the Indians had dug, apparently after dark, because the Schullers had not seen them digging. The Indians were never seen again.

It wasn't until several years later that a cave was discovered, about a mile from the Schuller's farmhouse. This cave was exposed when spring rains flooded the area. As far as I can learn, the cave was explored only once. It has since fallen in and no one knows if the Indians obtained the silver from the cave or dug it up.

This story has been in the Schuller family for over sixty years. If the Indian told the truth (and he had no reason to lie after he and his companions apparently took what silver they needed with them) either in the cave, or close by, a fortune in silver bars is still hidden.

IOWA

This treasure site should be of interest to a large number of people for two reasons. One is, the $11,500 that was found, lends credence to the fact that more is still probably in the area, because several local people remember the man they think hid the money and believe there is more hidden or buried on the property.

In 1965, twelve young boys found $11,500 under a floorboard in an old building on the property of Josh Rosenbeck, in the small community of Bayard, in west-central Iowa. The coins were auctioned off after a court ruling, for an estimated $18,000.

The reason it is believed there is more money hidden is, the owners in the 1950's were Fred Beardsly and his spinster sister. They were known to be semi-wealthy. Mr. Beardsly willed his part of the property to the Red Cross before his death in 1950. His sister willed her part to her niece.

The court case and controversy between the different people claiming the property, or parts thereof, caused nationwide attention to focus on the small town. From a treasure hunter's point of view, the correct thing to do is, obtain permission and give the old property a thorough search.

KANSAS

These two gold caches in Kansas were buried by the same party, but in widely separated places. Sometime during the 1870's, a group of miners was returning on foot to Missouri from a successful gold mining operation in the mountains of Colorado. Arriving at Bents Fort, they were told that Indians were on the warpath. Ignoring the warning, the miners pushed on, following the Arkansas River eastward.

Several days later, while making camp, they noticed their burros were nervous. The next morning the miners decided to run before Indians raided their camp. A few miles from their last campsite, the miners saw a band of Indians come into view, riding in a large half-moon circle, in front of them.

Realizing it was useless to try and get away on foot, the miners looked for a place to make a stand. A nearby gully seemed to offer a little protection. Just as the miners got into a position to defend themselves, the Indians charged but stopped and demanded the burros. Knowing they could not carry the gold without the burros, the miners refused this offer and dug in for a fight which was not long in coming.

After the Indians made several charges in which four of the miners were killed, the rest decided to bury the gold. When it became dark, the gold was buried in the gully. One man refused to go along with the plan that his friends suggested. Taking three burros, against the advice of his companions, the lone miner slipped out of the gully under the cover of darkness. The miners that were left behind were never heard from again. It is almsot certain they were killed by the Indians when their ammunition ran out. Today, this location is near the railroad tracks running between Cimarron, Kansas, and Choteau's Island.

The miner that had escaped, traveled by night and slept by day until he reached the junction of the Big and Little Arkansas Rivers. Feeling that he was safe, he decided to camp for several days. After the first night, he learned to his dismay, that he had stopped a short distance from an Indian camp.

Realizing he would be lucky to get away alive, the miner buried his gold at the junction of the rivers. Leaving the burros, he managed to slip away unseen by the Indians. After reaching his home in Missouri, the miner married and never made any attempt to return for his gold. So there are two caches of gold in Kansas, deposited several miles apart, by members of the same party, that have an estimated value today of over $3,000,000.

KENTUCKY

There is almost certainly a cache of gold coins buried on the old Anglin farm, at Pactolus, Kentucky, that has not been reported found.

A few years prior to the Civil War, the three bachelor brothers; John, Bill and Adrian Anglin, shared a large log house. It was well known to the Anglin neighbors that the brothers had money. They were known to be thrifty and saving, living for the most part off their farm products.

When most families killed three or four hogs in the fall, the Anglin brothers killed 18 or 20. They would sell most of the meat in addition to numerous cattle and corn crops. In this manner they each amassed a small fortune for the times.

Bill, the eldest, always took his money received from various sales to a country store in Oldtown, Kentucky, where he had it converted into gold coins. This he always did on Sunday, partly to keep from taking off from work during the week, and partly because he figured most people would be at church and would not learn or see how much money he had. Bill did this for several years, prior to the Civil War.

When news that the Civil War had started, reached the Little Sandy Valley that summer of 1861, Bill, knowing that soldiers would be coming through the area plundering and stealing anything they could, took his gold from its hiding place in the old log house and buried it outside. He went on foot and alone, his brothers said he was gone over an hour. Bill told no one where he buried the money and was never known to visit its location.

When the Civil War ended, Bill because of paralysis, was unable to go and get the money. He did not trust his brothers and never told them the location. After his death, the house and surrounding areas were searched, but according to family tradition, no money was ever found.

LOUISIANA

This Civil War cache of coins is almost certain to still be where it was buried because the man that helped deposit it tried for years to relocate the coins but failed.

In 1886, Dr. George J. Adams told the police of New Orleans a strange story of pillage and the burial of $30,000 during the Civil War. Adams had been a doctor attached to Company A, 17th Mass., Volunteers, during the Union campaigns throughout the South. On a foraging trip, Adams and two soldiers broke into a house at Magnolia Plantation, about twenty miles above New Orleans, on the Mississippi River.

After entering and searching the home, the three men found $30,000 that had been hidden in different places. $1,000 was in mixed silver, $1,800 was in silver dollars and the rest was gold coins. Afraid to enter New Orleans, where their company had been sent, and having no way to conceal such a large amount of money, the trio decided to bury the loot.

They selected a very large tree in a pecan grove, about a half-mile from the locks at the canal opposite Ewenville. Here they buried the money among the tree roots. Each man took a bearing and wrote down the directions.

They then joined their company, intending to return after the war for the money. But soon after burying the coins, the two soldiers were killed and Dr. Adams was wounded. After being sent home, the doctor suffered a long recovery in a Union hospital. It wasn't until 1886, that he was able to return to Louisiana to search for the hidden money.

When he returned to the pecan grove, he found that the older trees had been cut down. He tried for over a month to locate the exact spot. Finally realizing he needed help and that his money was running out, the doctor let several local residents in on his secret. After several more weeks of fruitless searching, they all gave up. There is no record of any recovery having been made, but somewhere about a half-mile north of the Ewenville locks, a small fortune in Civil War coins waits for a treasure hunter.

MAINE

There is an unusual treasure that probably is still where it was stored, about ten miles southwest of Portland, Maine, waiting to be found.

To some people, the idea of searching for Egyptian mummies might seem sacrilegious, but remember, the mummies have already been taken from their original graves, transported to the United States and are worth on today's collector's market, in excess of $12,000 each. Here is the story:

In 1857, and thereafter for several years, newspaper publishers in this country faced a severe shortage of rags, which were necessary to add strength and body to wood fibers used in paper sheets. As the shortage of rags increased, large numbers of small newspapers went out of business.

Augusta Stanwood, a printer in Portland, Maine, was greatly affected by this rag shortage. Realizing that he could go broke, Stanwood looked around for a much needed source of this ever increasing shortage of fiber. One night while drinking ale with a sea captain, Stanwood told of his troubles. The sailing man suggested using the cloth wrappings of mummies. (At this time the Egyptian grave sites were being exploited; artifacts, coffins and mummies were being sold by the thousands throughout the world.)

Stanwood made a deal with the ship's captain to obtain several dozen of these cloth wrapped bodies. When the shipment arrived, Stanwood stored them on his property (in pits to preserve them), about ten miles southwest of Portland. During the next three to seven years he used about half the mummies, putting their linen and cotton wrappings into his paper grinders. The pulp made a very good grade of paper stock.

About this time, the rag shortage (because of the Civil War and the capture of huge stores of cotton by the Union forces throughout the south) let up enough, that Stanwood did not need his mummies. After he tried to sell them and couldn't, Stanwood left the mummies in the pits on his property.

After Stanwood died, few people even remembered the mummies and they are, as far as can be learned, still buried on the old Stanwood property, about ten miles southwest of Portland, Maine. If one isn't afraid of ghosts, this unusual treasure would be worth thousands of dollars today.

MARYLAND

Although several authors have written about this treasure site during the last few years, I am adding a few new facts that were found through recent research.

$50,000 (not $150,000 as a few writers have stated) is believed to be buried in a shallow spot near Catonsville, Maryland. This cache was made about 1800. During the French Revolution, a wealthy merchant named Jean de Champlaigne, who owned a fleet of trading vessels, fled to the United States. After he was settled in Baltimore, he continued his shipping interest.

Having brought a considerable fortune with him, Champlaigne had no problems in starting a profitable trade with European ports.

During the period that Napoleon rose to power in France, he tried to cut off Great Britian's shipping. This act caused the United States (which had a profitable trade agreement with England), to close all its ports to French shipping. Napoleon ordered his ships to sink all American vessels they found sailing the Atlantic Ocean, and the whole fleet of Champlaigne went to the bottom.

This loss caused him to retire to his colonial home, which was surrounded by 20 acres of wooded land, on the old Frederick Road, outside Baltimore, and become a recluse, with only one black servant for company. Champlaigne finally went insane.

A short time before his death, he and the servant buried an iron chest which contained $50,000 in gold coins. After Champlaigne died, the servant was given the money that was received from the sale of the large home. His recorded remark at the time was, "If I could only remember where it was

buried that chest of money, I wouldn't need this. All I know is, it was not too far from the
According to public record, the chest has never been admitted recovered.

MASSACHUSETTS

ε buried treasure of Alden Culver in Massachusetts is little known. I obtained my first information concerning it from an old newspaper. This is one treasure that is almost certain not to have been found.

When Indian fighting was still going on in Massachusetts, Alden Culver was in so many Indian battles that it began to affect his mind. One day he dug his own grave on his farm near West Chesterfield, Mass. He showed the grave to a friendly Indian chief and asked him to see that he would be buried there with all his possessions, including an iron chest full of gold and silver coins. The chief agreed to do this.

A few weeks later Culver was found dead beside a pioneer road west of town. He had killed several Indians, whose bodies were scattered around him, before he died. It was assumed that Culver had come upon a war party and being half crazy, had attacked the Indians singlehandedly.

The friendly chief did as Culver had requested. He buried him with all his possessions, including the chest of coins. Then he marked a large flat rock nearby with this inscription: "Alden Culver, age ILVMO, of Chesterfield, Mass."

The key to the iron chest was kept by Culver's only daughter. When the daughter died several years later, the key was placed inside a gold locket and buried with her, next to her father. Since the two graves were the only ones in a large wooded tract, their location was lost.

It wasn't until 1936, that the two graves were mentioned again in any known records. During the summer of that year, when a school teacher at Chesterfield was telling a group of children the story of Culver, one of the small boys that had been listening to the story, remembered seeing the name and numbers carved onto a rock on his father's farm nearby. The boy told his father, who with six other people, went to the rock. But since no one knew how far from the inscribed stone the bodies were buried, nothing was ever found. The rock with Alden Culver's name and age carved into it, could still be seen a few years ago. With today's modern electronic equipment, the graves could be found.

To my knowledge, until now, the story has not been told or any searching done for the graves since 1936. Remember, there were no metal detectors during the 1930's; one needs to recall only that and search.

MICHIGAN

I will give two treasure sites in Michigan: No. 1. From the 1880's until 1902, a man named Porter Pritchard, lived on a small 30 acre island in Higgins Lake, in Roscommon County. Pritchard became known as the Hermit of Higgins Lake. No one knew why Porter isolated himself all those years. It was thought that he had murdered his wife and was hiding out, although no authorities ever checked on him.

The most widely accepted story is that Pritchard was a "bounty jumper" during the Civil War. Men were paid from $300 to $500 to take the place of any man that did not want to serve in the Union Army. It is believed Pritchard did this for three years to collect bounties in seven different states. If this is true, he came to the island with considerable money.

No one ever saw him spend any money except for food and tobacco. The money has to be still on the island, because Pritchard's body was found in 1902, in the dugout he used for a home. He had no money on his person. Since this is a small island, it would be a good place for a treasure hunter to spend a vacation searching for the missing cache.

No. 2— One of the most bloodthirsty Indians in American history was an Ottawa Chief named Pontiac. He always returned to Acole Island, in Orchard Lake, in what is now Oakland County, Michigan. Local legend was told for years that Pontiac buried a fortune in booty he obtained in raids against the white settlers in Pennsylvania and Virginia, on this island. This is highly possible, since Pontiac learned early in life, the white man's greed for gold and silver.

His orders to his warriors were always the same during a raid, "Take what you want, burn everything else and kill the prisoners." Since Pontiac made dozens of raids during his war on the whites, called Pontiac's Uprising, it is probable that he buried a large quantity of loot on Acole Island.

MINNESOTA

This treasure lead appeared in a newspaper for October 20, 1904, at Croakston, Minnesota: Thomas Fontaine, a farmer from Woonsocket, Rhode Island, moved to Mentor, Minnesota in 1901. A short time later he bought a farm a few miles east of Mentor. Fontaine had brought considerable money with him from Rhode Island and was considered well-to-do for the times.

During early October, 1904, Fontaine was hunting rabbits with a friend, Joseph Gullmette, also from Rhode Island. After they crossed the railroad tracks near Mentor, a family living in the area heard two gunshots. Since there were several hunters in the vicinity, nothing was thought about the two shots. The next day, Fontaine's dead body was found near the railroad tracks. The body had been mutilated almost beyond recognition.

Joseph Gullmette was questioned, but it was never proven that he had killed Fontaine. The treasure angle to this story is, it was common knowledge in the neighborhood that Fontaine carried large sums of money with him at all times. Since he did not trust banks, this would mean that he had a ready cash reserve which was accessible at his farm. This little known location would certainly bear further checking.

MISSISSIPPI

This buried treasure in Holmes County, Mississippi, has been searched for, but no reported find has ever been made. There are dozens of stories of southern citizens that buried their money or valuables during th Civil War. For different reasons, many of these caches were never recovered.

This treasure is firmly believed in by the descendants of the man that buried it. When Union General Sherman entered Newton and Holmes Counties, Mississippi, in 1864, his orders were to seize or destroy anything of value to the South. During his march to the sea, Sherman's men took not only livestock and food, but anything else of value they could find.

When he heard of Sherman's approach to his plantation, a wealthy man named Joseph Moore, in Holmes County, decided that the Yankees would not get his valuables. Gathering the family's money, silverware and other items, Moore placed them into two large iron cooking pots and buried them in an orchard back of the plantation house. As was expected, Sherman's army overran the farm, taking anything of value they could find.

But the two pots were not found. Moore died during the war, but he had not told his family exactly where the valuables were buried. After the war, the widely scattered family came together and searched unsuccessfully for the valuables. Permission to search for this one will have to be obtained from the present landowner.

MISSOURI

Because I have quite a bit of information on Missouri, I will give two locations for the state: Number one is on the Madre Vena Cave, located southeast of Pineville, on the Arkansas-Missouri border, and is supposedly the place where a great amount of bullion was stored. According to some early accounts, "It would require several mules to haul away the gold and silver there."

The bullion was presumably taken from the surrounding Ozark Hills, which due to the many underground caves in the area, have been the source of numerous tales of romance and legend. However, of the several stories concerning the Madre Vena treasure, the one about an unknown Mexican appears to be the most accepted, although the details may seem rather slight.

Just before he died, the Mexican said that a plat carved on a flat stone would show where the gold and silver hoard could be located. The stone was supposedly discovered around 1891, in the grave of one of three Mexicans buried near the entrance to the cave. A map was copied from the stone, which was then either lost or destroyed. Whatever happened to it, the stone hasn't been found since. Moreover, the map, which was the only remaining direct lead to the bullion, has mysteriously disappeared.

It could be that both the stone and the map are intact, although most accounts say the rock was destroyed. In any case, intermittent searches have been made for the treasure, and as far as is known, no one has found it. But it certainly is worth a try!

Number two concerns John Hickman, who ran cattle in the area of the Missouri, Indian Territory and Kansas borders. His exceedingly great wealth was believed cached in the ground since he had no faith in banks. When the Civil War broke out, foraging parties of both armies and guerrillas appropriated whatever they wanted.

Hickman was tortured several times in an effort to get him to reveal the hiding place of his money. In 1862, a Union foraging party found Hickman's body. It is not known whether soldiers or guerrillas murdered him. His treasure was never found and is believed to be along a point near Shoal Creek, in Newton County, Missouri.

MONTANA

Here is a little known treasure site in Montana that is relatively modern. There are people still living in the area that can remember this story of a cache of gold coins that were accumulated between 1868 to 1917.

About 1866, a man calling himself Alemzo Yerdon, went from New York to Montana and was one of the first men to find gold at Confederate Gulch, in Meagher County. He was popular with the women and soon became engaged to marry a wealthy widow.

On the day of the intended marriage, for some strange reason that was never learned, Yerdon simply walked into the nearby hills and became a hermit. He settled in a small cabin on Beaver Creek and worked several gold claims which paid him well.

Yerdon didn't trust anyone. He took his gold nuggets and dust to Helena, where he always obtained gold coins, which he buried near his cabin. During the freezing weather Yerdon bought his supplies on credit, saying his assets were frozen until the spring thaw. (This led to the speculation that his coins were buried.)

For over fifty years, Yerdon is supposed to have hoarded gold coins. He spent only what he had to and it has been estimated that he buried, in one or more places, over $100,000.

On New Year's Eve, in 1918, when Yerdon had not been seen for several days, a miner went to his cabin and found it completely burned. Yerdon's charred body was just in front of the door. The possibility of finding Yerdon's cache, or caches of coins made the property sell for $15.00 an acre instead of the customary $3.00 when his estate was probated in the Meagher County Court.

The homestead was sold at public auction in 1919 and only brought $1,000. There is no way of knowing for sure, but it is likely the gold coins were buried near Yerdon's cabin on Beaver Creek, because the only time he left his claims was when he went to Helena or bought supplies.

NEBRASKA

For a treasure hunter with a metal detector, to uncover one cache of coins in a particular location is considered good odds, but at the following site he has a chance to find from one to possibly 100 caches, ranging in value from $100 to $1,000. They are mainly in coins, although several would be in gold dust.

Three miles west of Plattsmouth, Nebraska, is a field of about ten acres that was a camping ground where gold seekers stopped for over twenty years on their way to California and other gold fields; also on their way back east.

Gold was discovered on Cherry Creek, in Colorado, in 1850. During the next few years a steady stream of hopeful men passed through Plattsmouth going west and coming back east. This was one of the last places to stop for supplies. Thousands of men outfitted here before going on to the gold fields. Merchants of Plattsmouth helped to fire the greenhorns gold desire by telling them: "A month out there and you can come back with a fortune."

The easterners listened with open mouths and paid in coin for supplies to mine the supposedly large amounts of gold for the taking in Colorado. For most of the greenhorns, the hard work of mining and not making over $3.00 a day, proved too much. True, several were lucky, but for the majority, all they wanted was to save enough to get home.

By 1859, several thousand of these disillusioned miners were returning to the eastern states. One such group of about 1,000 men camped at the usual place, three miles west of Plattsmouth. The ones that had gold or coins, buried it near their campsites. During the evening, several of the ex-miners decided to rob and burn Plattsmouth because of what the merchants had told them about the easy riches to be found in the gold fields, so that the eager greenhorns would buy supplies.

By the next morning, over 1,000 men had gathered with the intention of sacking the town. (Before leaving the campground, those that had not buried their gold and valuables the night before, now did so.) But someone had tipped off the townspeople, so when the miners reached the edge of Plattsmouth, armed citizens were waiting for them.

Before the ex-gold seekers realized what had happened, they were being driven to the Missouri River, where they were told to "Swim to Iowa and don't come back." With no choice but to swim, the miners crossed the river in any manner they could. They were told in no uncertain terms, not to return.

After all the miners had crossed the river, a large number of Plattsmouth's citizens went to the campground. One of them described the scene later: "The miners left wagons, horses, mules, mining tools, and all kinds of camping equipment. This litter could be seen for years, what the citizens didn't gather up and take home."

A few people know of the miner's caches of gold and coins but they didn't know where they had been buried. A few searches were made, but so far as is known, none of the gold or coins were found. Today, with a metal detector, a treasure hunter's chance of finding one, or several, of these caches are very good.

NEVADA

As I will do on a few states, since I have an abundance of information on them, I will give two locations of buried treasure:

Site number one, in Nevada, concerns a miner named James Fennimore. Locating in Nevada, Fennimore found a rich outcropping of gold on Sun Mountain, now Mt. Davidson, in Storey County, in 1858. Filing a mining claim, Fennimore took out just enough gold to live on. After about two years of mining, several large companies began to move into the area of Fennimore's mine.

These companies were buying all claims whose owners would sell. Fennimore, since he didn't care for the hard work of mining, sold his claim for a quart of whiskey and $7,500 in gold coins. After getting about half drunk, Fennimore decided to go to Virginia City. Afraid to carry the coins, he buried them near the mouth of his former mine. (He wasn't to vacate the claim for several days.)

After several days and nights of drinking in Virginia City, Fennimore went back to his former claim to get his belongings. Although he searched for several days, Fennimore was never able to find his buried coins.

This is a good location to investigate, because the people that obtained and developed the Comstock Lode bought Fennimore's claim and they are certain to have records of all the claims they bought.

Site number two tells of a cache of coins that is almost certainly still there, because the sister of the man to whom it belonged, searched several times but never found aything.

Samuel Vail and Robert Knox were two wild horse wranglers in Nevada, during 1867. Their permanent camp was about ten miles south of Hiko, in Pahranagat Valley. During the spring of 1868, they had a herd of several hundred half-broken mustangs that they were taking north to sell to the Mormon farmers.

When the camp was suddenly deserted and a few days later, Paiute Indians found a half burned saddle with the initials R. K. burned into it, the sheriff investigated. The body of Robert Knox was found in a shallow grave with a bullet hole in the head.

It was learned that Knox's partner, Vail, had tried to cash a check that had belonged to Knox. Vail was arrested, tried and sentenced to hang. While awaiting the hanging date, Vail wrote a letter to Knox's sister, telling her that he had buried $15,000 (joint earnings from selling the horses) in a fruit jar near where Knox's body had been found. Since he would hang, he wanted her to have the money. The sister searched the camping area several times, but never found the cache.

NEW HAMPSHIRE

Although this cache, or caches, have been searched for, there is no public record of anything ever being found.

The story begins in 1720, when a company of emigrants, sailing from Ireland to Boston, were stopped at sea by the notorious pirate Philip Babb (an aide and cohort of Captain William Kidd). When the pirate was recognized, one of the women on board, Elizabeth Fulton, who was expecting a child, delivered it as the pirates boarded the ship. For probably the only time in his life, Philip Babb was emotionally affected and asked the mother if she would name the baby for his dead wife.

Willing to promise anything under the circumstances, the mother agreed. Babb gave her a bolt of expensive green cloth as a gift for the baby, then sent the emigrant ship on its way.

The mother kept her word and named the baby girl Ocean Born Mary. The emigrants settled in the community of Londonderry, in southern New Hampshire. The baby grew up there and married James Wallace when she was 22 years old. Meanwhile, the old pirate, Philip Babb, had kept in touch with the Fulton family and sent expensive gifts from time to time.

Through politics of the time, Babb somehow managed to get a pardon and moved to the tiny village of Henniker, where he built a beautiful home. (The house has been restored and is now a tourist attraction.)

When Ocean Born Mary's husband died, she and her sons went to live with the old pirate. It is a matter of recorded history that Babb was wealthy and probably buried part of his gold near his home. He is also thought to have buried large amounts of loot on the tiny island of Appledore, one of the group known as the Isles of Shoals.

Babb was eventually killed by robbers trying to force him to tell where his treasure was buried. There is little doubt that a large amount of money is buried somewhere in the vicinity of the village of Henniker. If anyone searches for this treasure they might also look for garnets, as several of gem quality have been found in the area.

NEW JERSEY

For those treasure hunters interested in searching for pirate loot along New Jersey's coastline, they should read the book "Folklore and Folkways on New Jersey;" also the "Newark Daily Advertiser" for December 27, 1834.

Many of the Jersey beaches are located on outer islands, ranging in length from a few hundred feet to many miles. Legend has it that the vicinity of Long Beach and others were once the stomping grounds for pirates from many ports of the Spanish Main. They sought shelter from the rigors of the open sea in the secluded back bays of the islands.

Contrary to popular opinion, pirates did not bury their treasure in the sand dunes. Such locations were too obvious, as other buccaneers might come along and dig it up. Also, the winds shifted and changed the landscape almost daily. Instead, they usually buried their treasure back from the waterline; in the nearby forests; in the vicinity of a large tree; or rock; that could easily be remembered at a later time when they returned.

This story is of one little known location of pirate booty believed to be buried on Five Mile Beach: In the early days (1700 to 1750), there were no buildings on this beach except the lifesaving station on the south end. This station was manned for many years by a retired man named Captain Eli Barnett.

One morning in 1710, when Barnett was alone at his station, he saw through his telescope, a sailing ship heading for the breakers. The ship anchored off shore and a small boat was lowered. Eight men came ashore, took their bearings, then went into the sand dunes.

Sometime later, the men reappeared on the beach, and rowed out to the ship, which sailed away. Were these men checking to see if loot they had previously buried was still there?

For anyone interested, the old lifesaving station was near the south end of the beach. With the old type of telescope in those days, Captain Barnett couldn't have seen too far. It's worth a search.

NEW MEXICO

A treasure story that is unusual, happened near Lordsburg, New Mexico, in 1930. It is unusual in that the treasure was found then lost again during the same day.

About 1930, an aged Mexican known only as Juan, lived on the outskirts of Lordsburg. His source of a livlihood was cutting firewood. Each morning he would tell his daughter where he would be working, and return home that afternoon.

On the day he found the large Spanish treasure, he had told his daughter he would be working in the vicinity of Dogshead Peak. About mid afternoon, much earlier than he usually came home, Juan was seen riding a burro toward the house. He appeared to be ill so his daughter and neighbors took him to a doctor. Juan was in a coma and unable to speak by the time the doctor saw him. He had suffered a stroke.

The doctor noticed that Juan was clutching something in his hand. He finally got Juan's hand open and found several old gold coins of Spanish make. The doctor theorized that Juan had stumbled upon a cache of coins and the shock had been too much for the old man. Whatever the reason, Jaun never regained consciousness and died.

There has been an old treasure story told around Lordsburg for years, about a Spanish treasure of gold coins somewhere in the area of Dogshead Peak. This site could be worth looking into because Juan had a pattern he followed when he worked. Some oldtimer or family member in the area might still remember Juan and his working habits. Also, at his age, when he found the coins he couldn't have buried them too deep, if he reburied them.

NEW YORK

When a body was found floating in the Hudson River, near Beacon, New York, in March 1897, it took several days for the authorities to identify the dead man. His name was Ashel Bell and he was known as "The Hermit of Fishkill Mountain." He had a cabin, but also lived in various caves in the area.

When the hermit's estate was settled several weeks later, it came to $16,000 in cash and $10,000 in real estate. But the greater part of Bell's money was not in a bank or real estate, he had buried it somewhere near his cabin. His relatives knew of at least $30,000 that Bell had drawn from different banks shortly before his death.

Bell's gold is almost certain to be buried near where he lived, because he seldom left the Fishkill Mountains. As far as can be ascertained, no one ever found any of his hidden money. For those interested in searching, more information may be obtained in the March 1897 issue of "The New York Times."

NORTH CAROLINA

Since the price of silver keeps rising, it could pay some interested persons to check the following location:

In Macon County, in southwestern North Carolina, there is a rich deposit of silver somewhere in the Nantahala Mountains, that was known to the Cherokee Indians, but kept secret from the white men.

The story goes, that the first white settlers into the area found an old Indian whom the Cherokee called Sontechee, living at the mouth of a stream, now known as Factory Creek. At that point there was a large shelf of rock, partly covering the entrance to what was once a large cavern in the hillside.

The settlers wondered why the Indian had no squaw and lived apart from the other Indians and seldom left the cave's entrance. Sontechee was highly regarded by the Cherokee and was always supplied with whatever he needed. In time, the settlers learned why he lived alone and at this exact spot.

Sontechee had been selected by his people to guard the cave because somewhere back of the shelf in the mountain was a vast deposit of silver ore. This mine is believed to have been the source of supply for much of the metal used by the Cherokees in the making of various trinkets, which they prized highly.

Not wishing to stir up any trouble with the Cherokees, the early settlers made no attempt to explore the territory around the cave. With the passing of years, other settlers moved in and took over the Indian lands. Sontechee, the old guardian, died and the mysterious cavern was forgotten.

A few years later a big landslide sealed up the entrance to the cave. About this time, the finding of the remains of an old smelter, firebox, piles of cinders and large quantities of burned ore that had been buried near the cave's entrance, convinced the settlers that the Cherokees had a large mining operation going on for years, before the white men came to the area.

On Factory Creek, a short distance from where the cave entrance was, is an ancient water wheel built by the Cherokee Indians, of large hand-hewn logs. It was used to furnish power for the crude crushing of silver ore to be smelted.

Silver has been found in the area in small quantities, so maybe if the cave was reopened the rich deposit could be found. But so far, no one has attempted this.

NORTH DAKOTA

For the relic hunter interested in U.S. Army and Indian artifacts, the following listing of battles and forts will be helpful, if they visit North Dakota:

Fort Abercrombie, on the west bank of the Red River, about 12 miles north of the site of Wahpeton, was established in 1857. Supplies for this post were brought from St. Paul. When the Sioux went on the warpath in 1862, Minnesota settlers sought refuge here during a seven-week seige. The fort was abandoned in 1877.

Fort Rice, on the west bank of the Missouri, came next. General Alfred H. Sully's men cut cottonwood trees to build it in 1864. The fort housed four infantry companies. Fort Rice was dismantled in 1878, when Fort Yates, to the south took its place. Fort Yates was abandoned in 1903.

Fort Totten, near Devil's Lake, was constructed in 1867, and served until 1890. Fort Stevenson, on the Missouri, at the mouth of Douglass Creek, was maintained from 1867 until 1883.

Fort Buford was built in 1866, opposite the mouth of the Yellowstone River, on the north bank of the Missouri.

Established on the Red River, near the site of Pembina, Fort Pembina was maintained from 1870 until 1895. Fort McKeen, established in 1872, became, the same year, part of Fort Abraham Lincoln, garrisoned until 1891. It was from Fort Abraham Lincoln that Custer and his seventh Cavalry marched to death and disaster on the banks of the Little Big Horn, in 1876.

These early forts were established to protect the settlers along the frontier and to keep the Indians in order. It was after the Sioux outbreak in Minnesota in 1862, that General Henry H. Sibley was sent to punish the Sioux. In June of 1862, he headed his army west from Minnesota toward the Devils Lake region, where he arrived to find the Indians had gone south. He pursued them and on July 24th, engaged them in a battle at Big Mound, about seven miles north of the present town of Teppen.

They retreated and he followed them to Dead Buffalo Lake, northwest of Dawson, where on July 26th, another engagement was fought. Two days later he met them again at Stony Lake, northeast of Driscoll, but the Sioux retreated rapidly and there was no fighting. Moving on toward the Missouri, Sibley encamped on Apple Creek, seven miles east of the present site of Bismarck, near the mouth of The Sioux then fled across the river.

Sibley, all along the route, had thrown up defensive earthworks at each of his camps. All these camp sites which are not plowed under, have been definitely located under the direction of the State Historical Society.

OHIO

Although this cache has been searched for, no one, to my knowledge, has found it.

Just a few hours before General George Rogers Clark and his small army were to attack the Indian town of Old Chillicothe (now Oldtown, Ohio), Catahecass (Black Hoof), the Shawnee chief, waited for the report of his scouts to tell him of Clark's advance on the village. He had known for several days the attack was coming and while he waited he was remembering the coming of the white men, the beginning of the end for the Indian's way of life.

The first white men (so the stories said, that the old ones told) came in search of gold and silver; wild eyed men, wearing iron hats and carrying a stick that spat fire and death, calling themselves Conquistadores. Finding no riches in the Indian villages, they moved on north. Black Hoof could remember the French people that came after the Spanish, built their friendly trading posts and had gifts for the Indians. After the Long War between the whites (French and Indian War 1756-1763), the French people were forced to leave the Ohio and Illinois Valleys.

Then came the English traders, trappers and hunters. Footloose, carefree men, never permanent, always looking over the next mountain or crossing the next river. These men presented no problems to the Indian's way of life, some (like Simon Girty, one of Black Hoof's chief scouts) even accepted it.

It was the coming of the settler, moving deeper into the Ohio Valley, that presented danger to the Indians. His progress was slow, plodding and permanent. When he moved in with his family, built a cabin and tore up the earth with his plow, he meant to stay. This, Black Hoof could see,

172

meant the eventual removal of all Indians; they were pushed west, always west. The eastern lands were closed to them forever.

Late in the afternoon of August 6, 1780, Red Snake and Simon Girty brought word that Clark was only a few hours away. Black Hoof called a council of his sub-chiefs and told them what had to be done with their possessions. They were to hide everything they didn't need, burn the village, then leave and join their friends at Piqua Town. Black Hoof knew that General Clark was relentless, death and his name both, meant the same thing to the Shawnee.

In a short time the Indians had gathered a large pile of assorted tools, pans, kettles, furs, leathers and spare weapons. The heaviest and most valuable items were made of silver. There were arm bands, plates, earrings, necklaces, medallions, long bars and heavy "wads."

As soon as it was dark, the Indians began to move the silver and goods west to the large marshy area between the village and the Little Miami River. (A large part of this silver was also carried north of the village and buried.) One tree, a large oak, grew in this swamp. Black Hoof stood near this tree to supervise the hiding of their valuables. Each item was passed from hand to hand down a long line of warriors and squaws, then thrown into a large pool of stagnant water, of an unknown depth.

When everything was in the pool, it was covered with brush and set on fire. Black Hoof then led his people back to the village and they burned most of it and the surrounding area to the ground. Then the entire tribe (all but about a dozen warriors that had taken part of the silver a few miles north of the village to bury, and were to meet the others at Piqua Town later) started their march to the northwest for the village of Piqua Town, thirteen miles away on the north side of Mad River.

In his report, General Clark said that when he reached the village of Old Chillicothe, only a few buildings were still standing and he burned them. Since all the Indians were gone by that time, Clark knew nothing of the buried silver and goods. Clark then went on to Piqua Town where the Indians were routed, with several killed, the rest were scattered and afraid to return.

This treasure and the silver that was taken a few miles north and buried, were never recovered by the Shawnee. According to local residents, Indians have visited the area in years past, more to pay homage to their ancestors than to try and locate the treasure.

The oak tree is gone now, the marsh had been drained and is being cultivated. I can learn of no recent attempt having been made to locate the hoard. This is a perfect spot to use a deep seeking metal detector, as I believe the weight of the silver and goods have caused them to sink to bedrock during the last 200 years.

OKLAHOMA

In southern Oklahoma, a cache of gold coins, well worth searching for, waits for some lucky treasure hunter.

When the Civil War ended, Warren Mun had lost almost everything he owned. Sherman's March from Charleston to Goldsboro, North Carolina, had destroyed the farm Mun had worked for years to build. Salvaging a wagon, team of mules, a few household goods and his life savings, a quantity of $20.00 gold pieces, Mun loaded up his wife and small daughter and headed west.

Several weeks later he entered what was then the Indian Territory at Fort Smith. He then crossed the Texas Road north of Perryville and camped at the edge of a small canyon, just north of the South Canadian River. It was while he was camped here that a party of friendly Indians visited the camp.

After they left (Mun was not familiar with Indians and thought they were all killers), the family decided, since they could not outrun the Indians if they came back, that they would bury the gold until they were ready to move on. Years later, the daughter described the hiding place of the coins in these words, "My father buried the gold in a cavern beside a dripping spring. I don't know how much gold there was, but when my father took the strongbox from the wagon, I could not lift it."

Later that night, after burying the coins, Mun was joined by a group of strangers. Still fearing an Indian attack, Mun decided to travel west with this party, but becasue of the strangers, he was afraid to dig up his gold the next morning. Mun figured to go on to California and return for his gold after he was settled. But because of time, raising his daughter and building a farm, Mun never returned to Oklahoma.

Many years later, after Mun and his wife died, his daughter returned to Oklahoma to search for the gold. There had been so many changes that the daughter, after telling her story to local residents and not finding the coins, returned to California. So somewhere near a dripping spring, in a small canyon, a few miles southwest of Holdenville, in Hughes County, Oklahoma, near the Canadian River, is a cache of gold coins... waiting.

OREGON

The location of $75,000 in gold that was buried by an outlaw gang in southwest Oregon is scarcely known outside the state.

In 1851, while men were still eagerly going to California in search of gold, a strike was made in the Illinois River region at Josephine and Canyon Creeks, near O'Brien, Oregon. Gold was found in large quantities and the area became overcrowded. Several of the new citizens not too anxious to dig for gold, set up saloons, gambling halls and other enticements to separate the miner from his gold. Outlaws also preyed on the miners and stagecoaches.

One such bandit gang was made up of Jack Triskett, his half-brother Henry, Fred Cooper, Miles Hearn and Chris Stover. This outfit was probably the meanest in the area.

On August 3, 1852, the Triskett gang, fleeing from a number of robberies they had committed in California, rode into the mining town of Sailor's Diggings, near O'Brien. Since they were unknown in Oregon, they were treated like any other strangers. The gang visited a saloon and had a few drinks, ate a meal, then went out into the street.

While they were standing in front of the saloon, Fred Cooper, for no apparent reason, pulled a gun and killed the first man who walked by. At this time the Triskett gang seemed to go crazy. For the next twenty to thirty minutes, they went from one end of the camp to the other, killing anyone in sight. They killed seventeen (the number varies, some say twenty men were killed), raped two women, then stormed into the assaying depot where they took $75,000 worth of gold dust.

The gang then rode toward the northwest of town. A heavily armed posse was soon on their trail. Just outside O'Brien, the posse surrounded the bandits on a low hill. During the following fight all the outlaws but Chris Stover were killed. Stover was taken back to Sailor's Diggins but died a few hours later without revealing where the gold dust had been hidden.

Several questions remain unanswered concerning this indicent. Why did the gang shoot up the mining camp? It would have been much easier to have robbed the depot quietly. Why kill so many people? What happened to the $75,000? Was it hurriedly buried at the place the outlaws were killed? Or did they stop at a prearranged spot and hide the gold dust? This is a good location to check into.

PENNSYLVANIA

While this treasure site is legendary, there are enough known facts to support its authenticity. The story goes, that about 1697, a party of French Canadian voyageurs left New Orleans for the return trip to Montreal, Canada. They had been sent to transport a load of gold coins for the French governemnt to use in the fur trade in Canada. They left New Orleans on rafts, with provisions and several small wooden kegs. Each keg was filled almost full of gold coins, then a layer of gunpowder was placed over them. The kegs were then anchored to the rafts with nails and ropes.

The planned route was almost 2,000 miles. It went up the Mississippi River to the Ohio, then to the Allegheny, north on the Conewango to Chautauqa Lake, across this lake to Prendergrast Creek, then on to Montreal by way of Lake Erie and Lake Ontario. The complete trip could be made by water without any land portages.

The gold was to be delivered to His Majesty's Royal Governor in Montreal. It was to be guarded with their lives, the voyageurs were told. Regardless of the hardships received in such a trip, the valuable cargo was not to be taken by the hated English or the Seneca Indians. The party consisted of about twenty Frenchmen, two Jesuit priests, and several friendly Indian scouts. They made it up the Mississippi River to the mouth of the Ohio, where they are believed to have camped for several days. They repaired the rafts and built canoes to be used later on the more narrow streams farther north. As they traveled up the Ohio, the priests made maps and checked locations for forts and settlements to be built or started later.

They almost certainly stopped at the Shawnee Indian Village of Sonioto, at the mouth of the Scioto River, where Portsmouth, Ohio, is today. The Shawnee were good friends with the French. At the forks of the Ohio River, the party camped again before turning north up the Allegheny. They were now approaching the lands of the hated Seneca Indians. The bloodthirsty warriors would like nothing better than to scalp a few Frenchmen. A few years before, the Senecas had raided and killed over 200 French settlers in and around Montreal. The voyageurs wanted no part of this Indian nation, their worst enemy. They changed their planned route. It was decided not to make the trip up the Conewango, but to continue on the Allegheny to its headwaters. By doing this they might not contact the Senecas at all.

At the head of the Allegheny they could portage to the Genesee River, then go on north to Lake Ontario. After turning southeast, it is believed the Frenchmen reached a point near what is now Coudersport, Pennsylvania. They had been attacked by the Senecas several times during their trip up the Allegheny, but had fought them off. Realizing that Indian runners would bring enough warriors to annihilate them, the Frenchmen decided to bury the gold and continue the trip on foot to the Genesee River. They could return for the gold later.

The legend tells that they traveled to what is now known as the Valley of Borie, in Potter County. Near a large rock (big as a house), they buried the kegs of gold. The priests chiseled a cross into the rock as a marker. A crude map was made of the area, then the party headed back to the Allegheny. By traveling at night and hiding during the day, they finally made it to the Genesee River and on to Montreal. They reported to the Royal Governor that they had buried the gold near the head of the Allegheny River and had marked a large rock at the location.

The Senecas learned about the rock in the Borie area that had a strange carving, like two crossed sticks, upon it. Thinking that the carving was a religious totem of the French and therefore dangerous to them, the superstitious Indians never disturbed it.

Because of the war with the Senecas and the threat of the English, no record of the Frenchmen returning for the gold can be found. It is believed by many, that somewhere near the head of the Allegheny River, in Pennsylvania, is a buried treasure of gold worth over $300,000. It has never been reported found.

RHODE ISLAND

While Block Island is known to have been a pirate hangout in the early days, what is not generally known, is on what part of the island Joseph Bradish buried his immense treasure. I have an old book that states: "We buried ye money and ye jewels on the south point of ye island to the leeward." This statement was supposedly made by Bradish himself. This information narrows the search area for an interested treasure hunter.

The background of the Bradish treasure is this: an undetermined quantity of jewels and coin were buried on Block Island by Bradish and his pirate crew in April 1699. It was put there to escape seizure as proof of piracy against Bradish and his men, in case they were captured.

When the pirate crew dropped anchor near Block Island, Bradish sent several of his men to the mainland of Rhode Island to buy a ship. His own vessel, the Adventure, was no longer seaworthy.

Rhode Island, at any other time was a protected area for pirates, but when Bradish's men landed, a fervent anti-pirate campaign was going on. The pirates were recognized, promptly arrested and jailed. Hearing of the capture of his men, Bradish scuttled his crippled vessel and moved to the mainland. He intended to remain in hiding until such time that he could obtain another ship. But he was captured, taken to London, tried for piracy and hanged in 1700.

For anyone interested in searching for this immense treasure, remember, pirates always buried their loot above, or back from, the high water line and always used a tree, rock, cliff or hill as a marker. Also, remember Bradish's statement as to where the treasure was buried.

SOUTH CAROLINA

As I have done with information on several other states in this listing, I will give two metal detector or treasure sites in South Carolina:

One... This item appeared in a newspaper printed in Columbia, South Carolina, July 12, 1905. "The president, until recently, of the Darlington Trust Company and the Independent Oil Company, Keith Dargan, drank carbolic acid in the presence of his brother-in-law and died soon afterwards. A note was left, written by Dargan, saying he had appropriated company funds. It is reported that the shortage will be $800,000."

This would be a very good lead to investigate further by checking court records and newspapers in Columbia, South Carolina, of the period July-September 1905. There had to be follow-up stories on an embezzlement of this size.

Two... For those interested in searching for Civil War relics in South Carolina, they can be found in almost every county. All newspapers of the period 1861-1865, carried stories of the different Civil War actions within the state. Any historical society should have information on this conflict. Family histories, old diaries, letters, court records; all would be good sources to research for information on the Civil War in any particular area of South Carolina.

There is a published listing of 71 sites where Civil War action took place within this state, called "Civil War Battles," compiled by H. K. Melton. This small booklet is invaluable to the Civil War buff.

SOUTH DAKOTA

Near Rochford, in Pennington County, South Dakota, the old mines and homesteader's buildings are still to be found, by the side of the road, or hidden in the back country, preserved mostly by neglect. Of interest to the treasure hunter, is a long abandoned gold mining operation that took place east of Rochford, off a back road in Bloody Gulch.

Perhaps a dozen men worked here in the 1880's. The cabins these men lived in were still standing in 1980, beside a small mine, whose shaft is almost filled with debris. This mine was abandoned because it did not pay enough to work it during the 1880's. With the price of gold today, it could very well pay for an interested person to check this location.

Another mine called the Standby Mine, is close to Rochford and remains of it can still be seen. This mine at one time (1904), was well enough developed that a photo was made showing the mill and water trace. There was even talk at that time of a board of directors for the Standby Mine and others in the area.

The vicinity of Rochford would be of interest to relic hunters since there are dozens of old buildings and miner's shacks to be searched. Any of the streams would pay (at today's gold prices) to be checked. Several stories of buried caches of valuables are told in the area, but these will have to be investigated by the individual interested in searching for them.

TENNESSEE

This is a known treasure in Tennessee that could very well pay anyone to search for. The facts have been researched and proven to be true. Most authorities agree that the time of burial of this huge cache, was during the summer of 1863. Until the treasure is recovered the exact value will never be known, but according to the amount of looting done in the area by Union soldiers during 1863, it is generally given in excess of $1,000,000.

It was a time during the Civil War when the Union forces had been victorious and were engaging in a little publicized facet of the Civil War plundering. During their campaign, unscrupulous officers had accumulated a hoard of coins, jewelry, silverware and other valuables they had liberated from plantations and towns along the way.

By the time they reached the central area of Tennessee, the loot had grown to such proportions that it had to be transported on a special wagon and guarded by handpicked guards. About two miles north of the town of Lexington, Tennessee, intelligence scouts reported that a large force of Confederates were grouping for a counterattack.

Realizing that the quantity of loot they were transporting was too cumbersome to be saved in a running battle, the officers decided to bury it. The elite guard was detailed for the job and apparently it was an excellent accomplishment. There was plenty of time to bury all the treasure and conceal the diggings.

Within a few hours after the task was completed, the attack began and the Union forces were driven back. They recovered, but the next drive took the officers and guard far from their original campground, where they had hidden their loot.

Before the campaign was finished, the men that buried the wagon load of valuables were many miles from the treasure and the land was occupied by Confederate troops. When it was once again won by the Union, it was another army which never guessed they marched over a fortune.

When the Civil War ended, many of the original group were dead. The ones still living which were involved in burying this huge cache, could not return for the treasure because it would have been classified as contraband of war and the U.S. government would have confiscated it.

Able historians agree there is little doubt but that in the area two miles north of Lexington, Tennessee, a treasure worth in excess of $1,000,000 waits to be recovered.

TEXAS

Dozens of treasure stories have been written concerning different caches in Texas that would be of interest to treasure hunters. Several good treasure books are on the market dealing with Texas, but no author, or combination of authors, could hope to cover the entire state. There are always little known stories, usually true, of hidden, buried or lost valuables in any state, and Texas is no exception. The following information on a lesser known treasure site could be helpful to an interested person:

A successful rancher named John Hightower, and his wife, lived in the town of Kossee, Texas, during the late 1800's. Their ranch was located south of town. It was a known fact that Hightower was making money through livestock sales. He kept a safe in his home with money for operating expenses, but he is believed to have cached the greater part of his earnings somewhere near his house. This house was still standing in the late 1950's.

John made periodic trips to a large ravine near where he lived, usually after dark. After having been seen several times going or coming from this ravine, John's neighbors began to suspect that he was burying part of his money somewhere in the area. At that time, anyone that had any money, kept it at home or buried it.

John Hightower died about 1920. His wife died a year later. For years, it was local talk in the neighborhood, that Hightower had hidden his money near his home. It is a known fact that he was well-to-do for the times and did not keep any money in a bank. This is a very good location to check out, since, as far as it is known, no searching has been done.

UTAH

The location of silver mines in Utah, that need to be checked further are in and near the old ghost town of La Plata. This mining camp was built over a known deposit of silver, but the ore was in quantities too small to mine at that time.

Several discoveries of silver in Utah, have proven to be "spotty deposits", not really worth mining. However, the veins of silver under and extending out from La Plata, have proved to be very rich in spots. They run from north of Brigham City to northeast of Huntsville. La Plata is located on the veins, about eight miles north of Huntsville.

A chunk of galena was found between Huntsville and La Plata a few years ago, that weighed almost a hundred pounds. This piece of ore was just lying on a hillside. Prospectors that saw it, claimed it was the richest they had ever seen in Utah. A sample was sent to Salt Lake City, the assay report was 84% lead and 16% silver. The source where this rich sample came from has not been found.

With the ever increasing price of silver, it could very well pay an interested person to check out these "spotty deposits" around La Plata and Huntsville. The mother lode has to be somewhere in the vicinity.

VERMONT

A treasure story that should be of interest to those treasure hunters in Vermont, who think their state is short on sites, is the following location:·

During the days of sailing ships in New England, 1600 to 1800, the tall pines in Vermont, Massachusetts and New Hampshire, were in great demand to be used as ship's masts to hold the hundreds of yards of sails. Trees were cut, then taken by large sleds (sometimes as many as twenty or thirty horses or mules would be used to haul one to three of these huge logs overland) to the Merrimack River, where they would be rafted down to Amesburg, Salisbury and other seaports, usually ending up in Boston, the largest shipping port on the Atlantic seaboard.

According to information I have been able to obtain, one such logger that made a fortune for the times, dealing in ship's masts, was David Jarvis, who operated out of the headwaters of the Winooski River, in Vermont. During the 1730's and 1740's, Jarvis ran an extensive, if somewhat primitive, lumber operation. Jarvis, when he delivered a load of logs, would accept payment in nothing but gold coins. It was a known fact that he kept a large amount of money on the small farm where he lived when not in the woods.

This story has a ring of truth to it, because there were no banks and the entire area was sparsely settled. Also, Jarvis would have had to have money to pay his men, who were usually itinerant loggers. They would, in a large number of instances, work one season then move on to another camp. He also needed ready cash to buy timber tracts.

The local story in the neighborhood for years after Jarvis was killed in an accident while helping to fell a tree, was that he had buried a large part of his money on the farm. This would be a very good location for an interested treasure hunter to research through old records, some of which are still believed to be in existence.

VIRGINIA

While the story of a cache of approximately $58,000 in gold and silver coins and jewelry was written by an author several years ago, he did not have the letter (from one of the men that was involved in the robbery), of which I now have a copy. This letter was sent to the man that had been robbed, over a year after the Civil War was over. I quote:

"Kind Sir: I am in pain and upon my deathbed, I feel I must divest my conscience of a burden that has kept constant company with my soul shortly after we fought over the salt works there. Your son, Eli, fearing he would be hanged, made a deal with my first sergeant, Jack Harrington, to share your fortune with him, an amount of some $46,000 in gold and silver coins, $12,000 in jewelry and several gold watches. In return, your son would be helped to escape into Tennessee. Harrington murdered your son on the pretext that he was escaping."

"With my help, Harrington moved the cache and hid it in a saltpeter cave, about a quarter mile distant from the little town church. Harrington was killed in a blast while we were destroying the saltpeter caves before we left. I took a minie ball at the battle of Seven Mile Ford and have been unable to travel since. I had planned to return to Saltville and reveal the location of your money to you. But I am dying and I want you to know that I took no part in the murder of your son. Respectfully, Corporal Allen E. Brooks, late of the Fortieth Mounted Infantry, Army of the U.S., General Stoneman Commanding."

This letter was written September 11, 1866, The location of the cache is believed in or near a cave, locally called Harmon's Cave, near Saltville, Virginia, in Smyth County. This cache could be found by a persevering treasure hunter.

WASHINGTON

A little known treasure of $20,000 in Okanogan County, Washington, is still waiting for some resourceful treasure hunter to find it. From about 1900 to 1918, a Colville Indian, known as Chief Smitkin, lived between Omak and Colville. He was a successful cattleman. Sometimes his roundup would reach 600 to 700 head of cattle. This livestock was usually sold in Omak for a good price, always in gold coins.

Chief Smitkin was a stingy old Indian that did not trust the white man, or his banks, so he left his money on his ranch. The chief could not count very well, so he had his brother-in-law add up his money for him. At one time, shortly before Smitkin's death, he had over $20,000 in coins, mostly gold.

Smitkin always went to church at Saint Mary's Indian Mission at Omak. He would come alone, at night and just look at the church building. After his death in 1918, his neighbors theorized that the reason Smitkin visited the church so much was, he had his money buried nearby. Perhaps the chief thought the white man's God would protect his cache. In any event, the money was not found after Chief Smitkin died. It is believed that somewhere around the small Indian mission there is $20,000 still buried.

WEST VIRGINIA

A little known site of what could be called treasure today and certainly worth a small fortune, is two railroad cars filled with whiskey that were lost in the early 1900's. This location should be of interest to treasure hunting scuba divers:

The two boxcars are in New River, in the Hico-Fayetteville area. Local research could probably pinpoint the exact location. The whiskey, according to local information, has not been recovered.

Also of interest to those that want to check out metal detector sites in Fayette County below are the following locations:

Near Montgomery, in the bottom lands of the Kanawha River, was the location of a large Indian village. Relics from three different civilizations, dating back to 500 A.D. have been found.

On September 11, 1862, Confederate and Union forces clashed at Cotton Hill, with minor losses on each side. There was also a battle at Gauley Bridge, on November 10, 1861, with the Union forces suffering the heaviest losses. Near Fayetteville, are remains of breastworks that were used during the Civil War. Both armies occupied the town at one time or another. Two battles, one on September 10, 1862, and one on May 19, 1863, were fought there.

East of Boomer, on a ridge between Armstrong and Loot Creek, are many prehistoric ruins, made of stone. The walls are several miles long, and surround a large area.

On the east side of Jansted is the Half-Way House, a stop on the Kanawha Turnpike, from before the Revolutionary War until after the Civil War. This was a favorite stopping place for travelers.

Information on ghost towns in Fayette County, can be gotten at Fayetteville. Here are four that are ghost or near ghost towns: Drennen, Lockwood, Pax-town and Thurmond.

WISCONSIN

This location is in the Apostle Island group, just north of Wisconsin, in Lake Superior and the islands are considered part of Wisconsin. To substantiate the story, this clue to the treasure is in the British Army archives. I quote: "The payroll is buried somewhere along the shoreline of an island in the Apostle Group, in Lake Superior, believed to be Hermit."

A fact that is not commonly known, is that up until the First World War, the British army always carried a payroll for the men. In this manner the soldiers were paid regularly, no matter where they were in the world. This payroll was always carried by an officer and due to the character of some of the soldiers, the officer, while on a march, always walked off alone from the campsite, and buried the money until the soldiers were ready to move on the next day. The money was always well concealed, but was usually buried only a few inches deep.

On a cold, wintry evening in the 1760's, a contingent of British soldiers landed on Hermit Island. The men were told by their officers to walk and talk quietly and build no fires, because there were hostile Indians on the island.

The soldiers ate a cold meal, stationed a guard and the rest went to sleep. Early the next morning, the British troops were awakened by Indian war whoops. Most of the soldiers were still in their blankets, where they were slaughtered. Only a very few managed to escape.

The Indians threw the dead soldiers into the lake or fire, then the loot was divided and the indians left. The surviving men came out of hiding and found that the officer who had buried the payroll was dead, so only a brief search was made for the money. Afraid that the Indians might return, the survivors moved out quickly to the fort on the mainland.

The fort's commander organized a party to search for the payroll. A week was spent in looking, but no trace of the money was found. This is a good location to spend a vacation with a metal detector. The coins would be worth a small fortune today.

WYOMING

To my knowledge, this bulletin has never been published in any treasure magazine. I quote in part from this old newspaper clipping:

"One of the most famous lost mines in Wyoming is the Lost Cabin Gold Mine said to be located somewhere in the Big Horn or Owl Creek mountains." In 1919, the Wyoming Historical Society published an account of the Lost Cabin mine in the Society's "Miscellanies." Following is the story from that publication:

The Lost Cabin gold placers of Wyoming were discovered and worked for three days, in the fall of 1865, by seven men who came into the region from the Black Hills country. Five of the seven men were killed by the Indians; two escaped. The two who escaped brought away $7,000 in coarse gold. Since that day, no effort for the discovery of this locality has been successful.

The account given by Charley Clay, an old Wyoming pioneer (formerly of Douglas), now in Washington (March 20, 1894), is this, and it is delivered directly from the two men who escaped and gave him the gold to put in the safe at the Post Trader's store at Fort Laramie:

"In October, 1865, two men reached Old Fort Reno at the point which is now the crossing of Powder River, in a terribly weak and exhausted condition. They explained that they had belonged to a party of seven gold prospectors who came into the Big Horn Mountains on their eastern slope from the Black Hills of Dakota."

"They traveled along the base of the range, going south and testing the ground until they came to a park surrounded by heavy timber, through which ran a bold mountain stream, and which a few hundred yards below, joined a larger stream. Here they found rich signs of the yellow metal and at a depth of three to four feet struck bedrock, where the gold was very plentiful and coarse. They immediately camped, having tools and grub which they brought by two pack animals. Among their tools, they brought a big log saw and with that sawed enough logs to construct a flume. They also built a log cabin. The seven men, all working hard, finished their habitation and flume in three days and then began to work the gold in earnest."

"Late on the afternoon on the third day, they were suddenly attacked by a band of Indians and five of the men were killed almost instantly, the other two escaping to the cabin, where they held the Indians at bay till nightfall. In the darkness of the night, they succeeded in escaping without being seen by the Indians. They were on foot and took nothing with them but the gold, their arms and food. From this time on they traveled at night and hid themselves during the day. After three nights of rapid and continuous walking, they reached Fort Reno and told their story."

"The two men then went to Fort Laramie and spent the winter. Here Mr. Clay met them, and being clerk of the Post Trader's store, they gave him the gold for safekeeping. He put the gold in the safe until their departure.

They left in the spring determined to go back, and in order to better find the place, went to the Black Hills, (and) formed a new party to go over their old trail. In this expedition, some ten or twelve persons engaged and all were killed by Indians. For the next 12 or 15 years succeeding, it was unsafe to go into that region and prospect."

I hope this information will be helpful to interested treasure hunters in Wyoming.

FINIS

There is proof being shown every day that there is more realism to treasure hunting—and finding—than we experience in our dreams.

This nugget was found in Montana.

One type of gold bearing stream.

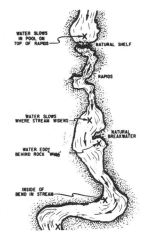
Typical stream. X—trapped gold.

Montana ledge with gold bearing rock.

Author panning gold.

TO ORDER OR RE-ORDER THESE BOOKS, CONTACT

MICHAEL PAUL HENSON
Post Office Box 980
Jeffersonville, IN 47131-0980

Phone Number
283-4164
Area Code 812

"Lost Silver Mines and Buried Treasures of Kentucky" $5.95

"Lost, Buried and Sunken Treasures of the Midwest" $5.95

"John Swift's Lost Silver Mines" $5.95

"Treasure Guide Series - Michigan and Ohio" $5.95

"Treasure Guide Series - Illinois and Indiana" $5.95

"Treasure Guide Series - Pennsylvania" $6.95

"Treasure Guide Series - Virginia and West Virginia" $6.95

"Treasure Guide Series - Kentucky" $6.95

"Treasure Hunt for Fun and Profit" $2.50

"Gold and Diamonds in Indiana" $2.50

"America's Lost Treasures" $7.95

"Tragedy at Devil's Hollow & Other Kentucky Ghost Stories" $10.50